CU00690638

Anxiety Anonymous
The Big Book on Anxiety Addiction

Dennis Ortman

Copyright 2015 by MSI Press, LLC

All rights reserved. No part of this book may be reproduced or utilized in any form or by any means, electronic or mechanical, including photocopying, recording, or by any information storage and retrieval system, without permission in writing from the publisher.

For information, contact:

MSI Press
1760-F Airline Highway, 203
Hollister, CA 95023
Orders@MSIPress.com
Telephone/Fax: 831-886-2486

Library of Congress Control Number 2015935542

ISBN 978-1-942891-00-0

cover design by Carl Leaver
cover photos: Shutterstock.com

Contents

Dennis Ortman, Ph.D.

Introduction

"Whoever can see through all fear will always be safe."

—Tao Te Ching

In our fast-paced society, living with stress seems normal. There is so much to do and so little time to do it. You may rationalize the stress as the inevitable price of ambition and success.

What you call stress is really anxiety. It is your fearful, nervous reaction to the many challenges of your life. That anxiety may escalate and persist to the point that you tell yourself: "I'm powerless over my anxiety, and my life has become unmanageable because of it."

If your anxious reactions become harmfully excessive and beyond your control, you have crossed a line. You have become addicted to your anxiety. You experience it as powerful as any drug, taking over your life.

Nancy's Story

Tonight was a special night for Nancy. She planned a surprise thirtieth birthday dinner for her husband Rick. It would be an intimate celebration for just the two of them. Nancy carefully decorated the kitchen with balloons and the table with candles and birthday dishes and napkins. She prepared his favorite meal of prime rib and lobster with mashed potatoes and shrimp cocktail. Nancy even baked his favorite cake, double chocolate. She wanted to have a romantic evening together, a celebration of both his birthday and their fifth anniversary. It was six thirty, and Nancy was just waiting for him to get home from work so she could shout, "Surprise!" She had it all planned out in her imagination, and everything was set to the last detail.

When seven o'clock came around and Rick had not yet arrived, Nancy caught herself beginning to worry. "He's often late," she thought to calm herself, resisting the impulse to call him. She didn't want to ruin the surprise or appear too anxious. A half hour went by, and still no Rick. Nancy lit a cigarette to relax herself. She kept telling herself, "There's no need to worry." Another half hour passed, and Nancy could not resist calling him.

No answer.

She called several more times, becoming more frantic with each voice mail. Nancy could not sit still and began pacing and looking for little cleaning jobs. Her stomach upset, she dreaded the thought of food. Her heart beat more rapidly, making her more anxious. She wondered if a heart attack was coming. Her head throbbed. "Why hasn't he called? Dammit!" she said to herself as she felt her anger rising. "He had better not be at the bar," and she had the passing thought he was having an affair. She felt like throwing the dinner in the garbage but restrained herself. "I could kill him," she thought.

Nancy paced more frantically, watching the clock, her worry escalating, "I hope he hasn't gotten into an accident." She had visions of his car crashed with him mangled inside. When the phone rang, she jumped to answer it, imagining it was the hospital calling to inform her of Rick's tragic death. It was only her mother, and Nancy quickly got her off the line, hoping to hear from her husband. "Something terrible must have happened to him to keep him from calling," she reasoned. Nancy began to pray and bargain with God, "If you bring him home safely, I'll never nag him again about his drinking."

As the time passed, Nancy felt more desperate and began calling the area hospitals, certain that Rick had had an accident.

At midnight, when Rick stumbled through the door, intoxicated and apologetic, Nancy flew into a rage. "How could you do this to me, and on your birthday of all days?" she screamed at him. Rick just stammered his apologies while Nancy berated him about his drinking and how it was ruining their lives. Rick sat down on the couch and soon passed out, deaf to his wife's worry and anger. Her relief at his safe return home was fleeting.

Nancy could not sleep or stop the deluge of thoughts that flooded her mind. She felt like jumping out of her skin. When her stomach continued to churn and her heart raced, she imagined she was having a heart attack and wondered if she should go to the hospital. Nancy tried to calm herself by pacing and by distracting herself with cleaning up.

But the worrisome thoughts persisted.

Rick had become intoxicated on so many occasions that she despaired he would never stop. She imagined him losing his job, going broke, and losing the house they worked so hard for. Her mind jumped to the future, and she saw them divorced and Rick dying of alcoholism. Because Rick was her soulmate, she envisioned herself never remarrying and living alone the rest of her life. She imagined herself dying young of heartbreak. "I hate how I feel. These thoughts are driving me crazy, but I can't help myself," she lamented.

Nancy realized that her husband was addicted to alcohol, but what she did not see so clearly was that she had her own addiction—to worry. She had the habit of worrying about so many things, not just his drinking. At some level, she knew that her anxious reactions were useless and even harmful. She may have told herself, "My worry doesn't change anything. What will happen will happen. It only makes me miserable." However, the harder she tried to control herself and the circumstances of her life, the more she failed to quell her anxiety, feeling even more out of control.

Such a sense of helplessness in the face of self-defeating behavior is the essence of addiction.

Anxiety as a Drug

As a psychologist, I meet with many anxious patients like Nancy. Nearly all have said, "I hate how I feel. What can I do to get rid of it?" They have tried many strategies, including therapy, and only found temporary relief. The anxiety usually returns with a vengeance. The anxious patient is fighting a battle within herself to get rid of what she does not like about herself. That battle of self-rejection cannot be won.

Another strategy is needed.

All of us feel anxious from time to time. Anxiety and fear are normal human reactions to a perceived threat. Our bodies are activated and energized to confront the danger by fight, flight, freezing, or fainting. Our minds anticipate the negative consequences and begin planning ways of escaping or avoiding the imagined catastrophe. Both fear and anxiety serve survival purposes. They help us stay alive.

Sometimes, the warning bells can become so loud and persistent that they impair our ability to live a happy, fulfilled life. Our brain is constantly on high alert, and we cannot relax. Often we cannot sleep, and our bodies feel wired. There is tension in our neck, back, and shoulders, as we prepare to face the imagined threat. Our heart pounds, and we have difficulty breathing. We feel dizzy and sweat profusely. Our minds race uncontrollably with thoughts of terrible things happening. A sense of doom enshrouds us.

When the levels of anxiety and fear interfere with our happiness and daily living, we suffer a clinical level of anxiety, called an anxiety disorder.

If you recognize that your anxiety has crossed that line where it begins to interfere with your happiness and wellbeing, you are not alone. There is an anxiety epidemic afoot. Research indicates that anxiety disorders are the most prevalent of mental/emotional conditions. More than a quarter of the adult population (28.8%) will suffer some form of clinically significant anxiety disorder in their lifetimes (1). A recent study of mental illness among U.S. youth revealed that nearly a third of our children (31.9%) meet diagnostic criteria for an anxiety disorder, with the average age of onset at six years (2).In our fast-paced, success-driven, high-expectation society, these numbers are increasing.

If you suffer from anxiety, whether a little or a lot, you may feel enslaved by it. If you thrash helplessly in its grip, you may be addicted to your anxiety. Here are some questions you can ask yourself to determine if your anxiety is addictive:

- Do you feel overwhelmed at times by a sense of danger and helplessness?

- Do you consider your anxiety excessive, even crippling at times?

- Even though your anxious reactions are painful and harmful, do you feel powerless to stop them?

- Does your preoccupation with safety interfere with your life?

- Do you seek desperately to control your feelings and the circumstances of your life?

- Does your need for control seem excessive, interfering with your relationships?

- Do you feel hopeless about finding a cure for your anxiety?

Without realizing it, your anxiety acts like a drug that excites, numbs, and possesses you. You probably don't think of it as a drug because you do not feel any pleasant high. You hate the distressful feeling and cannot imagine deriving any benefit from it. Nevertheless, anxiety acts like a stimulant, giving you an adrenaline rush. Under its influence, you are energized. Your body tenses, ready for action, either fight or flight. Your emotions run high, intense, fast, and furious. The physical, mental, and emotional excitement numbs you to any other disturbing thoughts and feelings. Your anxiety may disguise deeper hurt and be a way of self-medicating.

It also numbs you to joyful feelings. Your focus narrows to the perception of danger and the pursuit of safety, excluding engagement in other life-enriching activities. Your life shrinks. Caught up in anxiety, your emotional reactions seem beyond your control, making you feel powerless and possessed. You feel stuck.

Anxiety—it's a hard habit to break.

Steps to Wholeness

Appreciating the addictive quality of anxiety may open the door to a different way of finding relief and enable you to be more patient with yourself. Conventional therapy has been limited in helping because it does not reach to the deeper roots of anxiety in the human psyche. Therapy, including medication, addresses the symptoms and not the underlying cause in the human condition.

In the 1930s, it became clear that psychology had failed in treating alcoholics. Carl Jung, the renowned Swiss psychologist, announced the failure and the need for a spiritual conversion. He called alcoholics "frustrated mystics" who looked for the Spirit in the spirits. Bill Wilson, a hopeless alcoholic, found recovery outside the walls of traditional psychological treatment. He and Dr. Bob Smith founded the fellowship of Alcoholics Anonymous and formulated the Twelve Steps as the guideposts of recovery. They realized from personal experience that only a spiritual conversion through a Power greater than themselves could break the chains of addiction. They quickly added that no particular religious belief or church affiliation was needed, only an openness to the depths of experience and a willingness to work the program.

Over the years, the Twelve Steps of Alcoholics Anonymous has been a powerful tool in the recovery of countless alcoholics. It has a proven track record. Its success promoted its use by others in distress: those addicted to other drugs and their family members. Today, the same Twelve Steps are used for the recovery of those who gamble, overeat, over-shop, or suffer sexual addictions. Family members are also included in the self-help program. Recognizing the addictive quality of some mood states, Emotions Anonymous groups have emerged, following the spiritual/psychological guidance of the Twelve Steps.

The Twelve Steps of Alcoholics Anonymous can help relieve suffering from anxiety. You do not have to profess any religious belief to benefit from the steps, only be an open-minded seeker. The steps draw from ancient wisdom sources, offering practical guidance to live a good life in clear, simple, straightforward language. They assume that the addictive behavior is only a symptom of a deeper problem that must be addressed for a full recovery. Even though you may experience your nervousness as touching your core, it only hides who you really are.

In simple terms, the Twelve Steps invite you to stop, look, listen, and then consciously act according to your true self. This book is an adaptation of the Twelve Steps to the problem of anxiety.

What is the result of working the steps? You move from an anxiety-driven life to a value-directed life.

A Personal Note

Many strands of my life tie together in writing this book.

I have been working as a psychologist in private practice for over twenty years. Each day I sit and listen to my patients tell me stories of their suffering and their efforts to find happiness. Their stories are always unique, heart-breaking and heart-warming. Over the years, I observed how many of my patients suffer a variety of addictions, some acknowledged and others overlooked. Most come for relief from emotional and mental pain and hardly recognize the many ways they self-medicate with drugs and activities. I also noticed the increasing number of patients who complain of being in the grip of intolerable anxiety. Since 9/11 it seems fear has taken hold of our society and found residence in many of my patients. That fear possesses many like an addiction.

Before becoming a psychologist, I served as a Catholic priest in the Archdiocese of Detroit. I worked in several different parishes. Much of my work was one-on-one counseling with parishioners who came to me to unburden themselves of their guilt and be consoled in their sorrows. I spent many hours in the confessional celebrating the Sacrament of Reconciliation, experiencing the power of God's Word to bring them relief and challenge them to live a fuller life.

As a seminarian preparing for the priesthood, I had the good fortune to study Catholic/Christian theology in depth at the Gregorian University in Rome, the heart of Roman Catholicism. I also spent a summer in India, experiencing the richness of the Eastern culture and religious traditions. Over time, it dawned on me that the spiritual traditions of the West and the East are not as irreconcilable as I imagined. Both share a unity in the practical wisdom they offer to lead a good, wholesome life.

A third life strand has enabled me to unite the wisdom of modern psychology and the ancient wisdom traditions in an unexpected way. I grew up in an alcoholic family, struggling with my own worries about the wellbeing of my family and myself. I attended Al-Anon meetings and read about Adult Children of Alcoholics, learning how much I was personally in the grip of an illness called codependency. Participating in the Al-Anon meetings and reading the literature, I came to appreciate the power of the Twelve Steps to bring freedom and wholeness to my life.

This book is the fruit of my reflections on my own life experience and that of my patients.

How to Use This Book

This book is divided into two parts. The first four chapters of part one address the nature of anxiety and its disorders, their similarity to addictions, how they develop, and how they shape the personality. The second part has thirteen chapters which present an overview of the Twelve Steps and how each of the steps can be used as a practical guide to recovering from anxiety. Practices are offered as recovery aids. The case examples are composites of the stories of various patients, with details changed sufficiently to protect their confidentiality.

The fellowship of Alcoholics Anonymous gave birth to the Twelve Steps as a path to recovery. The steps were formulated from the experience of alcoholics who gathered with a common goal, to become sober and improve their lives. They gathered in small groups to share their life experiences and work the steps. Within the fellowship, they found support, understanding, and hope.

I recommend that you not use this book alone but in a group with others who suffer like you. Emotions Anonymous is a group of those who suffer various emotional struggles, including anxiety. They gather and work the Twelve Steps of AA in a way that applies to their particular problems. You can join such a group. Check out their website to see how the groups work and where they are located.

My dream is that groups emerge that use the Twelve Steps specifically for recovery from anxiety. I would call them Anxiety Anonymous groups. You may feel inspired to gather a self-help group yourself. You are not alone in your suffering.

If you do not join a group, you can benefit working with this book alone and using the exercises at the end of the chapters to aid in your own recovery. The steps need to be worked, not just thought about.

Family members can also benefit from this book. They can come to understand and accept their own sense of powerlessness to overcome the anxiety addiction of their loved ones. Ironically, you may even find yourself becoming sick with worry caring for your anxious loved ones.

Mental health professionals who treat anxious patients may benefit from the book's presentation of a new way to think about anxiety and its treatment.

Clergy and religious may appreciate the book's suggestions that spiritual practice can enhance psychological wellbeing. It also may provide you with a new way of looking at spirituality, presented in contemporary, this-worldly language.

The anxious addictive self is a fragmented self, broken into a million little pieces. Fear torments it and tears it apart. How can you put Humpty Dumpty together again? The Twelve Steps suggest a path to wholeness by finding your center. It is a way of gaining mastery over yourself, as expressed in the Tao Te Ching (3):

The Master sees things as they are,
without trying to control them.
She lets them go their own way,
and resides at the center of the circle (29).

My wish is that this book may aid you in finding your center in the midst of your swirling, anxiety-driven life. Living from your center is the way to a joyful life.

Note: Numbers in parentheses in each chapter, e.g. (1), refer to the Endnotes, which are given by chapter at the end of the book.

Dennis Ortman, Ph.D.

Part One
Anxiety as an Addiction

Dennis Ortman, Ph.D.

The Many Faces of Anxiety:
Living in a Dangerous World

"The only thing we have to fear is fear itself."

—Franklyn D. Roosevelt

"Is the anxiety I feel my friend or my foe?" When we are in the midst of an anxiety attack, with our heart pounding, stomach churning and mind racing, we only want the pain to stop. We experience, in those moments, our anxiety as the enemy, a demon we desperately want exorcized. However, when the agitation diminishes, we may glimpse how our anxious feelings can be a helpful ally.

The answer is that anxiety is both our friend and our foe.

Anxiety and fear, like all our emotions, are completely natural and serve a survival purpose. In fact, anxiety is a sign of intelligence. Animals never experience anxiety because they live by their instincts, entirely in the present moment. We humans, in contrast, possess a mental capacity to look both backward and forward. Looking backward, we learn from our experience. We then devise strategies to meet our needs beyond the blind pursuit of the instincts we share with the animals. We sense both the paths and obstacles to having our desires met in a world that competes for limited resources. Looking forward, we project into the future. We recognize potential threats to our wellbeing and make plans so we can survive and thrive.

Anxiety and fear signal danger. These reactions are hardwired in the brain from time immemorial. Because we live in a world fraught with danger, we were born with brains on high alert. With our intelligence, we are exquisitely sensitive to danger and our lack of control over our world, which can harm us in countless ways.

When the danger to our wellbeing is immediate and specific, we react with fear. We feel a surge of panic. Our attention narrows, and our body tenses to fight, flee, freeze, or faint in response to the perceived threat. We are ready to take immediate action.

When the threat is in the more distant future and less clear, the anxious mind takes over to identify and prepare for the coming danger. Because the future does not yet exist, the anxiety and accompanying worrisome thoughts imagine what can go wrong. Anxiety heightens our awareness of future problems and spurs us to make constructive plans of action to avert the possible crisis. The worry, the persistent replaying of negative thoughts, keeps us focused on the task at hand. As one patient told me, "Worry is my motivator."

Anxiety reveals the edge of our comfort zone. If we never experience anxiety, we may be too complacent and stagnant. We experience anxiety when we bump against and challenge our limits. It is a sign of growing pains.

Anxiety, worry, fear, and panic possess their own wisdom.

These unpleasant reactions arise from the depths of our wise minds. They alert us to the fact that despite all our efforts to pursue our desires and live forever, we live under the constant threat of losing it all. The specter of death haunts us. Despite all our striving toward enlightenment and gaining absolute control over ourselves and our world, we cannot dispel the darkness, mystery, and unpredictability of life. These painful emotional reactions compel us to look more deeply into our lives to find its meaning.

They are also steppingstones to humility.

There is a famous story from the Buddhist tradition that expresses well our sense of groundlessness and inescapable danger. It also suggests a way through it. A man runs through the jungle chased by a ferocious tiger. He reaches the edge of a high cliff and looks over the precipice. There is nowhere to go. To save himself from the pursuing tiger, he climbs over the edge of the cliff and hangs onto a vine. Looking up, he sees the tiger swiping at him with its claws and notices a mouse gnawing away at the vine. Looking below, he can hardly see the rocky ground because it is so far away. Then he notices a luscious red strawberry on the vine. He plucks it, takes a small bite, and says to himself, "Ah, what a delicious strawberry!" He escapes anxiety by engaging fully in the present moment.

Some Definitions

- Anxiety: sensing future danger with no clear target of fear.
- Fear: reacting to an immediate threat.
- Panic: fright over danger of bodily sensations.
- Phobia: fear of a specific person, place, or thing.

Anxiety and fear in the right measure enhance our lives.

Imagine a world without anxiety or fear. Would it be heaven or hell? If we are tormented by excessive anxiety, it may seem like a paradise. But think again. Without fear to restrain us, we would become reckless in our behavior. Sooner or later, we would ignore dangers and harm ourselves seriously, even fatally.

As any athlete knows, the right measure of nervousness keeps them sharp and focused to play the game. Keyed-up, attention narrowed, anxiety puts them in the zone for peak performance. Anxiety signals being stretched to the edge of our limits. Unfortunately, many of us experience intense levels of anxiety, worry, fear, and panic that interfere with our living and wellbeing. We experience our emotional lives as the enemy. The following is a sketch of anxiety over the edge. In clinical terms, these emotions are classified as anxiety disorders.

Panic

Larry, a Middle-Aged Man: First Panic Attack

Larry, a middle-aged man, reported his first panic attack: "I've always prided myself at being healthy and keeping myself fit. I go to the gym five days a week and watch what I eat. I'm fifty years old and have never missed a day of work because I was sick. I go to the doctor regularly for checkups and have always had a clean bill of health. I must admit I was mildly shocked when the doctor told me I needed hernia surgery. He described the procedure and how I would need general anesthesia but kept reassuring me that it was really no big deal. I scheduled the surgery for two weeks later.

One day, as I was driving to work, I suddenly felt overwhelmed with a sense of doom. I'd never felt that way before. I felt a tightening in my chest that concerned me and had difficulty breathing. My immediate thought was that I was having a heart attack. I tried to dismiss it, telling myself I had just had a physical. When my heart pounded more wildly, I really got scared and pulled the car off to the side of the road. I began sweating profusely and felt certain this was the end. My life flashed before my eyes. Before I passed out, I fumbled with the phone to call my wife who called an ambulance to take me to the hospital. She was as terrified as I was at that moment."

A panic attack comes on a clear day like a sudden, unexpected thunderstorm of fear. You are caught unaware by the suddenness of the lightning strike. Stricken with intense fear and dread, you feel strong physical sensations throughout your body. Your body is drenched with fear. You experience palpitations, pounding heart, chest pains, or accelerated heart rate that leads you to think you are having a heart attack. You tremble and sweat or feel chills and hot flashes. Experiencing shortness of breath, you feel like you are smothering. Your stomach churns with nausea or abdominal distress, and you feel as if you are choking. You feel dizzy, unsteady, lightheaded, or faint. Your panic-stricken body is energized to meet imagined dangers from within.

An out of control mind matches your body. Worries fill your mind that something catastrophic is happening to you, that you are dying, losing control, or going crazy. Your imagination runs wild. After the attack, you live in dread of being stricken again, unexpectedly, out of the blue.

Panic attacks drive more people to the hospital than any other anxiety disorder because the physical reaction is so powerful.

Agoraphobia

Jan, Career Woman: Reaction to Being Laid Off

Jan, a career woman, shared her reaction to being laid-off: "Work has been my whole life. For the past twenty-five years, I've been working as an office manager, moving up to become the executive secretary to the owner of a large company. My world fell apart when my boss, who had become a close friend, called me into his office to tell me that the company had been bought out. He was retiring, and I would be out of a job. I couldn't believe what he was telling me; it didn't seem real. We both cried, and he apologized profusely.

I fell into a deep depression. My husband tried to comfort me as best he could, but I was inconsolable. I stayed home and slept a lot. When the black mood began to lift, I ventured out of the house, trying to resume my normal activities.

Then, I noticed something else happening to me that was terrifying. When I was at the grocery store in the checkout line, I suddenly felt like I was choking to death. I couldn't breathe, and my heart was pounding. One thought occupied my brain, "I have to get out of here." I left the cart, desperate to get home. I cautiously tried to run errands, to resume a normal life, but panic set in and fear that I would have another attack. I became afraid of going out of the house. Over time, I gave up driving altogether."

For some, the world is a threatening place, and they are in constant search for safety. When you are afraid of crowds or the outdoors, you may feel like a helpless newborn thrust into a cruel world, wanting only to return to the comfort and security of the womb. When you venture out of your safe place, you are afraid that you may become overwhelmed with anxiety or panic and not get help. You always want an escape route to safety, which may not always be readily available.

Your life begins to shrink.

To cope with your fear of being exposed in a state of panic, you begin to restrict your activities. You avoid driving or going to grocery stores, malls, and restaurants. You may plead that your spouse accompany you wherever you go just to feel safe. Your medication is always at hand. You never venture far from home for long; your world begins to shrink, and you isolate yourself. You refuse more and more invitations from family and friends, hesitating even to answer the phone. Embarrassed, you don't want to explain your silly fear.

Phobia

Joe: Fear of Flying

Joe discussed his fear of flying: "I'm a big man, and because of my size, people have always respected me. But I have some secrets that I've been able to hide from everyone except for those closest to me. I'm terrified of flying, and I'm ashamed of that. It shows weakness. Even the thought of getting on a plane causes me to tremble inside and feel like I'm on the verge of a panic attack. People tell me that flying is safer than driving and how rare plane crashes really are, but all the reasoning in the world won't change my emotional reaction.

Many times flying for business would save me time and money, but I always choose to drive or take the train instead. My wife, who loves to travel, tries to convince me to get drunk or drugged when I get on the plane but to no avail. Even if I were drugged unconscious during the flight, the dread before the flight would nearly kill me.

I have another little secret that only my family knows. As a child, I was terrified of vomiting, of my insides coming out and me dying from it. Terrified of getting sick, I often covered my mouth in public and avoided my sick siblings like the plague. I watched what I ate and noticed any stomach rumblings. Any time my stomach hurt, I worried about vomiting. When I became anxious, my stomach hurt, which caused me to be more anxious, and my stomach to hurt more. It was a merry-go-round nightmare that kept me on the edge of panic. Fortunately, I haven't vomited in over 25 years, but the specter of it still haunts me."

All the threats to our life and limb are not only in your imagination. There are real dangers in your world, and you have been biologically programmed to identify and react to the threat. Everyone fears the possibility of something terrible happening. You avoid what you perceive as dangerous people, places, or things.

However, your fear of some object or situation may become excessive and seem unreasonable. You go out of your way to avoid it. If your avoidance does not cause too much inconvenience, you go about your business. If it interferes with your life and causes you distress or embarrassment, you may recognize it as a true phobia. Spiders, insects, dogs, or various animals may frighten you, and you just avoid them. You may fear heights, closed-in places, water, darkness, or storms, which may be a little harder to avoid completely. If you fear flying, driving, tunnels, or bridges, your life becomes more restricted in our fast-moving world. You may fear anything to do with blood, such as having an injection, blood test, or surgery, which can become a real problem when you require medical attention. Fearing sensations, such as choking, vomiting, or being sick may keep you often on edge.

All those feared objects and activities mirror the insecurity you experience inside about life.

Social Anxiety

Rodney: Fear of Being around People

Rodney commented on his fear of being around people: "When I sit at a table in a restaurant, I test myself. I hold the cup of coffee and watch how much my hand shakes. I notice that the more people around me, the more my hand shakes, and the worse I feel about myself. I'm afraid of exposing to others how nervous I feel around people.

I can't stand being in crowds or at parties. I think everyone is watching me, noticing how much I shake and judging me as a freak. I've declined more party invitations than I can count. If I feel obligated to attend some social gathering, the dread nearly incapacitates me. My stomach ties up in knots, and I imagine being humiliated. It's being humiliated I fear more than anything else.

I know how irrational my fears are, and I know when they all started. I was shy as a child and had terrible acne as a teenager. Kids made fun of my looks. My parents took me for all kinds of treatments to get rid of the acne. I've been self-conscious about my looks ever since.

As a teen, I found a magical way to cope with my anxiety. I drank. Before any gathering with family, friends, or strangers, I took a drink—and then several drinks. That was the only way I could relax. Over time, the drinks added up, and I began drinking to relax even when I wasn't going out. My drinking nearly cost me my job and marriage, so I stopped. I lost a friend in alcohol, a lifesaver in social situations. Now I am adrift, alone, and terrified around people, with no escape. The Valium my doctor prescribes barely gives me relief."

We are by nature social animals, living in and through relationships. Ironically, the most common type of anxiety is social anxiety, the fear of being embarrassed in a social situation. Many celebrities, such as Barbra Streisand, Donny Osmond, and Hugh Grant, experience overwhelming performance anxiety and push themselves to keep their careers going. Most everyone feels some nervousness being the center of attention.

However, your fear of being in some social settings may become crippling. You may, like many others, fear speaking in public, conscious of everyone watching and judging you. All eyes are on you. You may become extremely self-conscious eating in public or even urinating in a public restroom. Simple conversations with any stranger, such as sales persons or waiters, may cause you to shrink in fear. You fear making a mistake and appearing foolish. Of course, you want to spare yourself the embarrassment of others knowing that you're nervous and how inadequate you feel. A dreadful sense of being watched and judged negatively consumes you in social gatherings, which leads to an avoidance of being with people and a terrible loneliness.

Many with social phobias drink or use drugs to help them relax and end up with another problem, a chemical dependency.

Generalized Anxiety

Alice, a Housewife: Crippled by Worry

Alice, a housewife, related how worry cripples her: "Every morning I wake up with a sense of dread, thinking about everything I have to do and how little time I have to do it. Seldom do I enjoy a good night's sleep. When I do, I thank God. Usually, it takes me a long time to fall asleep because my mind runs through the day and all the things I did wrong. When I finally do get to sleep, I toss and turn, awakened by disturbing dreams I can never remember. I awaken before the alarm clock goes off, feeling weary, like I never slept.

I begin each day exhausted and worried about some impending doom. I feel so tense all the time, unable to relax as I begin my daily chores. My husband goes to work early, before I get up, and the kids are grown, living on their own. I am alone with my thoughts all day. They are such troubling thoughts that I pray constantly they will leave my mind before I go crazy. I think about my family most of all, wondering what they are doing. Then suddenly, I imagine my husband getting into an auto accident on the way to work or the children getting sick without me to take care of them. I call the children each day, just to be reassured that they are okay. The worry is so useless, dragging me down, but I can't stop it, no matter what I do to distract myself."

When the black cloud of worry follows you wherever you go, it blocks out the sunlight of happiness and peace. Your mind imagines terrible things happening to your family, your health, and your finances. You worry about the most trivial things, like your appliances breaking down, and cannot get the tormenting thoughts out of your mind. As hard as you try, you cannot escape the shadow of worry. It even invades your sleep and dreams.

Perceiving danger around every corner of your life, you live in a constant state of readiness to confront some danger, real or imagined. Neither your mind nor your body relaxes. You feel tense, restless, shaky, and fatigued. Your heart races like your thoughts, and your stomach and bowels mirror your mental distress. You may sweat, feel flushed, and have trouble breathing and swallowing. You always feel keyed up, are easily startled, and have difficulty concentrating. The worry exhausts you mentally and physically.

The symptoms of this generalized anxiety nearly overlap with those of depression. Both anxiety and depression are reactions to loss, the one anticipated and the other already suffered. Both manifest symptoms of poor concentration, sleep disturbance, and irritability.

Obsessive Compulsive Disorder

Jeff, a High School Student: Obsessive Thoughts

Jeff, a high school student, complained of obsessive thoughts: "The thought hit me as I was walking to my fourth period class that I was going to kill myself. The thought terrified me. I didn't know where it came from, and I couldn't get it out of my head. I was raised Catholic, and I go to church every week. I say my prayers daily, without fail, with a regular routine. I say three Our Fathers and three Hail Marys ten times each day. The idea of suicide horrifies me because I believe I would go immediately to hell if I killed myself.

When the thought of killing myself persisted, I prayed more each day the same prayers, hoping God would spare me this cross. I went to confession to tell the priest that I had this unrelenting thought and assured him I would never do anything to hurt myself because I was a religious person. The priest tried to reassure me and advised that I see a counselor, which I did. Talking with the therapist helped. The suicidal thoughts became less frequent, but the sense of dread that I could hurt myself and go to hell remained a long time."

The greatest loss of freedom occurs when your mind is possessed by unwanted thoughts, images, or urges. A stranger has moved in, and you cannot make him leave. Where can you go to escape your own mind? You are its captive, a prisoner. The thoughts are more intense and consuming than worry although not as pervasive. You may have specific, unshakable thoughts about harming yourself or others, of being contaminated, of doubting what you know to be true. You know these thoughts are irrational and somehow come from your own mind, but you cannot make them go away. The thoughts also frighten you because you imagine terrible things happening.

How do you find safety?

You establish rituals and routines to give you a sense of control over your uncontrollable mind. You find comfort in hand-washing, counting, checking, or repeating phrases, knowing full well that the repetitive behavior is excessive. You resort to magic and rituals to find safety in your threatening world. Those with severe obsessive-compulsive disorder can be so crippled by the condition that they need to be hospitalized.

Post-Traumatic Stress

Jennifer: The Terror Lives On

Jennifer discussed the impact of being molested as a child: "It happened so long ago that it surprises me no end how much I am still affected. I never told anyone what happened for many years and buried it deep inside, never to see the light of day. But when I was dating my future husband and he wanted sex, the horror of what happened to me as a child overwhelmed me. I had no idea why I became so frozen to his touch and began to tremble uncontrollably.

Then the terrible nightmares began. I dreamt of dark figures attacking me in my bed and feeling totally defenseless. The anxiety drove me to see a therapist who listened and made me feel comfortable when I wanted to jump out of my skin. Over time, the memories began to leak out in little drips and then in torrents. I saw that shadowy figure in my dreams as my stepfather who used to climb into bed with me and rub me under the covers. I remember feeling terrified and confused, knowing it was not right, something never to be spoken about. In fact, I remember him telling me it was our little secret.

I dug a deep hole in my soul to bury those memories, but they came flooding back when I least expected it. Suddenly, something reminded me of my monster stepfa-

ther, and I relived the horror of so many nights in my bedroom. Anxiety followed me everywhere, and I never trusted anyone, mostly myself. Danger lurked everywhere. Yet, I could not put my finger on precisely what the danger was, only that I was vulnerable and could be hurt. I could not relax, ever vigilant of being hurt.

Mercifully, over time, with therapy and medication, the nightmares faded away."

No one escapes life without being wounded, but some experience such deep wounds that recovery may take a lifetime. You may have experienced a severe life-threatening event that you cannot seem to get over. Many war veterans have been traumatized by the experience of combat. Your life, either psychologically or physically, may have been threatened by an auto accident, natural disaster, crime, or physical or sexual assault as a child or adult. Your partner may have cheated on you.

Ever resourceful, your psyche finds a way of surviving without your conscious effort. You numb your feelings and block off the painful memory, mercifully forgetting it. Yet, the lid of that black box of pain suddenly opens, and you are flooded with the memories and feelings of that forgotten event. You experience flashbacks and nightmares. You often feel anxious and depressed without knowing fully the cause. You avoid anything that may remind you of the traumatic event, activities, places, or thoughts about it. You begin to lose interest in life and detach yourself from it for your own protection. Your future seems dim, and you become watchful and alert for trouble to overtake you. There is no respite from your fear that you will be traumatized again. Your pain is buried under a blanket of anxiety.

More Definitions

- Panic Disorder: abrupt surges of intense fear with strong physical sensations.

- Agoraphobia: fear of having a panic attack in an unprotected place.

- Phobia: overwhelming fear of a specific object or situation.

- Social Anxiety Disorder: self-consciousness and anxiety in social situations.

- Generalized Anxiety Disorder: chronic worry about terrible things happening.

- Obsessive-Compulsive Disorder: consuming unwanted thoughts and behaviors.

- Post-Traumatic Stress: aftermath of terrifying, dangerous event.

Is anxiety and fear a blessing or a curse? It is both.

Anxiety and fear, the natural survival emotions, can be experienced along a continuum. These reactions, of course, can be beneficial in helping you to be alert to potential dangers and make plans for the future. Your intelligence makes you cautious when circumstances require it. However, your anxiety and fear can escalate to the point that it interferes with your living a full life. You feel threatened and helpless in specific situations or you sense danger around every corner and live in a helpless state of constant dread. You cannot escape your anxiety. It possesses you with the power of an addiction.

Many cope with their anxiety and fears by using alcohol and drugs to calm themselves. If that becomes a regular habit, they are at risk of developing another problem, a chemical dependency. Research shows that nearly 30% (28.3%) of those suffering from anxiety disorders also have a chemical dependency (1). We have no accurate numbers of those who self-medicate from time to time to manage their anxiety. There appears to be an overlapping of both anxiety and addiction, with manner of coping with anxiety and fear causing more problems than the discomfort of the feelings.

2

Addicted to Anxiety:
Trying to Control the Uncontrollable

"Ultimately we know deeply that the other side of fear is freedom."

—Marilyn Ferguson

Gripped by fear or anxiety, your first thought is a desperate cry, "Help me get rid of it!" You just want to escape. Anyone telling you to calm down infuriates you. "You don't understand what I'm feeling. I can't calm down," you protest. You feel possessed by the painful emotion, powerless to cast out the demon. You may be in such pain, afraid that you will die, that you prefer death to a continuation of the anxious suffering.

Body and mind both rebel.

Your body reacts with uncontrollable sweat, trembling, and tension. Your heart pounds, your breath shallows, and your stomach churns. Your mind mirrors your body, running wildly with terrifying thoughts. When you hear, "Just stop worrying," you want to scream. It is as senseless as someone telling a drug addict, "Just say 'no' to drugs."

If you consider for a moment your sense of powerlessness while under the influence of anxiety, you can understand the experience of an alcoholic who cannot stop drinking. In fact, anxiety, especially severe anxiety, is like a drug that captures and enslaves you. You cannot escape its influence as hard as you try even though you know the harm it causes you.

It begins to rule and take over your life. You start changing your habits and altering your routines to avoid becoming anxious. Before you know it, you build a lifestyle in the pursuit of a sense of safety to escape the dread of fear and anxiety. Surprisingly, you may even experience a subtle pleasure in the nerve-wracking chase after security.

The experience of anxiety parallels that of addiction to alcohol and other drugs. The following are characteristics of both anxiety and addiction:

- trapped in bittersweet excess;

- fooling yourself, nobody else;

- déjà vu all over again;

- wondering who's in charge;

- starved and power hungry;

- running away from pain and life;

- Hopelessly incurable.

Let me briefly explain how the experience of the alcoholic, as an example of an addicted person, overlaps with what you experience with anxiety.

Trapped in Bittersweet Excess

"One drink is too much, and a thousand drinks are not enough." That slogan from Alcoholics Anonymous expresses clearly what the alcoholic learns through bitter experience. But that truth is realized, normally, after a period of time. Initially, the alcoholic begins drinking like everyone else. Drinking helps him relax and enjoy his friends. He likes the way he feels, and others enjoy his company. It gives him pleasure. He discovers the mood and mind-altering effect of alcohol and begins to drink to relieve stress, to calm his nerves, and to make his sadness disappear. Alcohol becomes his faithful friend who accompanies him through all the joys and sorrows, the celebrations, and the trials of life. He only sees benefits from imbibing.

But the honeymoon does not last.

If an addiction begins to take hold, a subtle shift occurs in the pattern of drinking. The budding alcoholic starts to look forward to drinking on any occasion. When he drinks, he consumes more and more to achieve the same buzz. Without realizing it, he is developing tolerance to his drug, needing more to produce the same effect. Two drinks become four, which over time become six to twelve.

The mind changes with the behaviors. The reason for drinking shifts from wanting it to feel good to needing it to feel normal. Pain relief replaces pleasure-seeking as a motive. With the increased drinking and intoxicated binges, problems with family, friends, work, and health mount. At that point, if the alcoholic honestly faces himself, he admits that his drinking is excessive and out of control.

Sue: Lifelong Struggle with Anxiety

"I remember being shy as a child and afraid of going to school. I thought something terrible might happen to my parents when I was away from them. As I grew older and took on the responsibilities of life, my worries mounted. Now I worry about my children, my husband losing his job, and my health. I worry about the weather, the economy, and the silliest things, like the pipes breaking in the house. It's become too much for me. I realize that my worry is excessive, but I can't help it. My friends

tell me all the time that I have nothing to worry about, but their reassurances only make me feel worse, like something is terribly wrong with me for worrying so much."

Your anxiety may begin as a small seed in childhood, hardly noticed and easily reassured. You may have brief anxious moments that you attribute to a shy personality. But over time, those anxious moments may increase in both frequency and intensity. You find yourself worrying about more and more things that seem so trivial when you stop and think about it. You discover fears of animals, places, and situations that baffle your logical mind.

Your fear moves like a gathering storm. And you build dikes.

Just to feel safe, you develop more and more routines and avoid places and activities. Your discomfort zone expands, squeezing out moments of relaxation and happiness. You perceive your world as increasingly dangerous and yourself as helpless to protect yourself. You develop increasing intolerance for what you fear, avoiding anxiety-provoking situations. At some point, it may dawn on you that your anxiety is excessive, taking over your life like a cancer.

Fear rules your life, and you are not in charge.

Both addictive and anxiety disorders are marked by excess, although the pleasure of anxiety is minimal. Alcoholics drink more and oftener than others while those suffering from anxiety have more fears and more intense anxiety than most people. The excess spills over in many ways. Most of the addicted abuse several drugs. Like a shell game, when something interferes with their drinking, like a DUI, they switch to another drug of choice, like marijuana or Xanax. The symptoms of anxiety also cannot be contained. One patient of mine picked her skin as a child, pulled her hair as a teen, and cleaned excessively as an adult.

Fooling Yourself, Nobody Else

"Denial is not just a river in Egypt," AA reminds its members. Denial allows addictions to continue. Alcoholics are notoriously the last to acknowledge that their drinking is out of control and interfering with their lives. They rationalize their drinking, insisting on its benefits in helping them to relax and socialize. "What's wrong with having a couple of drinks?" they ask. Their family counts more accurately, recognizing that a "couple drinks" is really five or six.

Alcoholics are also masters at making excuses, blaming the hardships of life or the strain of their relationships for their need to drink. "What's wrong with getting away from it all for an evening?" they ask seriously. Again, the family sees more clearly the havoc of their innocent escape from the responsibilities of life.

The alcoholic may not ever remember, because of a blackout, their crazy behavior when intoxicated. However, those around them remember all too well. Even if the drinker, remorseful the day after, remembers what he did, he forgets it when the next drinking bout begins. Reminded of the turmoil he caused while intoxicated, he indulges in "euphoric recall" of the pleasure he felt while buzzed. Unfortunately, often only a catastrophe will awaken him from the slumber of self-deception.

Jake, an Ambitious Businessman: Wake-Up Call

Jake, an ambitious businessman, related: "Sure, I felt stress. Doesn't everybody, at least those who want to succeed in life? I ran my own business and pushed myself to be successful. My father taught me to work hard and reminded me that nothing worthwhile comes easy. I lived by that philosophy, worked hard, and never thought about the price my family and I were paying. My wife complained constantly about me working too much and being absent from the family. I reminded her how much she and the kids enjoyed the lifestyle my hard work provided.

My denial crumbled in an instant when I had a panic attack and thought I was dying. I went to the hospital, and the doctor told me it was my nerves. That was a wake-up call. I never realized how unhealthy my lifestyle had become in my obsessive pursuit of success and how much I hurt my family."

We live in a fast-paced, success-driven culture and have come to believe that a stressful life is normal and unavoidable. What we benignly call stress is really another word for anxiety. Our national delusion is that an anxiety-filled life leads to a productive life.

You may share that delusion and not recognize how that unacknowledged anxiety affects the quality of your life. You focus on your goals, making money, gaining status, or impressing others, not paying attention to its cost to you and your loved ones. Even if you do recognize the anxious driven-ness of your life, you do not want to give up the benefits of your hard work—until some emergency grabs your attention.

Our culture also stigmatizes mental illness and all addictions, believing them a result of moral weakness. You may share that delusion, which makes you reluctant to admit any problems with anxiety or to seek psychiatric help. That would be a confession of a personal defect, a humiliation. Instead, you minimize the suffering your fears and anxiety cause you. A calm façade hides the fright. You ignore your body's warning signs of distress and the pleas of those who love you to get help.

How miserable do you need to feel before you ask for help?

Both the addicted and the anxious ignore clear warnings signs from their bodies, their family, and their friends. Because they are so accustomed to their lifestyles, they do not want to admit a problem until some catastrophe, some collision with reality, awakens them to the harmfulness of their behavior.

Déjà Vu All Over Again

All addictions begin with "stinking thinking." After many experiences of the soothing effects of alcohol, a tranquilizer, the budding alcoholic begins to believe that she can find happiness in a bottle and cannot live without it. She continually tells herself, "I need a drink," whether she is anxious, sad, angry, or happy. She rationalizes many reasons for drinking. Over time, as the addiction takes hold, she becomes more preoccupied with the thought of drinking. It becomes her obsession. She begins to plan her life around drinking opportunities on weekends with friends or at home alone to chill out.

Her obsession with drinking spills over into compulsive behaviors. She develops drinking routines, going to the same bar every Friday evening, meeting the same people. Cocktail hour, with the same drink, mixed in the same way, happens every day at precisely 4:00 p.m. She may make rigid rules for herself to assure herself that she is not an alcoholic, never drinking alone or in the morning.

Slowly, she builds a lifestyle around her drinking and activities that include alcohol, such as bowling, golfing, or playing cards. All her friends share her passion for alcohol, enjoying the same rituals and routines, while her nondrinking friends fall by the wayside. Over time, the repetitions around alcohol become deeply engrained in the psyche, a habit difficult to break.

Jane, a Housewife with a Compulsion to Clean: Running on a Hamster Wheel

"I had the vague fear that if my house weren't clean and in order, something terrible would happen. I wasn't quite sure what that terrible thing would be, but I couldn't dislodge the thought from my mind. Morning to night I either cleaned the house or thought about doing it.

When guests were coming, I'd obsess for a week about how I would make time to clean so I wouldn't be embarrassed. I just could not relax during parties because I was always watching for what needed to be picked up and kept running around. When the children played, my sole thought, rather than enjoying them, was worrying about the mess they were making and how I would clean it up. I was exhausting myself NS felt like I was running on a hamster wheel."

Fearful and anxious, your life preoccupation is to feel safe and secure. Danger lurks around every corner. "I always imagine the worst so I will be prepared," you tell yourself. You obsess about dangers in social situations, encountering dreaded objects, or simply being exposed. You also obsess about what you can do to be safe. Worry becomes your middle name, and you find yourself constantly planning to prevent things from going wrong.

At times, you go to great lengths to avoid threatening thoughts or situations. You may develop routines and rituals to ensure safety, such as praying, counting, or cleaning, which become compulsive behaviors. You may lose yourself in your job or in playing some role in life instead of being yourself. Rules govern your life, giving you a sense of security. Without realizing it, the four Rs direct you: routines, rituals, roles, and rules. You begin to live your life on automatic pilot so that nothing is unpredictable. Fearing the unknown, you structure your life in such a way that there are no surprises.

You become a creature of habit, and eventually, its prisoner.

No one is more conservative in their thinking and behavior than the addict and the anxious person. Both survive in a cruel world by predictability, by repeating the same thoughts and behaviors over and over. Both find safety and security in their routines, which they believe will magically protect them. These habits become engrained with many years of repetition.

Who's in charge around here?

The alcoholic is a person of many disguises. When drinking, he may appear rowdy, rude, and rebellious, but when he is sober, another person emerges who is often remorseful, sad, and broken. Dr. Jekyll by day, he is transformed into a drinking Mr. Hyde by night.

In reality, most alcoholics are sensitive people who feel overwhelmed by life. They live with a sense of helplessness, possess a tragic sense of life, and rage against their lack of control. Most have suffered traumas and struggle to find a way to cope. The remedy they stumble upon to gain a sense of control over their life is alcohol. Alcohol, they imagine, will save them. And it does, for a brief moment.

As the illness progresses, what the alcoholic imagines will save him begins to enslave him. Seeking control over his life through alcohol, he begins losing control. When he starts drinking, he is never sure when he will stop. He may restrain his drinking from time to time, but, eventually, the loss of control is more frequent and devastating. Initially, he tells himself, "I can stop whenever I want," but as the failed attempts pile up, he admits, "I can't stop," and may resign himself to a life of misery. He may perceive the harm he causes himself and those he loves by his drinking, but he feel powerless to quit. When the urge to drink comes, he cannot resist it. When he takes the first drink, he cannot predict his last. Alcohol has taken over his life. As the saying goes, "First, the man takes the drink; then, the drink takes the drink; and finally, the drink takes the man."

Jeremy, Self-Proclaimed Worry Wart: Give Me Back My Life!

Jeremy, a self-proclaimed "worry wart," complained: "I can't understand myself. I worry about the most ridiculous things, but I can't help it. I know that what I'm worrying about is irrational. In fact, it's downright harmful. I'm so miserable with my worrisome thoughts. I can't stop my crazy mind from running away with itself. The crazy thoughts keep me awake at night, and I feel so exhausted the next day. Give me back my life."

The core of anxiety is a sense of helplessness and lack of control in the face of perceived danger. Because you were born with an exquisite sensitivity to danger and likely suffered many hardships because of it, alarm bells go off when you sense a threat. The danger may be real or imagined, often exaggerated, yet you react with the same emotional intensity. Like painful withdrawal symptoms, when you approach something you fear, a loud, nerve-wracking alarm sounds that makes your body tremble.

Once your panic, worry or anxiety begins, it gathers momentum like a large snowball tumbling down a mountain, growing larger and gaining speed until it crashes at the bottom. Only physical and mental exhaustion can stop your frightful episode. You realize how irrational and harmful your anxiety and worry are, yet the anxious urge seems irresistible. You may try many strategies to regain a sense of control over your emotional life, such as thought stopping, relaxation techniques, or distraction, but nothing really works. If you are fortunate, you may turn down the volume a bit, but you can never still the roar of the avalanche.

The core of both anxiety and addiction is the loss of control. At some level, both the addicted and the anxious individuals realize that they are under the influence of a power greater than themselves, but they feel powerless to disengage. Both see themselves as help-less victims in life.

Starved and Power-Hungry

Alcoholics Anonymous describes alcoholics as "self-centered in the extreme," whose trouble is caused by "the misuse of willpower." Feeling so helpless and out of control, the alcoholic craves power and control.

When he first begins drinking, the alcoholic discovers the magical quality of alcohol to transform his moods and personality. He enjoys the pleasurable feeling of intoxication and escaping painful reality. With time and experience, he finds in alcohol the means to control his mind, mood, and world whenever he wants. Alcohol is his personal genie in a bottle.

If he desires escape from unwanted thoughts, he takes a drink to alter his mind and transport himself into another world. If he feels overwhelmed by feelings of sadness, anxiety, or anger, he drinks to numb himself. He has the power to "make the world go away" if there is something about his life or his circumstances he does not like. He proclaims alcohol a wonder drug, the elixir of life.

As the alcoholic's drinking increases and the addiction takes hold, the miracle drug that freed him begins to control him. The instrument he used to master his world now enslaves him. That bitter truth is hard for the alcoholic to admit. He cannot tolerate the disillusionment and giving up the drug he depends on. Instead, he redoubles his efforts to control his life, his drinking, and those around him. He blames others for his problems and attempts to change his drinking pattern. As his efforts at control inevitably fail, he feels defeated. His low self-esteem drives him to try harder to exercise power and control. He drinks more.

And the vicious, downward spiral continues.

Melanie: Control Freak

"What I hate more than anything else is the unknown. So, I try to manage all the details of my life. I keep everything in my life neat, clean, and orderly. I live a life of tidy routine and find comfort in predictability. I'm careful not to let anyone interfere with my routines and schedules. Otherwise, I become too anxious and upset. I know the future is unknown because it doesn't yet exist. I'm not stupid. Yet, I have the notion that if I could control the future I would be perfectly happy."

How do you find safety and security when you are anxious? You likely try to exert control over your life, and possibly over others' lives. Scratch the surface of a "worry wart," and you find a "control freak."

Fear and anxiety arise from a sense of helplessness, of lacking control. Your only defense against feeling overwhelmed in a world experienced as dangerous is to take charge of your life. You try to create safety zones for yourself in your rituals, routines, and rules. You attempt to eliminate unpredictability, letting the three Cs govern your life, that is, an unending search for certainty, clarity, and control.

Your mind is your chosen instrument of domination. You obsess about what can go wrong and make plans to prepare yourself for any possible catastrophe. You see worry as your powerful ally even though it exhausts you. Your brain, always on high alert, causes you to scan your environment for possible threats. You take evasive action, avoiding any situations or activities that make you feel uncomfortable. You expect others to follow your safety program, reprimanding them for their recklessness or for interfering with your routines.

All your exhausting efforts to control your life and your world inevitably fail. Unexpected, unwanted events always happen. Your fear and anxiety spike in reaction. That only reinforces your sense of danger and makes you redouble your efforts at control. You continue fighting for power and control until you either collapse or give up your fearful illusions.

Anger resides close to the surface in both addicted and anxious persons. They are angry that they have so little control over their lives. To compensate, they attempt to control their own lives, others' lives, and their environment. Their friends and family sense the aggressiveness in their efforts to control them and may rebel. Their rebellion only fuels the addicted and anxious persons to redouble their efforts.

And the vicious cycle of power-seeking escalates.

Running Away from Pain and Life

Alcoholism arises from suffering and is a means to relieve suffering. Most alcoholics, contrary to popular belief, are sensitive souls searching for something more in life. Imagine the joy when drinkers discover in alcohol a power greater than themselves to relieve them of their suffering and give them some pleasure. It offers a quick fix, a magical cure. It eliminates the need to work at developing coping skills, which require so much time and effort. And it works, at least for a moment, until the ravages of addiction cause their own brand of pain.

Pain grabs our attention and makes us focus on relief. Exquisitely sensitive to pain, alcoholics make it their life mission to avoid pain. Finding a solution to the problem of pain in alcohol, they devote themselves more to the pursuit of drinking, building a lifestyle around it. But as the drinking itself, the hangovers and backlash, cause more pain, the urge to escape through the bottle increases. Over time, attention is withdrawn from the responsibilities and activities of daily living. In the desperate desire to escape pain, they avoid living fully. The alcoholic becomes imprisoned in the narrow confines of the bottle.

Lisa's Social Anxiety: Having to Get Out of the Room

> *"It's too uncomfortable for me to socialize in a group. I think everyone is watching me, judging how I look and every move I make. Sometimes I feel a panic attack coming on and simply have to get out of the room. So, I spend a lot of time alone playing computer games. I suppose my anxiety protects me from the danger of being rejected by people. That would be too painful to bear."*

You may think to yourself, "I hate feeling anxious and would do anything to get rid of it." Consciously, you hate your anxiety, but unconsciously, you may love it. That probably sounds ridiculous to you. "How can I love anything so painful?" you ask.

Consider for a moment the benefits of your fear and anxiety, the pleasure they afford in a sense of safety. They alert you to danger so that you can protect yourself. Your painful emotional reaction serves to protect you from the risk of an even deeper hurt, for example, social rejection, health threats, or even loss of life. Your anxious reaction wakes you up to danger and protects you from harm. Your obsessive negative thoughts also fill the void of uncertainty, which can arouse a more intense anxiety.

Your sensitivity to danger and preoccupation with being safe can begin to dominate your life. Your pursuit of safety and security narrows your focus of attention to what can harm you. Danger lurks everywhere.

For protection, you begin to build walls around yourself. The walls of your enclosure are routines, rules, rituals, and play roles that exclude the unpredictable. Living according to the four Rs, you also exclude novelty and creativity. Your anxious avoidance of pain results in your world shrinking, your happiness fleeting. Your walls of safety imprison you in a very tight, dark place, isolated from a full life. What do you lose? The joy, happiness, and spontaneity of life.

Imagine attending a symphony, but instead of taking in all the sounds of the orchestra in concert, you hear only the drum. Your attention is riveted exclusively on the drum beat. What would your experience of the concert be like? How much enjoyment would you feel? Could you tell anyone about the beauty of the music? Anxiety focuses your attention on the drum beat of danger, shutting out the other beautiful sounds of life.

"Avoidance" is the middle name of both addicted and anxious persons. Both are exquisitely sensitive people who have difficulty coping with life. Easily overwhelmed, they develop survival strategies to maintain their wellbeing. They find relief from the unavoidable pain of life by numbing themselves with a drug or withdrawing from uncomfortable situations. Numb to pain, they also feel no joy.

Hopelessly Incurable

"Once an alcoholic, always an alcoholic," advises AA to its members. Alcoholics Anonymous suggests that alcoholics have an allergy to alcohol and a disease for which there is no cure. However, there is a simple solution to the immediate problem: do not take a drink. "It's only the first drink you have to worry about," AA reminds it members.

If an alcoholic believes she is cured, she risks not being vigilant about her vulnerability to relapse. Most alcoholics, after many failed attempts at social drinking, come to believe that they are life-long drunks. They realize that they have a chronic illness, like diabetes, that requires making a lifestyle change. Their challenge is not merely to remain sober but to have a quality sobriety, a wholesome, enriched life. Bitter experience teaches them that their alcoholism is a relapsing illness requiring constant attention.

Alcoholics remain hopeless about a cure but hopeful about recovering a life worth living.

Rebecca, An Elderly Woman: Lifelong Anxiety

"With each passing year, I lose hope for being completely cured of my anxiety. I've been anxious as far back as I can remember. As a child, I was self-conscious and terrified of going to school, leaving my parents. I imagined something awful happening to them and being an orphan. In high school and college, I shied away from dating, believing that no one would find me attractive. Even now, I am crippled by my self-consciousness whenever I am around people. I have read self-help books, practiced breathing and relaxation techniques, gone to therapy, and taken medication. Sometimes, my anxiety recedes into the background, and I have a glimpse of hope. But it always returns. At this point in my life, I don't believe it will ever go away completely."

When you finally admit to yourself you have an anxiety disorder and seek professional help, you have hope that therapy and medication can bring you relief and even a cure. You begin to notice patterns in the changing levels of your anxiety, the ebb and the flow, the periodic relapses. With some attentiveness, you may learn what situations or thoughts trigger your emotional responses. You observe your tendency to catastrophize events, to imagine the worst, and to obsess about the future. The brief successes give you a glimmer of hope that you can finally overcome your anxious temperament. But after brief remissions, the anxiety returns, like a cancer. Its persistence astounds you. The more you fight the feeling, the more you encounter defeat. Eventually, you resign yourself to live an anxious life, without hope for a cure.

From that sense of hopelessness, like a phoenix arising from its ashes, your recovery can begin.

Anxiety, like addiction, fills a void which you never consciously knew existed. Both arise from a sense of helplessness and an effort to gain control over your life. Both compensate for an intolerable sense of emptiness and give you an identity. One patient who suffered the pains of anxiety for eight decades acknowledged, "If I weren't anxious, I don't know who I would be." Her anxiety had become such a familiar companion that she imagined life would be more lonely and frightening without it. She also developed a security-seeking lifestyle around her anxiety, withdrawing from any activities that stretched her beyond her comfort zone. Clearly, the roots of both anxiety and addictions grow from a common soil.

3

The Addictive Process: Planting the Seeds

"Love what you were born with. Fear is what we learned here."

—Marianne Williamson

Our nature and culture provide the fertile soil for addictions and anxiety to flourish. At birth, seeds of happiness and suffering are planted within us. The right conditions allow these seeds to grow. The proper measure of love and guidance enables us to grow into happy, mature adults. Without the needed love and guidance, the seeds of suffering begin to grow like weeds, choking off our life and happiness. The flowers of suffering can be hardy plants that thrive in the harshest conditions of life, conditions of emotional and spiritual deprivation. In our time, addictions and anxiety have taken root, arising from and causing untold suffering.

What nourishes the growth of addictions and anxiety?

- Seeking happiness and holding on too tightly to what satisfies our needs.

- Insecure childhood attachment to our parents.

- A sensitive, shy, inhibited temperament.

- Society's great expectations, fueling the chase after power, success, and status.

Born for Happiness (1)

What is more precious than a newborn child? What can compare to his innocence and freshness?

When a child is born we witness a miracle, the miracle of a new life that gives us hope for the future. We marvel at his beauty and wonder what life may hold for him. A child is pure potential, uncontaminated by the world. We wonder what will be his road to happiness and what he will suffer along the way. What will life teach him? In our loving gaze at this newborn child, we see promise for the future.

This precious child is also a bundle of biological needs that cries out to be cared for. A child's vulnerability inspires our care. We want to hug the newborn and protect him from the world that we have discovered as adults can be cruel. We want to spare this innocent child from suffering and allow him to grow naturally into a happy, wholesome adult. This helpless human with so much potential is yet unaware of itself and the world.

As his caretaker, we understand his biological needs for safety and security in a threatening world. He cannot protect himself and is completely dependent on us. We appreciate his need to gain a sense of power and control over his own life as he matures and begins to shape his own life. By loving him wholeheartedly, we try to nurture his need for affection and esteem.

A child is completely dependent on us to care for these basic biological needs. We respond the best we can, realizing that we are not always the loving parents we hope to be. If we overlook any of these basic needs of the child, the needs do not disappear. Instead, they grow in intensity.

The wondrous resourcefulness of a growing child leads him to find ways of satisfying these basic needs. He will find a way to feel safe and secure in the world, often by clinging to loved ones or pursuing his own interests. He will learn ways of gaining power and control over his life, perhaps through defiant rebellion. He will look for ways to meet his needs for affection and self-esteem in the ways he interacts with others. Lacking a developed self-consciousness, a child spontaneously pursues the satisfaction of his instinctual needs in order to survive. At an early age, he begins to develop his own emotional programs to seek happiness and avoid suffering.

These emotional programs for happiness begin to develop before the birth of conscious living. A child does not freely choose his path to happiness. He merely responds to the urgency of his instinctual needs. If he is raised in a good enough environment, these needs are satisfied in a spontaneous, natural, and balanced way. However, if he experiences some deprivation of any of these needs, he pursues what is lacking with emotional intensity, causing a lack of balance in his life. The need for security, power, or affection may take on an exaggerated importance and become an unconscious preoccupation. A child naturally compensates for what is missing in his life.

The emotional programs for happiness, unconsciously pursued, shape the child's interests as he grows into adulthood. He may become fixated on the pursuit of security, power, or affection to the exclusion of other values. Relationships and his health may suffer as a result. These pursuits may assume an addictive quality in their excessiveness, repetitiveness, and powerlessness to overcome. He may even begin to find his identity in the blind pursuit of these needs. Anxiety arises as he faces the possibility of these needs not being met. His anxieties also express what he values most and fears losing.

Insecure Attachment

A child is born completely helpless, dependent on his parents for survival. He cannot feed, clothe, or shelter himself. His parents care for his every need, not only his biological needs but especially his emotional ones. Without love and affection, a child cannot thrive and grow to emotional maturity. Because of his utter helplessness and dependence on his caregivers, a child is hard-wired, like other animals, to form an attachment bond with his parents. That bond keeps the child emotionally engaged with the parents and elicits their nurturing.

Parenting is a fine art, more an art than a science, requiring maturity, wisdom, and generosity. It requires maintaining a fine balance between many opposing behaviors. It is like keeping a violin string at just the right tension to produce beautiful music, neither too loose nor too tight. In the midst of change, parents need to guide their children by being neither too strict nor too lax. Children require calm direction in negotiating the many challenges of life. Regarding intimacy with their children, healthy, emotionally stable parents are neither too distant nor too close. Children develop a sense of confidence and self-esteem through the non-intrusive loving attention of parents who maintain balance. Balanced parents do not indulge their children's every desire, spoiling them, nor do they deprive their children of what they need to be happy, which would make them into angry children. Instead, they make wise decisions about what would most benefit their child.

Who can be that perfect parent?

No one! The perfect parent does not exist. All parents fail to some degree to be attuned to the constantly changing needs of their children. Normal failures, causing frustration in the child, help the child develop resilience and tolerate the inevitable frustrations of life. However, parents' neglect of the physical and emotional needs of the child causes a severe strain in the attachment bond that the child has with the parent. Preoccupied with their own problems, parents may not see their children crying out for attention and care. For example, parents may struggle with substance abuse, a death in the family, job loss, or some serious illness which causes them to be absent or inconsistent. They do not provide the safe base the child needs to explore his world and mature, and the security of the child's world is shattered. The child becomes overwhelmed with anxiety, feeling helpless in a hostile world. The once secure attachment of the child to the parent is ruptured, flooding the child with anxiety. If the emotional or physical abuse or neglect is extreme, these children are traumatized and disabled in forming intimate relationships throughout their lives.

How does a child cope with these inevitable failures?

Children are amazingly resilient and resourceful. They cope by adapting to the needs of the caregivers in an attempt to maintain a semblance of the attachment bond. Some children compensate for their insecurity by becoming compliant children who are obedient and cause no problems. They are ruled by anxiety, feeling helpless and fearing abandonment. They have difficulty asserting themselves and fear being on their own. They wish to be cared for in relationships. They grow up to become dependent personalities who constantly seek safety in their love relationships. They believe: If I go along with you, you will love me and not hurt me.

Other children become so distrustful, believing they cannot count on others, that they withdraw into their own worlds. These are the invisible, the lost children. They can spend hours playing alone, appearing not to need their parents' attention. They become self-sufficient adults who deny their emotional needs. They find their identity in performance, while disengaging in relationships. They seek safety in their freedom to pursue their own interests. They believe: If I withdraw from others, no one can hurt me.

A third group become defiant children, simmering with anger at their needs not being met. They are scapegoats who express the family's rage. They rebel against the rules and seem to bond with others through the glue of anger. However, in reality, they fear closeness and depending on others. Beneath their angry façade, they feel a sense of powerlessness. As adults, they become workaholics and perfectionists who find safety in power and control over others and their environment. They believe: If I have power and control, no one can hurt me.

When the attachment bond between a child and his caregivers is strained or ruptured, the seeds of mistrust for any intimate relationship are sown. Insecure attachment is fertile soil for the development of an addiction.

One way to think about an addiction to alcohol, drugs, or anxiety is that it is a substitute intimacy. If personal relationships are too painful and unreliable, we may seek a secure relationship with the drug of our choice or familiar mood state. Our drug or mood can always be counted on to give us a predictable result, to calm us when agitated or energize us when down. We come to love our drugs and moods which give us immediate pleasure and help to avoid pain.

Kate: A Young, Newly Married Woman

"I get obsessed with cleaning the house and become enraged when my husband leaves messes. I hate the way I react, and I feel like I'm destroying the best thing in my life. I've always been a neat freak, having to keep everything neat and orderly. It's helped in my job as an executive secretary but not in my personal life."

After a few weeks of therapy, she admitted, "I believe the real reason I came for therapy is because I've always felt so distant from my parents. My father drank, and my mother stayed in her room. I grew up feeling so lonely and unwanted. And now I won't let myself get close to anyone, even my husband, whom I love dearly."

Insecure attachments from childhood do not end there. They continue throughout life.

We learn to compensate for our insecure feelings with anxious vigilance. We also tend to reproduce in our relationships what we experienced growing up. It is called repetition compulsion, whose purpose is to gain mastery over a painful experience by reliving it with the hope for a different result. Of course, the strategy does not work. Instead of easing anxiety, it heightens it. The sense of helplessness from childhood becomes intensified as we repeat the same pattern of unsatisfying, insecure relationships through adulthood.

Sensitive Souls

Our innate temperament is the garden for flowering addictions. No one is born, pre-destined genetically, to become alcoholic. There is no identifiable alcoholic personality type that evolves into a problem drinker later in life. Instead, many factors that lead to inner suffering and the urge to relieve that suffering make the alcoholic want to drink. Alcoholics experience an inner civil war that makes them want to lose consciousness of the pain. They discover, to their delight, that alcohol anesthetizes them.

What are some of those warring inner factions?

Carl Jung, the renowned Swiss psychologist, called the alcoholic a "frustrated mystic." Working with alcoholic patients, he observed that the craving for alcohol was equivalent to a deep spiritual thirst for wholeness. His alcoholic patients were sensitive souls who felt broken by life and undertook a frantic search to fix themselves. They sensed many competing desires, desperately sought satisfaction, and always wanted more from life. He described them as emotionally sensitive, wounded, and searching for new life. In alcohol, they found the spirit that was missing, giving them temporary relief. It gave them a sense of power and control in an uncontrollable world.

Yet over time, that angelic spirit became a demon that tormented and further tore them apart. It reinforced their sense of powerlessness. In their thirst for wholeness, the alcoholic mistakenly sought nourishment from spirits (alcohol).

Ken: A Sensitive Patient

"My family and friends have complained to me that I'm too sensitive. I hate to admit that's true. As a child, I remember countless times when my feelings were hurt by other kids. I couldn't stand any teasing. I took everything so personally. If a teacher corrected me, I broke into tears. If my parents showed any disappointment in me, I wanted to hide in a hole. They didn't need to punish me. A frown would stop me from doing whatever I was doing. My older sisters knew how sensitive I was and teased me mercilessly. I cried more than anyone I knew and was so embarrassed about it. I learned to hide my tears, stifling them until I could break down in private. Because I was so sensitive, the world seemed a cruel place to me."

Those who tend to become anxious have sensitive minds in sensitive bodies. Even small amounts of stress jumpstart the mind to worry and the body to tension. They react with intensity to the smallest disruption in the predictable flow of their lives.

They have an interior early warning system that is on high alert for danger. Their brain is hard-wired to detect threat, both within and without. They are attuned to any changes in their bodies that might suggest an impending illness or malfunction. A more rapid heartbeat, indigestion, or tightness in the chest may signal a coming heart attack. The dangers from the outside world are legion, hiding in high, closed-in, dirty, crowded places. Any change in their environment, or even in their routines, may foreshadow some disaster on the horizon.

The psyches of the anxious-prone appear selectively attuned to darkness, rather than to light, to what can go wrong, rather than right. They are easily aroused, physically and mentally, by unexpected changes in their bodies and environment. Any novel or unexpected event quickly knocks them off-balance. Any change is threatening because their immediate reaction is to assume impending danger, not delight. They are easily startled and tend to dwell on the negative, having difficulty quieting noisy thoughts of doom.

Those who are so easily aroused tend to alternate between two diametrically opposed emotional reactions. They attempt to shut down their emotions, becoming timid and inhibited. Or they become flooded with feeling, fearful of drowning and unable to control the emotional storm. Inside, they feel out of control, at the mercy of a constantly changing, threatening environment.

My sensitive patients lament, "I wish I weren't so sensitive and could be like everybody else. I feel the pain so deeply."

I respond, "I know you think of your sensitivity as a curse. Perhaps, it is also a blessing. You have an exquisite sensitivity that enables you to perceive things others do not. Most people live in a narrow range of sensitivity. You sense the outliers, what is going on beyond the awareness of most people."

"How can that be a blessing?" they protest.

"It opens you to a larger world. You see more clearly so you can be compassionate with the suffering of others, to pain they don't even acknowledge to themselves," I suggest.

Those with anxiety-prone personalities tend to be introverted, inward-looking.

Gerald: Introverted Experience

"From as far back as I can remember, I never felt like I fit in. I felt out of place, like a stranger in a strange land. It was as if I lived in a bubble, looking out at the world and everything going on around me, not being involved. Most of the kids ran around and played with each other during recess, but I walked around alone daydreaming. In high school, I was considered a geek. I enjoyed going to the library to read science fiction. Bored in class, I used to doodle and draw pictures. Kids mocked me because I was so uncoordinated and clumsy. I hated phys ed. I never dated and had only a few friends, who were nerds like me. We talked about our interest in science fiction and computers. I spent most of my day in my head, making up stories, living in my own fantasy world. It was no surprise that I went to college and became an English professor."

Others may see quiet introverts and think something is seriously wrong with them. Introverts do not love social gatherings, small talk, and gossip like everybody else. Crowds and loud parties overwhelm them. Their interests are unique and absorb most of their attention. They seem mysterious and aloof as if they are hiding something. Others may even think they are cold or arrogant.

They are, however, only valuing their privacy. As introverts, they naturally focus their energies inward, rather than outward, in socializing, more interested in their internal thoughts, feelings, and moods than events in the outer world. They can be quite sociable when they want to be but can only take so much socializing. It drains them to be around people too long, and they withdraw into their own worlds to revitalize themselves. It is not that introverts do not enjoy other people or lack social skills. It just takes too much energy, and they quickly lose interest in idle conversation. They enjoy their own company and pursuing their own interests even if others do not share them.

Introverts can suffer terribly for being different. The American culture is extraverted. Three-quarters of Americans have an extraverted temperament. They focus on fitting in, sharing their thoughts and feelings with others, and being social animals. They enjoy parties and having many friends. Being alone makes them uncomfortable. Being with others in conversation energizes them. In our democratic culture, the majority rules, and there is pressure to conform to the lifestyle of the majority, "keeping up with the Joneses."

The introvert in our culture is in the minority and often misunderstood and criticized for being so different. The pain of being misunderstood further fuels the fires of anxiety. Life is difficult. Painful events occur which impress upon us that terrible things can happen over which we have no control. We suffer the death of a parent or sibling, an illness that separates us from our family, or the divorce of our parents, and we are overwhelmed by a sense of helplessness. If we are sensitive and introspective, we dwell on the fickleness of fate and our vulnerability. We may rage at our lack of control over our lives, seeking to relieve the pain with alcohol or drugs or burying it in anxious preoccupation.

Sensitive souls appreciate more than anyone the cruelty of life.

Great Expectations

America is the "land of the free and home of the brave." Our country was founded by adventurous and pioneering men and women motivated by high ideals of liberty and justice for all. Our Puritan ancestors undertook an errand into the wilderness, attempting to create a society based on Gospel ideals. They were idealistic, rugged individuals who believed that everyone had the "inalienable right to life, liberty, and pursuit of happiness." They had fled the poverty and oppression of their homelands and wanted to form a free society where "all men are created equal" and could advance through hard work and initiative.

The United States of America became a beacon of light, hope, and freedom for the world. Millions of immigrants came to America to share its pioneering spirit and prosperity. When they arrived, they were greeted by the Statue of Liberty with raised light and plaque that proclaimed (in the words of Emma Lazarus):

"Give me your tired, your poor,
Your huddled masses yearning to breathe free,
The wretched refuse of your teeming shore,
Send these, the homeless, tempest-tossed, to me:
I lift my lamp beside the golden door."

Some came fleeing poverty, prejudice, and religious persecution in their homelands. Others sought adventure and wealth. Still others were captivated by the democratic spirit. Most came with great expectations for a new life. America's vast land and natural resources offered opportunity for those who lived poor, oppressed lives. The enterprising spirit of the American people developed America's natural resources through technology and industrialization, making it the wealthiest nation on earth. Its prosperity was considered a blessing from God for its dedication to the ideals of freedom and justice for all under the protection of the law. The dream of unlimited progress gave all the new arrivals hope.

The light of promised freedom, justice, and prosperity did not completely dispel the darkness, though. In the shadows lurked the desire for unlimited power and glory that became the seedbed for both addictions and anxiety. The refrain from the song by Queen expresses well that dream: "I want it all, and I want it now."

The song begins with the "I." Our society glorifies the individual and the pursuit of personal happiness and wellbeing, proclaiming, "Be your own person. Take charge of your own life." That is a noble ideal as long as others are included in our pursuit of happiness, as long as our interests do not end with the "I."

Unfortunately, glorifying the individual can easily slip into a narcissistic self-obsession that ignores others and the common good. We then become a nation of separate, self-seeking, self-centered individuals competing with one another for limited resources. Self-obsession, the "big ego," underlies all the addictions, according to Alcoholics Anonymous. Another name for addiction is "self-will run riot." Anxiety also arises from a preoccupation with ourselves, with our safety and security, in a world perceived as threatening.

What defines the "I"? Our "wants." We live in a culture that promotes the satisfaction of personal desires. Advertising seduces us with its subliminal messages. The fantasy of pleasure-seeking, self-indulgence, and consumerism, that the more we possess the happier we become, takes over our thinking.

Slowly, we begin to think that our wants, what we merely prefer, become needs. Enter a slippery slope. Needs degenerate into cravings. We develop a sense of urgency to fulfill our every desire. We believe we cannot be happy unless our wants and needs are met. We may even develop a sense of entitlement that we deserve to get what we want. Addictions happen when we become so attached to some desire for pleasure that we sacrifice everything for it. Anxiety arises when whatever we come to believe we want and need is threatened.

What do we want? We want "it," something impersonal and material. Our culture promises material prosperity for those who are willing to work hard for it. We define the "it" in our striving for achievement, money, status, power, and success. We live in an it-driven, Id-driven culture. Our strivings express our instinctual needs for safety and security, power and control, affection and self-esteem. Fear takes hold when we perceive our needs threatened and feel helpless to protect ourselves. The more we think we need, the more vulnerable we feel to losing what we value. Then, anxiety takes hold.

How much do we want? We want it "all." The future holds endless possibilities for us Americans. We keep our eyes looking forward, rarely backward, searching for ways to build a better life. Ambition drives us to pursue our dreams, and hope keeps us optimistic about realizing them. Such ambition often leads to greed for more: more money, more power, and more possessions. The aversion to being ordinary and accepting limits leads to restless pursuits and a lifestyle of excess.

When do we want it? We want it "now," not later. We Americans rush to get somewhere, to achieve something. The need for speed controls us. A noisy restlessness holds us. Our fast-paced culture does not allow us to rest and relax with what we have and who we are. We always want more and are impatient to get it. We can't wait, for fear we will fall behind, waste time, and not reach our goals. The competitive race for achievement produces nervousness, a fear of failing and not reaching the finish line. So, we push ourselves, often beyond the breaking point.

Alcoholics are restless, impatient people, mirrors of our culture. They want a quick fix. Alcohol provides that magical, instant cure for all that ails them.

Brandon: High School Student Suffering from Social Anxiety

"I was always so shy and self-conscious that I was afraid to approach other kids. I felt like an outsider. Because I was a good student, I put my energies into my studies. I pushed myself to be the best in every subject. Every night I studied for hours. Before every test, my stomach was in knots. After the test, I went over and over every question, just to reassure myself that I answered right. I died a thousand deaths awaiting the grade on an important exam. I didn't just want an A. I wanted the highest grade in the class. If I didn't get it, I felt like a failure and pushed myself even harder for the next exam. I thought I had to prove myself over and over again. I came to realize that getting the best grade was my way of feeling important, getting some recognition, and fitting in. No wonder grades became a life-or-death issue for me."

High expectations for achievement and success start a chain reaction in the anxiety-prone psyche. First, we think, "I must do well to feel good about myself." Secretly, we believe we are defective because of our nervous condition. We are not like other people. Next, we set high standards for ourselves without considering if they are realistic and reasonable. Third, the worry about failing motivates us to work hard, without awareness of the cost to our wellbeing. Fourth, if our standards are excessively high, which they tend to be for perfectionists, the odds of our not succeeding are also high. Then, when we do not achieve our goal, we feel like failures. That only reinforces our negative self-image. Finally, we push ourselves even harder to do better the next time.

Where can all this lead? We repeat the cycle until some catastrophe or awakening occurs.

Dennis Ortman, Ph.D.

4

The Addictive Personality:
Self-Will Run Riot

"We fear violence less than our own feelings.
Personal, private, solitary pain is more terrifying than anyone else can inflict."

—Jim Morrison

Alcoholism and addiction are equal opportunity illnesses. Anyone can develop a drinking or drug problem. No personality type is more predisposed to become addicted or is immune to it. Researchers have tried unsuccessfully to establish an alcoholic gene or an alcoholic personality to predict that someone will drink excessively. Their efforts failed.

Researchers and those in recovery discovered that once the addiction takes hold it shapes the personality in predictable ways. The thinking, emotional responses, and behaviors of an addicted person follow a predictable pattern. These progressively ingrained reactions become habitual, shaping the personality and character. The final outcome, the destiny, accurately expressed by Alcoholics Anonymous, is insanity and death.

Anxiety, like addiction, shapes the personality along well-worn paths. We know that certain temperamental traits, such as sensitivity to danger and introversion, predispose individuals to develop anxiety conditions. Painful life experiences and lack of consistent parental support contribute to the emergence of anxiety disorders in those who are genetically predisposed. However, once the anxiety disorder takes hold, physical sensations and perceptions of oneself and the world shift. Ways of thinking, behaving, and reacting emotionally take a negative turn. These reactions become ingrained over time, habits hard to break. The physical and emotional impact of unchecked anxiety can be devastating and life-threatening. You feel powerless in the grip of this anxiety.

If you are overwhelmed with fear and anxiety, you may exhibit these personality traits:

- You feel vulnerable and self-obsessed in a dangerous world.

- You are exquisitely sensitive to danger and find pleasure in guarantees of safety and security.

- You feel powerless and work desperately to gain control over your life.

- Your thinking and feeling are biased toward the negative.

- You become childlike in your pursuit of safety and security.

It's All about Me and No One Else

Alcoholics Anonymous has been so successful in helping so many because of its clear-sighted understanding of the power of addiction to shape and ruin lives. The AA Big Book (1) states: "Selfishness—self-centeredness! That, we think, is the root of our troubles" (p. 62). Drinking to get intoxicated is a selfish act. No one or nothing else matters when an alcoholic is in the midst of a binge. All cares and responsibilities are cast aside. All the pleading of family, friends, and concerned others meets deaf ears. As the addiction progresses, the alcoholic becomes more self-centered, living only for the party. Consuming alcohol becomes the organizing principle of his life, leaving little room for anyone or anything else.

The consequences of progressive alcoholic drinking inevitably lead to isolation. The Steps/Traditions Book (2) states: "Almost without exception, alcoholics are tortured by loneliness. Even before our drinking got bad and people began cutting us off, nearly all of us suffered the feeling that we didn't quite belong (p. 57)." The self-centered, exclusive consumption of alcohol drives others away and reduces the alcoholic's social world to himself, his drinking buddies, and his bottle. The drinking leads to a lonely existence, which in turn becomes the excuse for more drinking. The cycle continues until some collision with reality motivates recovery.

Bottle-induced loneliness results in feelings of emotional insecurity. The alcoholic tries desperately to connect with people to relieve his painful isolation. Unwittingly, he connects in immature and self-defeating ways. "Either we had tried to play God and dominate those about us, or we had insisted on being dependent on them" (p. 115), the Steps/Traditions Book observes. Driven by insecurity, he either tries to dominate others, making himself feel powerful, or he becomes dependent on them, indulging his sense of helplessness.

The anxious, like the alcoholic, become self-absorbed. If you are ruled by anxiety, threats abound within and without. Because you feel so threatened, powerless, and vulnerable, you become preoccupied with finding safety. Some may accuse you of being selfish because you pay so much attention to your own comfort, to feeling safe and secure. But they do not understand how tormented you feel, how desperate you are to take any measure necessary to escape the sense of doom. You must think about yourself to survive, even if it means ignoring others. Feeling so insecure in your own skin and among others, you scan your environment and your own body for signals of danger.

High School Student Brian: Body Arouses Anxiety

"Working out used to be my way of relaxing. That all changed when one of my classmates suddenly died of a heart attack. At the funeral, I felt panic for the first time in my life.

I've always been involved in sports and love keeping in shape. When I resumed my cardio-vascular exercise in the gym after the funeral, I sensed my heart beating rapidly and struggled to breathe. I thought I was having a heart attack and began to panic. I felt dizzy and had to sit down. I thought I was going to pass out and never wake up. I'd exercised like that a thousand times and knew my reaction was irrational, but I couldn't stop the panicky feeling. The idea popped into my head that I was becoming a hypochondriac."

Likewise, Rachel, a woman suffering from social anxiety commented:

"Whenever I attend a party, my nerves are on edge. I can hardly control the shaking inside and hope no one sees me trembling. I'm embarrassed by my fear in crowds. I look around the room and am jealous at how easily people talk with each other. Thoughts freeze in my brain, and words stick in my throat. I feel like such an idiot. I imagine everyone looking at me, noticing my awkwardness, and secretly laughing at me. I wear my anxiety like a scarlet letter on my chest.

My only comforts at parties are my drink and my husband. I keep my glass full and hope I don't embarrass myself by drinking too much. I just want to drink enough to be relaxed. I also keep my husband close as someone to lean on and bail me out of uncomfortable silent moments in conversation."

Over time, your anxiety isolates you. You become increasingly self-conscious, monitoring closely what you sense in your body and what other people might be thinking about you. You are hyper-alert for any danger signals, unable to distinguish clearly if the threat is real or imagined. Nevertheless, the discomfort is real and disconcerting. You criticize yourself for being so nervous. "What's wrong with me that I can't control my nerves?" you ask yourself. You see your fears as irrational and berate yourself for letting them rule your life. When you are around other people, you imagine they are watching you and judging you critically. Again, you condemn yourself for being so self-conscious and thinking you can read other peoples' minds. To protect yourself from their imagined negative judgments, you withdraw more and more into your own world.

Addictions and anxiety color relationships. Alcoholics and anxious people become preoccupied with self-preservation. They see themselves as weak, powerless, and vulnerable. They hate these qualities in themselves and find ingenious ways to hide their insecurity. Projecting their low self-esteem, they view others has hostile, judging, and threatening. To protect themselves, they withdraw into their own worlds, either drinking or isolating themselves with the few people they lean on for safety.

Running in Circles

Alcoholics seek pleasure and avoid pain at all costs. The Steps/Traditions Book observes: "Instinct run wild in themselves is the underlying cause of their destructive drinking" (p. 44). Alcoholics, in their self-centeredness, want to indulge their needs. They want immediate gratification, and without limits. They want it all and want it now. Everything they do is marked by excess, drinking, playing, and working hard.

However, the unrestrained pursuit of pleasure, chasing the "high," over time takes a demonic turn. Drinking for the fun of it becomes drinking just to feel normal. As tolerance builds, it takes more alcohol to get the same intoxicated feeling and to dispel painful withdrawal. The physical, emotional, and spiritual damage mounts up with each drinking binge. Relationships suffer and begin to fall apart.

Drinking for pleasure becomes drinking just to survive, to avoid pain. The pain comes not only from hangovers, but from the wreckage caused by the drinking. The Steps/Traditions Book comments on this shift: "Our lives have been largely devoted to running away from pain and problems. We fled from them as from a plague. We never wanted to deal with the fact of suffering. Escape via the bottle was our solution (p. 74)." Running away from pain and problems through drinking becomes a way of life over time. "Avoidance" is the alcoholic's middle name. Yet, pain and problems do not disappear when ignored. They grow in intensity and cause more suffering, which becomes another excuse to drink more.

Like the alcoholic, the anxious person has a sensitive mind in a sensitive body. Your brain is on high alert for dangers, and your body is tensed for defensive action. You cannot relax. If you do, you fear something terrible will happen. So, you are always prepared for the worst. Your anxiety is your drug. You imagine that the anxious state of hyper-vigilance will keep you safe in a world that constantly forebodes disaster. The future especially keeps you on edge because it is unknown. The unknown hides tragedy, not treasure. You imagine the worst, not the best. The glass is never full, or even half-full, but always in danger of being emptied and broken.

Margaret: Lifelong Worry Wart

"I always have something to worry about. It's my job and identity. When the kids were young, I worried about them being hurt somehow. So, I became an over-protective "helicopter" parent. My husband could not reassure me that the kids would be okay if they went on some trip or even crossed the street. I was compelled to worry. When they became adults, I talked with them every day, just to make sure they were okay.

As I grew older, my concerns shifted. I worried about my health and my husband's health. Every ache and pain forecasted some life-threatening illness. I knew the anxiety was irrational, that it kept me from relaxing and enjoying life, but I had this superstitious belief that my worry would somehow prevent the disaster I feared."

Your anxiety and worry numb you to the pain of life. In fact, they may disguise a deep, unhealed trauma you have not yet acknowledged. As much as you hate the uncomfortable feeling, it soothes you with its familiarity and promise to prepare you for trouble. Your anxiety, your drug, gives you the illusion of safety in a threatening world. It helps you, in your mind, to avoid a greater pain. With your mind in high alert, you avoid many situations, like crowds, plane rides, and public speaking, which make you feel uncomfortable. Avoidance gives you the illusion of safety, which offers a measure of pleasure, but the fearful avoidance restricts your life and deprives you of many more possible enjoyments.

Addictions and anxiety provide brief moments of pleasure. Alcohol gives a brief "high," while anxiety and worry provides a magical sense of control over dangers. Mostly though, they both serve to protect those who are sensitive from the pain of life. Both shape the personality to pursue a path of avoidance to escape pain and suffering. In the process, though, much is lost. The restricted life becomes an unfulfilled life, sacrificing many life-giving activities and leading to more suffering.

Power Distortion

Alcoholics Anonymous described alcoholism as "self-will run riot." The Steps/Traditions Book adds: "Our whole trouble had been the misuse of willpower. We had tried to bombard our problems with it (p. 40)." Alcoholics want power and control over their lives. When they run into problems, they use their mind and mood altering drug to make the world go away. If they experience some uncomfortable feeling, like sadness, anger, or anxiety, they can make those emotions disappear in an intoxicated fog.

With the repeated use of their drug, alcoholics become "control freaks" who try to manage every aspect of their lives with the judicious use of alcohol. Encouraged by the illusion of control, they try to manage the lives of those around them. They can become irritatingly self-righteous and domineering.

As the alcoholic indulges his fantasy of control, the addiction begins to tighten its grip on his life. Believing he is exerting power over his life by drinking, the alcoholic allows the bottle to enslave him. Gradually, he loses his ability to choose to drink. He drinks because he needs to in order to avoid painful withdrawal symptoms and to feel normal. Even with many bitter experiences of loss of control drinking, the alcoholic stubbornly insists that he can control his drinking, stopping whenever he wishes. He may even attempt to prove to himself and others that he does have control by changing drinks, times he drinks, amounts he imbibes. He may even have periods of abstinence, for example, giving up alcohol for Lent. Nevertheless, the illness progresses relentlessly, decreasing the alcoholic's ability to choose. A well-known adage expresses this progression: "First, the man takes the drink; then, the drink takes the drink; then, the drink takes the man."

Like the addict, when you are overwhelmed with anxiety, you feel out of control with your life. The core of anxiety is the experience of lacking control in a threatening world. You readily admit your sense of powerlessness. You see how anxiety paralyzes you, preventing you from doing many things you desire. The word *can't* becomes your mantra. Because you feel so uncomfortable, you do not venture out of the house or mingle with people. You avoid planes and driving on the expressway. You stay away from high and closed-in places. You feel like a passive, helpless victim of your anxiety.

Your sense of being out of control propels you to make desperate efforts to regain control over your life. You make active choices to avoid people, places, and things that make your nervous. You try to take control over situations to lessen your anxiety. You make rules around the house and at work about "the right way" to do things. You may even become a perfectionist and be admired for the quality of your performance. Others may accuse you of being a "control freak." They do not understand how much you need order and predictability to feel safe. In your private life, you engage in rituals and routines to feel secure. You clean, count, and check to make sure everything is in order, just to keep your anxiety at bay. Even worry can become your imaginary friend who magically protects you.

George: A Perfectionist from the Quality Control Team

"I'm perfectly matched for my job at the factory checking parts. I have an eye for detail and imperfections. I can spot a mistake a mile away. My bosses love this personality trait, but my coworkers hate it. It makes more work for them. For even the smallest flaw, they have to remake the part over and over again.

My wife hates that trait, too. I keep everything at home neat and orderly, which drives her crazy. She calls me a 'damn nitpicker.' If there is a mess around me, I feel a sense of panic. I imagine myself falling apart."

The alcoholic and the anxious obsess about power and control. Both experience a sense of being out of control, which is frightening, and attempt to regain control through the use of their drugs, alcohol or anxiety. The more they indulge their drug use, the more they feel powerless, which confuses them. To compensate for their powerlessness, they desperately try to control their environment and details of their lives. They easily overcompensate for their sense of powerlessness and become "control freaks."

A Negative Turn

There is no such thing as a happy drunk despite the popular presentation of the relaxed, carefree, congenial drinker. The Steps/Traditions Book presents a more accurate, sober picture of the alcoholic as suffering emotional insecurity, with the most common symptoms of "worry, anger, self-pity, and depression...guilt and self-loathing (p. 42, 45)." He feels depressed about the losses of his family, job, friends, and health due to his uncontrolled drinking. In reality, the alcoholic hates himself for all the pain and sorrow he causes himself and others but feels powerless to stop. Even though he may try to hide his shame and guilt from himself and others, misery overwhelms him. He may drink to hide his shame and blame others for all his problems. Alcohol may temporarily anesthetize him, but suffering follows him like his shadow.

Alcoholics suffer from distorted thinking that takes them on a path to destruction. They are "victims of a mental obsession" (p. 22), believing that they can find happiness and escape the vicissitudes of life with alcohol. As the addiction deepens, their lives become more and more organized around the pursuit of alcohol and "chasing the high." They rationalize to themselves and others countless reasons for drinking, because they are sad, happy, angry, stressed out.

They also live in a fantasy world, trying "to create reality out of bottles (p. 100)." Their memories become selective. Experts at "euphoric recall," they remember only the wonderful, fun times when partying with their friends but forget the hangovers, trouble, and embarrassment that followed. They remember the drink and not the drunk. Even if confronted with irrefutable evidence, they deny any connection between their drinking and any trouble in their lives.

If you are anxious, like the alcoholic, you suffer from low self-esteem. You judge yourself harshly for having a condition you did not choose, cannot control, and are unable to cure. The stigma of mental illness haunts you. You see yourself as weak and defective, asking, "Why can't I handle my problems like everyone else? What's wrong with me?" Embarrassed about showing any nervousness that would broadcast your perceived character defect, you try to project an image of calm and control, but inside, you feel your stomach churn and your mind race. When others see signs of your fearfulness, you feel exposed, and a red-faced shame shows itself. Further, you may sense that your anxiety disguises a boiling cauldron of other unacceptable feelings, which you keep buried in secrecy and shame.

Negative, catastrophic thoughts fill your mind, which make you think you are crazy. You experience time as your enemy. The future holds uncertainty, which causes you dread and worry. You fill in the blank of the unknown, nonexistent future with your imagination. You imagine terrible things happening, the worst case scenarios. Better an imagined, certain catastrophe than a completely unknown future. "What if" ideas overshadow your thinking. You monitor closely your present situation and see danger around every corner. A cough signals pneumonia. Your partner's looking away means rejection. A dip in the stock market forecasts a depression.

The past never remains the past for you because you ruminate about what you did wrong and how you could have done better. "If only" thoughts echo through your mind. You cannot silence the constant barrage of critical thoughts about yourself. The sun never shines brightly for you, and you see only clouds and storms.

"Fear is the darkroom where negatives are developed," the AA slogan astutely affirms.

Weighed down by the negativity, you manage to find ways of lightening the load through magical thinking. You convince yourself that worrying will stop something bad from happening. It also prepares you for the worst, which you believe is inevitable. You may also engage in rituals and routines that you believe will protect you from the dangers of life. So, you make sure your desk and wardrobe are in impeccable order. You check the doors numerous times to feel safe. When you feel your life in chaos, you make up personal rules to bring order and predictability. You follow strict routines at home and work, insisting that others also follow your lead.

Betty, Elderly Church Lady and Negative Thinker

"I was shocked when the pastor asked me to run for the parish council. I felt unworthy, but too frightened to refuse. What would he think of me? When I was elected, I could not believe the results, believing it had to be a mistake. A friend in the parish called to congratulate me, but I only felt embarrassment and told her I didn't deserve it.

Because I've been so terrified of speaking in public, I didn't know how I could contribute at the meetings. At the first meeting, the chairperson asked each of us to introduce ourselves. I shook inside. Sweat stained my blouse, and I avoided making eye contact with anyone. I sensed everyone staring at me, feeling sorry for me. I could only stammer a few words and never looked up for the rest of the meeting."

Addictions and anxiety shape feeling and thinking in a negative direction. The glass is half empty (and leaking) for the addict and the anxious person. Both feel intolerable shame for their conditions, worry about discovery, and hide behind a façade of being normal. They are persecuted by a harsh inner critic who reminds them relentlessly of how defective they are. Their thinking is also skewed. Both live in fantasy worlds of their own making. The alcoholic imagines he can drink with impunity, while the anxious person ruminates about catastrophes past, present, and future, which he attempts to avoid by worrying, rituals, and routines.

Becoming a Child Again

The Steps/Traditions Book reported a study by psychologists and doctors of a group of problem drinkers in the early years of AA. Their conclusions shocked the AA members at the time. The researchers concluded that "most of the alcoholics under investigation were still childish, emotionally sensitive, and grandiose (p. 123)."

After an initial protest, the AA membership has come to acknowledge the accuracy of these observations. Those in recovery learned how much their personalities were formed by their years of drinking. Driven by unreasonable fears and anxieties, they developed a false pride to compensate for their deep emotional insecurities. Like children, they became self-centered in the extreme, seeking the immediate gratification of their desires. They ignored responsibilities to family, friends, and work, seeking only to escape pain and problems in the bottle. They avoided anything unpleasant and indulged their fantasy to create a carefree life and make the world go away in their intoxicated state. In short, the alcoholic regressed to become a child again in his obsessive pursuit of pleasure.

Anxiety disorders shape the personality along similar lines as the alcoholic. Those in the grip of anxiety become preoccupied with self-preservation. The desire to be safe and secure, like a child, drives their thoughts, feelings, and behaviors. They feel helpless in a hostile world, without mature resources for protection. Dangers lurk everywhere, mostly imagined and exaggerated. The anxious begin to withdraw from life and responsibilities in their obsessive search for safety. Like the alcoholic, they engage in magical thinking, imagining terrors and creating an illusion of safety through worry, rituals, routines, and rules. Feeling powerless, they attempt to control their environment and others for their own needs, for a sense of security. In short, the anxious individual regresses to become a child again in his obsessive pursuit of safety.

The experience of anxiety makes the sufferers feel like helpless children. They experience anxiety as

- a bully who dominates their thoughts and feelings;
- a liar who distorts the truth, exaggerating dangers;
- a baby who demands constant attention and comfort:
- a thief who robs them of peace and happiness;
- a warden who takes away their freedom of movement;
- a runner who invites them to flee discomfort;
- a charmer who seduces them into magical thinking and the illusion of control; and
- an artful dodger who makes them avoid intimacy with themselves and others.

Effective treatment for addictive and anxiety disorders requires an accurate diagnosis and an appreciation of the root cause of the disturbance. Often, what appears to be the problem is not the problem, only a symptom. Alcoholics Anonymous has been successful because of its clear-sighted view of the real issues of alcoholics. The Big Book states: "After all, our problems were of our own making. Bottles were only a symbol...Self-centeredness is the root of our troubles...At heart, we had all been abnormally fearful (p. 103, 62, 123)."

The alcoholic needs to address the character defects which underlie and arise from his habit of drinking. In a similar way, the Twelve Steps of AA can assist the anxious in their recovery because the steps address the personality defects that arise from and support the anxiety disorder. The fearful reaction is not the problem, only a symptom of the problem whose roots are found in an immature personality.

Part Two
Recovering Your True Self
Through the Twelve Steps

Steps to Wholeness:
A Lighthearted Dance

"There is no hope unmingled with fear and no fear unmingled with hope."

—Baruch Spinoza

What is the view like from the top of a mountain? If the mountain is high enough above the clouds, you can see forever. The sky appears an endless expanse of blue, encircling you and holding you in its spaciousness. The cool, clean air hits your face. You feel refreshed, fully alive. The bright sun illuminates everything, making every tree, waterfall, and rock stand out in clear detail. On a cloudless day, you can look down at the lush green and stark brown earth. Hills, valleys, and rivers divide the land, and you can distinguish nature's footprints. From this perspective, heaven and earth are one, in perfect harmony. At this height, even the darkness of night does not overwhelm or frighten you. The moon and stars cast a pale light that makes everything seem mysterious and intriguing.

What is the experience of being trapped in a cave? You feel claustrophobic, gasping for air. The walls close in upon you, and you feel its prisoner, unable to escape. You have nowhere to go, so you dwell on your own thoughts, which turn to ideas of gloom and helplessness. Because of the darkness, you cannot see the walls, or even your hand in front of you. You can only feel the unrelenting hardness, roughness, and jaggedness of your prison. Darkness envelops you. It is not a comforting darkness that invites sleep but a bone-chilling blackness that threatens to take over your life. Your body tenses, and your heart rate increases. Peace and relaxation elude you. If a shaft of light happens to appear briefly through an opening, it reveals the hopelessness of your situation. You are alone, trapped, and helpless.

Weighed down, Broken by Fear

When you have an addictive or anxiety disorder, you feel trapped in the cave of your psyche, with no hope of escape. You lose contact with others and become lost in your own thoughts. They are desperate thoughts, making you feel like a prisoner of your mind. You feel broken inside and hate yourself. Only your imagination can carry you outside the confines of your mental cage. What do you imagine? Terrible, catastrophic losses even if you are released from the cave. Your world shrinks as you attempt to find a measure of safety by withdrawing from everything and everyone that frighten you. Darkness, heaviness, and gloom reign.

Indeed, that is a desperate picture of someone in the grip of a serious addiction or anxiety condition. Unfortunately, too many feel a sense of hopelessness because of their suffering. The Steps/Traditions Book expresses accurately the power of self-centered fear to take over your life: "The chief activator of our defects has been self-centered fear—primarily fear we would lose something we already possessed or would fail to get something we demanded. Living upon a basis of unsatisfied demands, we were in a state of continual disturbance and frustration. Therefore, no peace was to be had unless we could find a means of reducing these demands (p. 76)." Notice that a glimmer of hope is offered in acknowledging and letting go of the self-centered demands at the root of fear.

Self-centered fear and anxiety tear you apart in many ways. First of all, you hate the anxiety because it is so painful and try desperately to get rid of it. Of course, that is a war you cannot win. You cannot eliminate emotional reactions that are natural to you. In the futile attempt to do so, you end up hating yourself.

Next, you become preoccupied with escaping fear and finding safety and security. In the process, you isolate yourself more and more. You see others as critical judges, enemies, rather than helpful friends. You become defensive, on your guard, in the company of others.

Third, the division between yourself and others deepens as you try to control your environment and others to feel safe. Others resent your efforts to control them and your unfair evaluation of them as hostile and threatening.

Finally, you begin to see the world and life itself as a hostile. You withdraw more and more from meaningful activities and ignore any opportunities to make the world a better place. Your fears put you at odds with yourself, others, and life.

Is there a way out of the cave? When you suffer from self-centered fear and anxiety, without knowing it, you are holding on too tightly to your life. You fear losing what is precious to you. The weight of worry crushes you.

An old Jewish tale suggests the remedy: "It was taught in the name of Rabbi Meir: When one comes into the world his hands are clenched as if to say: the whole world is mine and I will inherit it. And when one takes leave of the world his hands are open as if to say: I have not taken from the world a single thing (1)." Learning not to grasp so tightly and learning to surrender give relief from the suffering of fear.

Light-hearted Dance Steps

The Twelve Steps are more like lighthearted dance steps than an arduous climb up the mountain of enlightenment. You move yourself to music, a soul music that comes from the heart. It arises from deep within you, beyond thoughts and words. Listening closely to yourself, you hear the sweet music from your core, your true self. You also recognize the discordant music that does not disappear, the noise of your addictive, anxious mind. The heavy music of your anxious mind will continue to try to drown out the softer tones. With practice, you can learn to ignore the noise and not let it guide your thoughts and feelings.

There is a back and forth movement with the music. With some dance steps you move back to observe yourself closely. You sense the subtle longings from your heart. You begin to trust your own wise mind. As you become more intimate with yourself, you also listen more attentively to others, becoming aware of their spoken and unspoken desires.

With other dance steps you move forward in action. You act courageously for the benefit of others as you learn your own and their deep needs. There is a natural rhythm and flow to these steps. If you follow the rhythm closely, you experience harmony and wholeness within yourself and in your relationships. Beauty shows itself in all your dealings.

As you progress through the Twelve Steps, you have different dance partners. At some points, you embrace your true self and listen to its wisdom. At other times, you engage your addictive, anxious mind, attempting to learn its wisdom without letting it control you. You meet your faults, respect them, and try to learn from them. You may take a few steps with your inner critic, listening with amusement to its ranting. Finally, you dance with your Higher Power, by whatever name or idea you consider it. That is the Source of the goodness that transforms your anxious life.

By paying close attention to all your partners you enrich your life, and a surprising harmony emerges. All the parts fit together; nothing is excluded. Truth, beauty, and goodness shine forth.

Dancing to the music, you keep the beat. To stay in rhythm, you need to pay attention and stay in the moment. You need to feel the music, getting out of your head and into your body. It is easy to become distracted and lose the rhythm and mood of the music. If you think too much, you will lose the beat. If you keep looking around, you will lose the beat. If you do not focus on moving in synch with your partner, you will lose the flow of the dance.

Your effort, too, must be focused, neither too tense nor too loose. If you are tense, you cannot move easily with the music. If you are too loose, you cannot sustain a coordinated effort. To be a graceful dancer, you must develop the capacity to trust yourself and engage fully in the present moment.

The anxious and the addicted have particular difficulty staying in the present moment, trusting themselves, and not getting lost in their thoughts. They are out of tune with the natural rhythm of life.

Sermon on the Mount: A Word to Worriers

The Twelve Steps of Alcoholics Anonymous are not new. They embody ancient wisdom. Two thousand years ago Jesus spoke from a mountaintop about how to live the good life (2). In His sermon (Matthew 5:1-7:29), He singled out those who were caught up in worry about what they are to eat, drink, and wear. Jesus is portrayed as the new Moses, presenting the new law written on the heart. He is also a sage who offers wise advice to those trapped in the cave of anxiety. His advice is clear and straightforward, reflecting His mountaintop views. He encourages and models seeing life from a larger perspective, with a higher consciousness.

What advice does He give the worried? First, He begins by shocking you with some crazy ideas to get your attention. Jesus proclaims that you are blessed, happy, when you are poor in spirit, sorrowing, lowly, persecuted, and insulted. That contradicts all your natural instincts and society's way of being happy. You expect to find happiness when you are rich, successful, powerful, and praised, not the opposite. Jesus adds that those who hunger and thirst for holiness, show mercy, are single-hearted and peacemakers are the truly happy. In other words, those who care more for others than themselves find joy in life. If you are anxious and preoccupied with your own safety and security, what Jesus says startles you.

Next, Jesus asks that you look around and observe your world. He said, "Look at the birds of the sky...Learn a lesson from how the wild flowers grow." Nature can teach you if you just pay attention. Jesus observes that the animals and plants do not toil or worry, yet they flourish because of God's care. Whether or not you believe in God, some invisible life force or energy in the universe appears to sustain it. Trusting in God's or the universe's care can reassure you in your anxiety.

Third, Jesus appeals to commonsense: "Which of you by worrying can add a moment to his life-span?" Worry is useless. It does not change reality. What will happen will happen, no matter how much we worry about it. As the song goes, *Que Sera, Sera.*

Next, Jesus extends his commonsense thinking: "Enough, then, of worrying about tomorrow. Let tomorrow take care of itself. Today has troubles enough of its own." He reasons that worry is worse than useless. It drains your energy to confront the problems that inevitably face you each day. His advice: Live fully the present moment. Stay in the today, not the tomorrow. The problems of tomorrow may not occur if you pay close attention to what you are doing today. Jesus' message clearly contradicts your anxious tendency to dwell on what might happen in the future.

Fifth, Jesus points out something that may not be so evident to you when you are caught up in anxious thinking. Anxiety is the fear of losing something important to you. You become anxious only about what you care about, ignoring what holds no interest to you. Jesus says, "Remember, where your treasure is, there your heart is also." He invites you to pay close attention to what you are anxious about. It reveals what you treasure, hold precious in life.

A soul-searching question is implied in this statement: "What do you treasure most in life?" Is it your health, wealth, status, power, affection, self-esteem, or some relationship? What you fear losing shows what you value and, perhaps, cling to. Your attachments become evident. Jesus further warns that you may be worrying about the wrong things, about "earthly treasure" rather than "heavenly treasure," about material comfort rather than spiritual wellbeing.

Finally, Jesus ends with another piece of crazy wisdom: "My command to you is: love your enemies, pray for your persecutors." When you are in the grip of anxiety and fear, enemies abound within and without. Your physical sensations, your negative thinking, uncomfortable persons, places, and things pose threats to you. You see enemies and persecutors everywhere. Jesus tells you to love what you naturally want to hate, even love the anxiety itself. Your anxiety makes you view the world as a hostile place, full of danger. You can achieve freedom by viewing your life from a larger, mountaintop perspective, transforming enemies into friends through the power of love.

Jesus asks some pointed questions:

- Why do you worry so much?

- What does your worry accomplish?

- What do you worry about?

- What do you treasure most?

Jesus proposes a program of action similar to the Twelve Steps. An AA slogan summarizes the steps: "Trust God; clean house; help others." Jesus and other religious traditions say the same thing in different words: "Pray; fast; give alms."

Jesus instructs: "Whenever you pray, go to your room, close your door, and pray to your Father in private." Quite simply, He invites you to be quiet and listen, rather than rattle on with words. You are accustomed to having racing thoughts, worries and obsessions. If you can quiet your mind and enter deeply into the silence, you may be surprised at what you discover. You may encounter a presence that brings you peace and joy.

Jesus also comments on the power of this prayer: "Ask, and you will receive. Seek, and you will find. Knock, and it will be opened to you." In prayer, you experience a Power greater than yourself that can heal you.

When Jesus talks about fasting, He is referring to more than giving up food. He is speaking about house-cleaning, becoming aware of your faults and uprooting them. When anxious, you are preoccupied with getting away from dangers and do not look inward. You quickly judge persons, places, and things as dangerous to you and run away from them. You may not see clearly the emotional affliction you cause yourself by indulging your faults. Jesus says: "Stop passing judgment...Remove the plank from your own eye." He gives specific advice about the need to acknowledge the roots of anger, lust, lying, and selfishness deep in the heart, and take action to correct these faults, replacing them with love and forgiveness.

Almsgiving implies more than handing out money. It means extending yourself in love. Jesus clearly teaches: "Treat others the way you would have them treat you." How do you want to be treated? You certainly want to be treated with respect, kindness, compassion, and generosity. Others, of course, want the same consideration. However, preoccupied with self-preservation, you may not look beyond yourself to see others in need. You can become trapped in your anxious self-obsession. The way of freedom is to leave the cave, become involved in the world, and learn to love. In the end, it is only love that casts out fear.

The Power of Paradox

When you are fearful and anxious, you live in a dark mental cave, confined by four walls. Your thinking is narrowed, and you have a one-track mind. You are preoccupied with threats and neatly divide your world into the dangerous and the safe. Your thinking is black and white, either-or, because you are so focused on danger or not-danger.

Experiences of past hurts reinforce your tendency to be cautious. If your anxiety is severe enough, your danger zone is relatively large, your safe refuge small. Constantly threatened, you feel the need to be ever-vigilant and discriminating between what may help or hurt you. Your mind is rarely at rest, just to feel relatively safe.

Under the influence of anxiety, your mind is at war with itself and the world. You may judge yourself harshly because you feel so anxious, considering yourself defective and weak. You want to get rid of uncomfortable feelings and thoughts about yourself, becoming impatient when your efforts fail. The vicious circle of self-loathing then deepens.

With your brain on high alert, you detect dangers everywhere. You experience your world as hostile and believe you have to fight for survival. You actively flee persons, places, and things that make you feel uncomfortable, with the result that your life shrinks to a small safety zone. You separate yourself for security, becoming ever more isolated. The walls of your mental cave become even more confining.

How can you escape the dark mental cave of your anxiety? There is only one way: by going to the mountaintop. From those heights, you experience openness, spaciousness, and clarity, seeing everything in a new light. Alcoholics Anonymous has many slogans regarding recovery that invite a mountaintop experience, an alternative consciousness and way of living. These slogans express an open-minded, both-and way of viewing life that confronts the narrow-minded, either-or thinking of anxious cave dwellers. The following are some of the most popular phrases:

- From weakness (adversity) comes strength.
- We forgive to be forgiven.
- We give it away to keep it.
- We suffer to get well.
- We surrender to win.
- From darkness comes light.
- From dependence we found independence.

These statements, like the beatitudes of Jesus, express a hidden wisdom in a surprising way which contradicts your ordinary thinking and expectations. If you take them seriously, they jolt you and make you question yourself. They are called paradoxes, which mean "a union of opposites." What you think cannot go together is intimately related.

Paradoxes challenge reason and society's standards of behavior. In particular, they challenge your anxious desire for certainty, clarity, control, and logic. They confront your either-or thinking that makes you feel broken and separates you from others. You cannot fully grasp their meaning, but sense their truthfulness at a deep level you cannot yet understand.

The paradox invites you to search your soul for its deeper meaning, as it resonates in your heart, not your logical head. It suggests that you embrace what you despise, your own anxiety and what you perceive as threatening. Its message is clear: all is connected, everything belongs, and all is one. Beneath the brokenness, there is an underlying wholeness. At a deeper level, everything radiates from a Center, a Source.

To live the wisdom of the paradoxes of recovery requires unlearning the familiar and learning something new. As Albert Einstein said, "No problem can be solved by the same consciousness that caused the problem in the first place." On the one hand, you need to give up your reliance on your logical, either-or thinking, on your sense of normal, and on your efforts to control. You need to learn to trust your heart, question your assumptions, and accept unconditionally yourself and others. The steps will aid you in this conversion process, which is the only path to healing.

Using Medication

Many people take medication for their anxiety. However, you may have some reservations, such as the following:

- "All medications have side effects. I don't want the added problem of side effects I don't want. I don't want to be like a zombie."

- "Who knows the long-term effects of taking medications? I don't want to take the chance."

- "I don't want to introduce something artificial into my body. I want a natural solution so I can be myself."

- "I don't want to become dependent on medications for the rest of my life. Some of them are addictive, and I don't want to become a drug addict."

- "Taking medication means I can't solve my problems myself. I don't want the social stigma of being on drugs."

Since I am not a medical doctor and have no expertise with medications, I consulted with several of my psychiatrist colleagues to find out their approach in treating anxiety disorders. They said they recommend that the patient take medication when their anxiety is so severe that it interferes with their daily functioning. The patient might feel overwhelmed much of the time, cannot concentrate, and have trouble sleeping. These psychiatrists begin by prescribing an antidepressant, specifically, a Selective Serotonin Reuptake Inhibitor (SSRI), such as Zoloft, Paxil, Prozac, or Lexapro. These medications can help with anxiety, but they are slow to take effect. If the patient is so distressed that he needs immediate relief, they prescribe a Benzodiazepine, such as Klonopin, Xanax, or Ativan, to be used as-needed and on a short-term basis. They warn the patient about the risk of addiction with these medications and, generally, do not prescribe them to patients with a substance abuse history.

In deciding whether or not to take any medication, you need carefully to consider the benefits and risks. The psychiatrist will try to match you with the best combination of medications and right dosage to maximize the desired therapeutic effect and minimize the adverse side effects. Getting the right medication and dosage may take some trial-and-error, requiring patience on your part. Medication can help to reduce the intensity of your anxious symptoms so that you are calm enough to work on your life problems.

There is no magic pill to make your troubles disappear. Life is difficult and uncertain. Anxiety will naturally arise in the face of perceived dangers. However, working the steps can help you use that anxiety for your benefit, and not let it cripple you.

6

Defeated: Facing the Pain

Step 1: "We admitted we were powerless over anxiety—
That our lives had become unmanageable."

"There is a crack in everything. That's how the light gets in."

—Leonard Cohen

Frightened, you arrive at the dance hall with the big sign above the door: "Recovery Hall." You hear the inviting music from within and see all the others laughing, walking in. Your fear and anxiety have been such constant companions that you hesitate to leave them at the door and just walk in.

Perhaps for a long time you have been battling your anxiety, without admitting how much it has crippled your life. You may not have recognized that your discomfort was being caused by anxiety, thinking it was just the usual adjusting to the stress of life. "Everyone feels stress these days," you tell yourself. You may not have recognized how much energy you put into coping with your fears, trying to get rid of them, avoiding uncomfortable situations. Your life became choked-off, walled-in. Your job has suffered. Your family and friends have wondered what was going on with you. Now, the pain has become unbearable. You acknowledge your suffering and cry out, "Please help me."

"We admitted..."

When you are anxious, preoccupied with self-preservation, you lack a sense of "we," of fellowship with others. Like the alcoholic, you feel a terrible sense of isolation with your condition. You do not feel like you fit in because you think of yourself as abnormal, and you tend to withdraw from social interactions for safety.

The good news: You are not alone in your suffering.

In our fast-paced society, anxiety disorders are the most prevalent mental/emotional condition. Over a quarter of adults and nearly a third of children experience clinical levels of anxiety at some time in their lives. At any given time, forty nine million Americans, young and old, suffer crippling anxiety. Anxiety is epidemic.

Reasons Not to Admit

Despite sharing the condition with so many, you likely resist admitting to yourself and others the depths of your pain. Denial afflicts you, like the alcoholic. There are many reasons for this denial. First, as much as you hate your anxiety, it may not be apparent that you benefit from your condition. "How can that be?" you ask. If you have been anxious most of your life, that mood has become familiar to you. It has become a habit of thinking and reacting that gives you a predictable sense of security. You identify yourself as an anxious person, not knowing who you would be without worrying. Worrying also gives you a job that keeps you from extending yourself in other activities and thinking about other more painful emotions. Your anxiety also may cover up the pain of a deeper woundedness you are not yet ready to acknowledge.

Second, you may feel ashamed of your condition. Out of ignorance and fear, society stigmatizes mental illness. It is frightening because it is beyond comprehension and control, revealing the dark side of human nature. You may share society's illusions about it, secretly thinking yourself "crazy." Not understanding your fearful apprehensions and considering them irrational, you wonder what is wrong with you. You view your anxiety as an intolerable sign of weakness, even a character defect. To avoid feeling even more abnormal, you hide your fears from others behind a cool, calm, composed facade.

Third, society's high expectations for achievement and success, the need for adjustment to constant change, and the rapid pace of life lead you to believe that the stress you feel is normal. "Don't you have to push yourself to get ahead in life? Isn't everyone in a rush?" you rationalize. Preoccupied with the pursuit of your goals, you ignore the warning signs, the irritability, the restlessness, the distractedness, and the sleeping problems. You dismiss these signs as the expected price of a full, successful life—until you get a wakeup call.

Randall: Unexpected Panic Attack

"I always wanted to be my own boss and have my own business. When the opportunity came to buy a grocery store, I jumped at the chance. I worked long hours but loved it. I admit I felt tired a lot and had some sleepless nights, but I didn't think anything of it. My wife worried about my health because I was working so hard. She's a worry wart, always obsessing about what can go wrong. Unlike her, I'm an optimist, pushing myself to achieve more. She talks nonstop about problems, while I withdraw into my cave and think about things. I never realized how much my overwork was driven by anxiety until I had a panic attack and went to the hospital. The doctor told me it was my nerves and that I was on the verge of burnout."

"We were powerless over anxiety…"

You did not cause your addiction. You cannot control it. You cannot cure it. Only utter defeat, after repeated failures to manage it, awakens you to your powerlessness.

From the Ashes of Defeat

No one deliberately chooses to be addicted. Over time, through painful experience, you discover you are in its grip. Alcoholics Anonymous defines alcoholism as a disease that affects the body, mind, and spirit. It describes alcoholics as "the victims of a mental obsession…a compulsion," "smitten by an insane urge," and suffering from "an allergy of the body."

That describes you well as a prisoner of your anxiety. Instead of an allergy of the body, you suffer a disease of the brain. Psychiatrists describe this disease as a "chemical imbalance," affecting your mood, thinking, and behavior. Your brain is sensitized in the extreme to threats and mobilizes automatic self-protective reactions. You are easily startled, often feel on-edge, and tend to worry about even the smallest matters. You may even blame yourself for your high-alert brain.

I tell my patients, "You did not choose your condition, and your condition does not define you as a person."

Even if you can admit that you did not cause your addiction, you make exhausting efforts to manage it. Alcoholics engage in almost comical behaviors to convince themselves that they do not have a problem. They change the type, amount, timing, setting, and frequency of drinking to prove that they can drink socially, like everyone else. But such efforts inevitably fail, sometimes with devastating results.

In a similar way, when you are overwhelmed with fear and anxiety, you desperately try to keep yourself from feeling overwhelmed. You create rituals, routines, and rules to give you a sense of security. You avoid persons, places, and things that make you uncomfortable. However, all your white-knuckled efforts to manage the uncertainty and unpredictability of your life inevitably fail. The unexpected always happens. The defeat leaves you thrashing about with a sense of powerlessness.

All addicts hope for a cure. Alcoholics fantasize that one day they will be social drinkers, like everybody else. Hope for a cure springs eternal until they hit bottom. Then, they either give up in despair or admit their powerlessness over alcohol.

Karen: Powerlessness

"My parents first took me to therapy when I was seven years old because I was so frightened to leave them for school. Since then, I have tried every therapy imaginable to shake off this dreadful anguish I feel almost constantly. I've participated in group therapy and joined Toast Masters to help with my social anxiety. Doctors have prescribed over a dozen different medications in every possible combination. One never to give up, I became a self-help junkie, reading books on recovery from anxiety, joining yoga and meditation classes, doing massage therapy and acupuncture. I even tried drinking myself into oblivion for a period of time.

Nothing has worked. I'm left feeling more defeated and powerless than ever, close to giving up hope I'll ever be cured."

"That our lives had become unmanageable."

Alcoholics generally do not take the first step on the road to recovery until they "hit bottom." Often, it takes some catastrophe, like the loss of a marriage or job or health, to wake them up to the consequences of their drinking. They may admit struggles in their lives, "like everyone else," they rationalize.

They are blind, however, to the connection between many of their problems and their drinking. Instead, they blame others, the circumstances of their lives, or rotten luck, and avoid looking at how they may be the cause of their own misery. Before they consider the bold and frightening leap to recovery, they must come to believe that the problems drinking causes outweigh the benefits.

The unmanageable erupts regularly in the life of the anxious. You tend to be a "control freak." You only feel safe when your life and everyone around you follow you're a predictable agenda. Unfortunately, the world and others do not always dance to your tune. Sickness strikes. Accidents occur. Loved ones die. With these unexpected turns of events, you rage out of control. You drown in the storm-tossed sea of your emotions of fear, dread, and panic. So, you redouble your efforts to regain your sense of security and control.

An anxious person is like a man who builds a wall around himself. He is surrounded by bricks. Every time he feels uncomfortable, for whatever reason, he cements a brick in place for protection. As the years pass, he is assaulted with more and more threats. In response, he lays another brick. At first, the wall is knee-high, and he can see around him and step over the wall. Eventually, it is waist-high, and he has more trouble moving out of his fortress. Then, the wall is over his head. He feels safe, but the wall is becoming a prison, restricting his sight and movement. Finally, he completely encloses himself in the secure confines of the brick edifice his fear has constructed. He cannot move, sees only darkness, and has trouble breathing. The anxious seek recovery only when they realize how much life they lose in exchange for feeling safe. As the AA slogan puts it, "Change only happens when the pain of holding on is greater than the fear of letting go."

The Value of Pain

Our natural instinct is to seek pleasure and avoid pain. The first step, like all the steps, asks you to act contrary to your natural desires. You want to avoid and rid yourself of the discomfort your anxiety causes you. Perhaps you have suffered under the bondage of fear and anxiety for many years, feeling desperate to escape. This step invites you to embrace your anxiety, accept it, and learn from it. Such an approach presents an alternative path to freedom.

What would your life be like if you never felt pain? Initially, you might think it would be heaven on earth, a dream realized. Your life would proceed pleasantly without the distraction of pain—until you injured yourself. You might not even notice you hurt yourself because you feel no pain to alert you. You do not seek treatment. The cut may become infected and eventually cost you a limb, or worse, your life. You may become afflicted with an infinite variety of illnesses and not even know it. Without treatment, the simple sickness could become complex, damaging vital organs, and again costing you your life. We ignore the signs at our own peril.

Physical pain, as much as we hate it, serves a survival purpose. It alerts us to harm that requires attention. Pain grabs our attention and launches us on an exploratory search to find its cause. When we understand the cause, we can discover the proper remedy.

Emotional pain serves a similar survival purpose, to protect our psychological wellbeing. When you feel anxious, depressed, or angry, it is a warning sign that something is out of balance in your life. Of course, you hate the discomfort of these feelings and wish they would magically disappear, but these emotional reactions are symptoms of some deeper problem that is calling out for attention. Neglecting to address that deeper problem can put your long-term happiness at risk. Taking the pain seriously and exploring the causes can lead to growth.

The fearful and anxious reactions are powerful signals of danger. What would life be like if you never felt fearful or anxious? Perhaps you imagine a life of perfect peace and tranquility. Think again. If you did not have these reactions to warn you of impending danger, what would stop you from stumbling into dangerous, even life-threatening situations? What would restrain you from reckless behavior? You would not take steps to protect yourself. Eventually, your recklessness could cost you your life.

The approach of the first step is to face the pain of your anxiety, admit your powerlessness to overcome it, and acknowledge how it has affected your life. Accept your brokenness. That is the first step toward freedom. As the refrain to the Leonard Cohen song, *Anthem*, states, "There is a crack in everything. That's how the light gets in."

The Facts of Life

Psychological treatment was not invented a hundred years ago with Sigmund Freud, only a modern version of it. Perhaps the greatest psychologist the world has ever known lived 2600 years ago in a faraway land. He was a gentle, sensitive person, groomed by his father to become a king. His father pampered him and tried to protect him from the cruelty of the world. Yet, the curiosity of this young man drove him beyond the palace walls where he encountered the suffering of the sick, the aging, and the dying. Compassion was born in him, and he resolved to dedicate his life to the relief of suffering. He left the organized religion of his day because it was too pietistic, ritualistic, and dogmatic and undertook a personal search to find the path to freedom from suffering. He went off to fast, pray, and study the wisdom of the elders, but found no answer. He then spent time in silence, listening to his own experience and confronting his demons, and realized his own truth. His contemplation awakened him to become a scientist of the mind and a healer of the heart. His name was Siddhartha Gautama, also known as the Buddha, which means "the enlightened one."

The Buddha taught that all our troubles, all our anguish, arise from our desire for our life to be other than it is. He proceeded to describe the facts of life, as he experienced them. He told his followers not to believe authority, the traditions, or even his own word, but to trust their own experience. He suggested four facts of life.

The First Fact: Life Is Suffering

That seems obvious enough because we know we will get sick, grow old, and die. We cannot hang on to our loved ones and possessions. Yet, we have an inner drive to avoid the pain of life we know is inevitable.

The Buddha told a story about a man who was struck by two arrows. The first arrow was the pain of living a physical life in a body that decays and dies. That arrow cannot be avoided. The second arrow was the suffering the man caused himself by his reaction to the first arrow. That suffering was brought on by his refusing to accept the fact of human pain. That refusal caused him mental and emotional anguish.

Buddha added that there is a benefit in embracing the suffering of life. It can open our hearts to compassion and joy.

Your normal anxiety about the inevitable suffering of life increases when you refuse to accept painful losses. You may also refuse to accept your condition. You hate your anxiety disorder, but your hatred does not take it away. It only makes you feel worse and degenerates into self-loathing. Acceptance of your powerlessness over your condition frees you to put your energy into what you can change about your life.

The Second Fact: Life Is Change

Look around and observe how everything eventually changes. Day turns to night and back again. The seasons rotate every year in an ongoing cycle. We change each moment as we grow older, and hopefully wiser, in our journey to death. Our lives are a continuous dying to new life. Each moment passes away into something new. Our lives are like a flowing river that keeps moving to a destination that is in the unknown future. Each day, each moment, we adjust to the changing circumstances of our lives.

Adjusting to constant change generates distress for you. Your ultimate fear is of dying, losing your life. Each passing moment over which you have no control is like experiencing a death. The future is uncertain, causing you more anxiety. You tend to imagine the worst when something is unknown, excluding the possibility of the best occurring. Constant change keeps you on edge because you feel so powerless to comprehend and control it.

To create a false sense of security, you hang on to the regrets of the past and worries about the future. However, living fully in the present moment, open to the flow and pulse of life, is the only path to peace.

The Third Fact: The Self Is Open

The third fact frightens you, and you wish it would be different. Stop for a moment and reflect on your experience of yourself. Little remains the same. The molecules of your body continuously exchange with the molecules of the environment. Thoughts, feelings, and sensations within you rise and fall. Even your sense of who you are changes over time and in different situations. Who are you really?

In your anxious state, the idea of an open, fluid self may be intolerable. For the sake of security, you want things fixed, orderly, and predictable. So, you construct an identity for yourself, play roles, and tell yourself stories about yourself. You may use a variety of adjectives to describe who you are. Somehow, you think you can capture the essence of who you are by these fixed ideas about yourself.

Deep down, if you listen to your experience, you sense you are more than your thoughts about yourself. You are even more than what others say about you. You are not an object for all to analyze and categorize. You are a person, free and open to new experiences, to surprises. Only breaking the bonds of your narrow-minded view of yourself will set you free.

A Fourth Fact: Thoughts and Feelings Are Empty

I would like to add a corollary to the third fact regarding the open/empty self. Your thoughts and feelings have less substance than you tend to give them. They rise and fall, come and go. Your thoughts and feelings are not indisputable facts about the state of being. They are only what you are thinking or feeling in the moment as you react to your immediate experience. I tell my patients, "Your thoughts and feelings are like clouds. They are passing mist. Sometimes it seems a storm front has settled in and does not move. But the storm always passes. The thoughts and feelings come from you, but they are not you. You are the blue sky."

Watch the Flow

When you are anxious, you tend to give your thoughts more weight than they deserve. You live by the illusion that your thinking can save you from every danger. So, you always want to be prepared. You worry about the future, imagining that all your pessimistic expectations will inevitably come true. You may also think that by changing your thinking from negative to positive you will be happy. You believe in the power of thinking to alter reality, but, inevitably, you are disappointed, and your anxiety deepens.

I recommend that you change your relationship to your thoughts and feelings, rather than make the futile and artificial effort to change them. You cannot effectively manipulate yourself into thinking and feeling differently. Your thoughts and feelings emerge from a stream of consciousness with deep unconscious roots. They come and go in an endless stream. Nevertheless, you are always free to decide how much weight you give the thoughts and feelings and how you decide to act on them. There is no irresistible thought. You only think that. And you can decide not to act on the urgent thought or feeling.

You can take three different attitudes to your ongoing stream of thoughts, feelings, and sensations. First, you can try to stop the flow by ignoring them or distracting yourself with other thoughts and activities, but the pressure builds, and the unwanted thoughts and feelings erupt with a vengeance. Or they seep through in indirect ways, influencing your behavior without your awareness. For example, when you worry about something, you mentally try to redirect the flow of your consciousness.

The second approach is to jump into the stream of consciousness, give up any effort to manage the flow, and risk drowning. In the midst of a panic attack, you feel powerless to resist the urgent rush of threatening thoughts and feelings, and are overwhelmed.

The third approach, the only really effective one, is to become an observer of the flow of your thoughts and feelings. It is like standing back and watching a waterfall without trying to dam it or jump in. With practice, you can learn to become an astute observer of yourself and the ongoing flow of thoughts, feelings, and sensations. Taking in the information, you learn from the flow and then decide how to act in your best interest.

The Paradox of Suffering and Health

The first step suggests the paradox: "We suffer to get well." Your natural instinct tells you to avoid the suffering in any way possible. You want to get rid of the discomfort of anxiety. To achieve that, you wear yourself out trying to control your thoughts and feelings, your environment, and other people. Eventually, you become exhausted and want to give up in despair.

Acknowledging your powerlessness over your anxiety and embracing it to learn more about yourself, opens the door to new life. Pain propels you to undertake a personal journey in search of healing and a deeper wisdom. The suffering, if accepted, opens your heart to personal responsibility and compassion for yourself and others.

The book of Chinese wisdom, *Tao Te Ching*, expresses clearly this truth:

Failure is an opportunity.
If you blame someone else,
there is no end to the blame.

Therefore, the Master
fulfills her own obligations
and corrects her own mistakes
She does what she needs to do
and demands nothing of others (79).

In the midst of your failure and sense of powerlessness to manage your anxiety, you have a choice. You can give up in despair and blame others, your circumstances, or fate for your misery. You can choose to remain a victim of your anxiety. Or you can shift the focus to yourself and take responsibility for your own life. You can look seriously at your own life, over which you have power, and make decisions based on your deepest desires and true values. In surrendering to the powerlessness over your condition, you can begin to take charge of your life.

Practice: Join a Support Group

You do not need to suffer alone. Your anxiety may drive you to withdraw from social interactions to feel safe. You may be embarrassed by your anxiety and want to hide it from others. You can easily become a prisoner of shame, which will only increase your sense of painful isolation.

The best way to overcome fear, of course, is to face it, particularly if you are self-conscious about being exposed publically. Learn from alcoholics in recovery who discovered the benefit of joining a fellowship with other alcoholics. Gathering with others who suffer from anxiety, who can judge you? The group can become your safety zone. Feeling misunderstood by "the normals," those in the group can offer support, empathy, and understanding. You can learn from others what helps them to cope, and you can break out of your obsession with self-preservation to assist the group. The power of the group can give you hope for healing.

The following is a sampling of various support groups for the anxious:

Emotions Anonymous and Anxiety Disorders Anonymous follow the Twelve Steps of Alcoholics Anonymous and provide support for individuals suffering from a variety of mental and emotional health issues. The peer-led support groups help the participants face their emotional struggles and work toward recovery and personal growth.

A variety of support groups have arisen to assist you with your specific anxiety disorder: Agoraphobics in Motion, Beyond OCD, Social Anxiety Support Group, Panic Disorder Support Group. Many of these groups have specific meetings for women, men, and teens.

Recovery International is a mental health self-help group led by experienced non-professionals aimed to help those having difficulty coping with life. The program is based on helping you to use your cognitive resources to increase your self-control, self-confidence, and determination to take positive action in your life.

Toastmasters International is a nonprofit educational organization that sponsors clubs to help its members develop skills in public speaking, communication, and leadership. It can be a valuable forum for those who have anxiety about public speaking, the most common fear.

Practice: Journal on Your Powerlessness

Anxiety, like all addictions, interferes with you getting to know yourself. You become so preoccupied with the anxious discomfort and efforts to avoid it that you disconnect from yourself. You may even begin to identify with the anxiety and imagine that it defines you as a person. Remember, your anxious reactions come from you, but they are not you. They arise automatically from your emotional programming from childhood. They come from the surface of who you are, not the depths.

A good way to become more aware of yourself and less identified with your mood state is to become an observer of yourself. That involves simply learning to pay close attention to yourself, to your thoughts, feelings, sensations, and behaviors.

A good practice to develop self-awareness is to keep a diary of your daily reactions to events. Make it your own personal anxiety diary that can help you put your reactions into a larger perspective. You can review that diary at any time and notice the ebb and flow of your reactions. Thoughts, feelings, and sensations are always in flux, and therefore, cannot define you as a person.

Begin the process of journaling by purchasing a notebook. I recommend as a first entry that you spend some time thinking about how your anxiety has affected your life and then write down what you learn. Reflect on two questions: How am I powerless over my anxiety? How has my life become unmanageable because of it?

The first question: How am I powerless over my anxiety? The core of anxiety is the sense of being out of control in a threatening world. Undoubtedly, you make efforts to manage your anxiety to lessen its grip on your life. How much pain has your anxiety caused you? Allow yourself to feel the emotional distress of your fear, panic, and anxiety. Open yourself to the physical discomfort, the tension, you feel in your stomach, chest, and head. Observe the disturbing thoughts of terror, self-loathing, and relentless danger. How much do you hate your fearful reactions? Allow yourself to feel the intensity of your aversion toward your anxious reactions and toward yourself for having them.

Consider for a moment all the strategies you use to escape or eliminate the anxiety: distracting yourself, running away from threatening persons, places, and things, leaning on rituals and routines, attempting to control others and your environment. Note also your recovery work: reading self-help books, participating in individual and group therapy, taking medications.

Have all these efforts succeeded in controlling or eliminating your anxiety? Have your failed efforts awakened in you a sense of powerlessness?

The second question: How has my life become unmanageable because of my anxiety? Your anxiety makes you feel out of control with your emotions, thoughts, physical sensations, and behaviors. In the grip of fear or panic, you feel overwhelmed. You become paralyzed, focused on relieving the pain. How does your anxiety affect your daily living? What activities have you given up? Think of what you used to do and how you felt before the anxiety began to take over your life. You may feel like a failure, judging yourself harshly, because of your condition. How has your self-esteem suffered? Has your poor self-image caused you to withdraw even more?

Because your anxiety is so overwhelmingly distressful, you undoubtedly have undertaken many strategies to cope. What do you do to manage your anxiety? How much time and energy does it take just to get by? What energy and interest are left to pursue those activities that make you feel alive? Does it feel like you or your anxiety is controlling your life?

What will it take for you to regain control over your life? You discover the answer to that question in working the steps.

In the first step, you become intimate with your pain. You experience it fully, without running away from it. Recognizing how much your fear and anxiety have taken over your life and all your failed efforts to control it, you admit your powerlessness. That heart-felt admission is the first step on your journey toward recovery of your lost and broken self.

7

Hope Springs Eternal: Night Music

Step 2: "Came to believe that a Power greater than ourselves could restore us to sanity."

"Those who are willing to be vulnerable move among mysteries."

—Theodore Roethke

You embraced the pain of your anxiety and survived. It was a difficult dance with a partner you shunned. But through the dance, you came to a realization of your powerlessness over your anxiety and an acknowledgment of how it has harmed your life. Disillusioned, you now know you cannot find refuge in yourself alone. Your efforts to rid yourself of your fears have failed. Anxiety has defeated you. That defeat now launches you on a search for a sanctuary, a place of safety greater than yourself. The crack in your longed-for self-sufficiency moves you forward.

Where do you find refuge in a world you perceive as dangerous? Feeling insecure, you look for a strong, reliable dance partner who can protect and nurture you. That partner has been invisible, absent to you in your anxious fog. You wander the dance floor in darkness, not knowing where to look for that reassuring partner. Music of the night plays, haunting and seductive. It expresses your mood, your conflicted feelings. Admitting your powerlessness was liberating, yet frightening.

Coming to the dance, you see a glimmer of hope on the horizon. Like the alcoholic, you may struggle to believe. Your desires for certainty, clarity, and control make faith in a Power beyond yourself frightening. If you are already a believer, you may think your fear condemns you as a person lacking faith. True faith should dispel all fear. A deep longing for that Power greater than yourself to rescue you from your fears also possesses you.

Katherine: Struggles with Faith

"I was born a Catholic and suffered from obsessive-compulsive disorder since child-hood. Being Catholic and having OCD worked well for me for many years. I had an innate fear of hell, which I calmed by throwing myself into the prayers and rituals. I never missed Sunday Mass, prayed the Rosary daily, and attended devotions to Mary. I also went to confession every week.

When I was in my twenties, I began to despair because my OCD got worse, despite all my religious practices. I began to question God and lost my faith. How could a good and loving God allow me to suffer like this?

I'm still searching, but haven't found the answer yet."

"Came to believe..."

The step from admitting powerlessness to believing in a Higher Power is a daunting one. It may defy your natural instincts to live life reasonably on your own terms. Let me present a view of faith that may respond to some of your objections. Believing concerns

- a journey, not a destination;
- the unknown, not the known;
- letting go, not hanging on;
- living from the heart, not the head;
- opening, not closing;
- here and now, not then and there; and
- a lifestyle, not a belief system.

A Journey, Not a Destination

Coming to believe is an ongoing process that is never complete. It begins with the desire to believe and may take many twists and turns before you arrive at a decision of faith. You may find yourself hesitant to take that leap of faith for many reasons. As a reasonable, even scientific-minded person, you do not want to sacrifice your intellectual integrity, accepting what you cannot understand. You will not tolerate blind obedience. You may have been scandalized by the behavior of churches and supposedly religious people who do not practice what they preach. Talk about God may not make sense to you, and you do not see any connection between faith and your emotional problems.

Whatever your reservations, you do not need to rush to belief until you are ready. All that is required is an open mind and heart and a willingness to search for a deeper truth in life.

The Unknown, Not the Known

As an anxious person, you have an exquisite sensitivity to the unknown, the uncertain, and the unpredictable. You know life is a mystery beyond your control. All this uncertainty makes you nervous. To avoid discomfort, you create the illusion of security by manufacturing fixed ideas about how your life is and should be. You construct many plans and projects to make your life predictable. You look for guarantees that nothing will go wrong. Even though you are temperamentally primed to believe in mystery, you choose to live on the surface of life in the realm of the known.

Faith invites you to look deeper, beneath the surface of everyday life, into areas of the unconscious. Believing draws you into the darkness of the unknown that is beyond your understanding and control but from which all knowing arises. It is a journey to the Center and Source of life, which is shrouded in mystery. Despite your anxiety with the unknown and your desire for solid ground, you know that you cannot completely shrink the mystery of life into what you can manageably know. You sense that being comfortable with the unknown, the unpredictable, and the unfamiliar is essential for you to be free from your fears.

Letting Go, Not Hanging On

You cannot make faith happen. You cannot force yourself or anyone else to believe. Instead, you have to open your mind and heart to the mystery of life, to the completely new and unexpected revealing itself. That requires letting go of many of your assumptions about how life should be.

If you are anxious, you have many unacknowledged beliefs. "Life holds many dangers. The worst always happens. You have to be on guard. You cannot trust others." For the sake of security, you believe you need to hang on tightly to these beliefs. To make room for faith, you have to surrender these fixed ideas and open yourself to the possibility of surprise and wonder.

Living from the Heart, Not the Head

Faith does not contradict reason, but you cannot reason yourself to believe. The mystery of faith goes beyond the thinking mind and engages you at a deeper level. You believe with your whole person, your mind, heart, and soul. It requires a wholehearted trust, a heart-consciousness that engages you at all levels of who you are.

As much as you think your frightful emotions dominate you, the truth is you are a prisoner of your pessimistic thinking. You are lost in your thoughts about terrible things happening. Preoccupied with these negative ideas, you become disengaged from yourself. Your thinking mind analyzes, judges, manipulates, and distances you from yourself and others. Your chattering thoughts distract you from the subtle whisperings of your heart. You do not trust what you cannot understand or control. At some level, you may sense that you are addicted to your negative way of thinking and feel powerless to change it. You long to live from your heart, not your head, knowing that is the path to a richer life.

Opening, Not Closing

Faith involves a journey to the mountaintop where you can see forever. It is a new state of consciousness open to the fullness of life, where you see that everything belongs. Nothing is excluded. Even what you fear and despise can be incorporated into your path to a wholesome life.

Living in the mental cave of your anxiety, you exclude experiences and activities you judge threatening. In the name of safety, your world shrinks. The leap of faith can seem frightening because it means giving up what you think you need to be safe. You may wish for the courage to leave the confines of the cave and search for the path that leads to the mountaintop. Faith beckons you forward to face your fears and open your mind and heart.

Here and Now, Not There and Then

Many of you despise religion because it takes you out of the world. It promises heavenly rewards in the afterlife. The mission of believers, then, is to endure the trials and tribulations of the present life with the hope of a better life later.

That is a distortion of authentic faith. Believing involves being fully engaged in the present moment which reveals the divine presence. It means taking this life seriously, making this world a better place, as the path to happiness. The eternal is found in the everyday, here, now.

Your anxiety prevents you from living fully in the present moment. You live more in your mind than in your body. Where does your mind go? It flees the discomfort of the present. It retreats to the past in second-guessing yourself and accumulating regrets. It also flies to future, worrying about all that can go wrong. The distress of regret and worry may awaken a longing in you to enjoy the present moment, a necessary condition for faith.

A Lifestyle, Not a Belief System

Believing is not simply a matter of professing a creed, of saying, "I believe in God." Many of you reject religion because so many professed believers do not practice what they preach. They talk about the God of love but live in hateful ways. They preach the golden rule but live self-centered lives. Commonsense says that you get a more accurate reading of what someone believes by watching the feet, not the lips.

Authentic faith is more about action than words. It is embracing a way of life guided by a belief in the Ultimate Source of Love. The Dalai Lama expressed this beautifully when he said, "My religion is kindness." Genuine faith overflows in a life of virtue which is its true mark. Coming to faith will require you to give up your anxious self-obsession with safety that interferes with you freely loving others.

"...that a Power greater than ourselves..."

Where do you find your security in life? Your sense of powerlessness and your anxiety launch you on a safety mission. In the search, you face disillusionment. Many have failed to protect you. Much has given you a false sense of security.

Mark: Personal Search and Bible Church

"My father was a mean drunk. He used to beat all us kids. We were terrified of him. Our mother was afraid of him, too. She never tried to stop the beatings because he would hit her, too. At a young age, I knew that I could not trust the powers that be.

As insecure as I felt about myself, I kept looking for love—but always in the wrong places. It seems that all the girls I dated were as troubled as I. They drank a lot, were demanding, or cheated on me.

I was about ready to give up on relationships completely when a friend invited me to his Bible Church. I accepted the invitation with many reservations. What a surprise I experienced at the lively service! The people were so warm, welcoming, and happy. I participated in a Bible class and began reading the Bible for the first time. What I read made so much sense to me. I think I found in the Bible a sure guide for my life."

Where's the Power?

Feeling so powerless, where do you find that Power greater than yourself on which you can rely? Your search can take you in many directions. You may put your faith in three different places: in your own perceptions, in reason, or in God.

You may look out at the world and tell yourself, "What you see is what you get." You observe nature in all its splendor and terror. The beauty of one season replaces another. Storms, earthquakes, and tornados come and go. All the species battle one another for survival. New life erupts in the wake of death and destruction. You trust your perceptions, believing there is nothing more than you can observe.

You sense the natural power of nature, some life-force that keeps all alive and in motion. However, you cannot see, touch, hear, smell, or taste that life-force, only see its effects in the world. Further, you cannot tame or name that indescribable energy. In your anxiety, you fear becoming its victim. So, you try to make peace with the world, living in harmony with the mysterious life-force.

You may also look within yourself, intuiting a hidden power. You have the power of reason that sets you apart from all the other creatures in the world. You believe in the God of reason and see humanity as its divinely inspired messengers. With the power of reason, the human race invented science and technology which enables it to manipulate nature for its own purposes. You have the innate power to create beauty in art, to make free choices, to give yourself in love. You can understand deep truths and communicate with others, building community. No one can deny the grandeur and glory of being human.

Nevertheless, your optimism hits a wall with your anxious suffering. You feel defeated. Even with the power of your reason you cannot overcome the torments of anxiety.

As a religious person, you may look beyond yourself and put your faith in God, the Supreme Being. That is the conventional approach of traditional religion which has consoled people for millennia. Religion arose to answer the question of the meaning of life in the shadow of death. The answer given: a God of justice and love will reward you in the next life for your good deeds and punish you for your sins.

You relish the clarity and certainty of the system, but may object that for many it leads to blind obedience. Many believers become like sheep. Further, you may also be disillusioned by many professed believers who live with hypocrisy, bigotry, and self-righteousness. Believing in God may cause you to give up any faith in yourself, increasing your sense of powerlessness over your life.

There is an alternative to these three approaches.

The Paradox of Power

Listening closely to your own experience, you can discern a power that is completely within you, yet utterly beyond you. It feels like a power greater than yourself. In quiet moments, if you pay attention, you sense deep urgings for love, truth, goodness, and beauty. The struggles of daily life often obscure and interfere with you realizing your deepest desires. Yet, these desires and occasional glimpses of something more persist. There are moments when you feel fully alive even in the midst of your anxious nightmare. You experience the joy of the birth of a child, the beauty of a sunset, the thrill of an accomplishment.

Do you ever wonder how you survive the torments of fear without falling apart? What keeps you together?

Laura: Search for Inner Peace

"I grew up in an abusive home, feeling powerless and anxious. My life has been a constant search to fill that void, to do something to overcome my sense of inadequacy. I pushed myself to be the best in school. I graduated college and went to law school. I felt like I had a calling to be a divorce lawyer and help women who had been abused by their husbands. I fought tenaciously for them, sensing I was also fighting for myself.

Then, a colleague put a crazy idea in my head, 'Why don't you run for judge in the family court?' She recognized my passion for justice, especially for the underdog. To my great surprise, I won the election. At last, I found myself doing what I was truly meant to do. I have compassion for the children who are abused and neglected, and now I can do something to help them. I discovered a power within myself just to be myself and make a difference in the world."

That power within yourself is your true self that is hidden by the clouds of your anxiety and fear. You are not your condition even though you feel like it is swallowing you up as a person. Your recovery involves coming home to yourself, discovering who you really are deep down, beneath the stormy surface of your anxiety. Deep down you discover wisdom, peace, and power.

Yet you do not own or create that power within. Another paradox: it is yours, but not yours. It comes from a Source beyond you, yet within you. It is a divine, sacred presence that you may call God. You are "made in the image and likeness of God." His life dwells within you. You are one with God, yet not God. In coming to know yourself, you discover the Divine, the Ultimate Reality, at the heart of your being. In searching for God, you come to know yourself at the deepest level. As the great saint Teresa of Avila said, "You find God in yourself and yourself in God."

Taking the first step, admitting your powerlessness over your anxiety, prepares you for the second step. It opens your mind and heart, motivating you to search for a power greater than yourself. As AA states, "Religion is for those who are afraid they'll go to hell. Spirituality is for people who have been there." Your experience of hell makes you long for heaven. From your despair springs hope for new life.

"...could restore us to sanity"

Your anxiety, like any addiction, makes you feel insane. You realize that your frightful thoughts are irrational, but you cannot dispel them by efforts to be reasonable. You argue with yourself, berate yourself for your silly fears, and try to think of something else. You imagine that worry will magically make everything better. Nothing works. All your concerted efforts to rid yourself of the dreaded anxiety only make you feel more defeated, more broken. You are in over your head. The AA slogan echoes in your mind, "Insanity is defined as doing the same thing over, and over again, expecting different results."

Finding Your Center

How can you restore your sanity? The key word is *restore*. You seek to recover something that was lost, to find your original sanity, which is hidden behind the cloud of your anguish. That may seem surprising to you. You felt crazy with anxiety for as long as you can remember. In fact, you define yourself as an anxious person. That is who you are. You have never known a time when you were not fearful.

Beneath your anxious façade lives a sane person. Your true nature is wholeness, health, clarity, and peace, which has become misshapen by your anxious state. Your anxious mind is like a glass filled with muddy water. When the glass is shaken by fear and fright, the silt from the bottom fills the whole glass. No light can shine through the muddy water. As long as you are agitated, the dirty water remains stirred up and opaque. When you learn to calm yourself, the sediment settles to the bottom of the glass. The water, then, becomes clear, and light can shine through. The natural state of your mind is clean, fresh water through which the bright light of truth radiates.

Patients come to me in distress, seeking change. They are surprised when I tell them my view of therapy. I explain, "Therapy is not a self-improvement project, about creating a better version of yourself. Instead, it is about allowing yourself simply to be yourself and removing any obstacles to you being your true self."

Recovery involves letting the muddy waters of your agitated emotions settle. The calming permits the natural wisdom, strength, and compassion to shine forth. It releases the power of your true self.

Holly: Inner Strength

"I surprised myself that I didn't fall apart when the doctor told me I had breast cancer. Cancer runs in our family. My grandmother and father died from it. From as far back as I can remember, I lived in terror of getting sick. I constantly monitored any physical aches and pains and imagined they were signs of a growing tumor. My mother was a hypochondriac, and her constant worrying and obsessing about health didn't help. I came to believe that it was my fate to die of cancer.

When the doctor told me after my CAT scan that the lump on my breast was malignant, I amazed myself at how calm I was. I was determined to fight the cancer and talked with the doctor about the plan for treatment. I dug deep within myself. I don't know where the strength and hope came from."

The following practices can help you connect with yourself at a deeper level:

Practice: Journal on Your Anxious Reactions

Keeping a journal helps you to stay close to your experience. When you are anxious, you tend to get lost in your negative thinking and lose perspective on your life. You stray from your immediate experience. Making a commitment to journal regularly can break the cycle of your obsessive thinking.

Relax for a moment. Ponder your experience. What is it like for you when you feel anxious? Spend some time reflecting about your anxious reactions, which are personal to you. Then, write what you observe about yourself.

Notice first the physical sensations you experience when anxious and where you hold the tension in your body. Your body holds the accumulated pain from a lifetime that your mind tends to forget. Do you have headaches? Do you feel dizzy or lightheaded? Do you feel tension in your in your neck, shoulders, or other muscles? Does your heart beat rapidly or do you feel pressure in your chest? Do you experience shortness of breath, a choking feeling? Do you feel distress in your stomach, knots or churning or loose bowels? Do you sweat or blush? Do you feel irritable, restless, or fatigued? Do you feel shaky and tremble?

Thoughts accompany these physical sensations. Observe them closely and notice the repeating pattern. What do you tend to worry about: dying, the health of yourself and your loved ones, being judged in social gatherings, failing in performance? Do you tend to ruminate about the past, reviewing critically what you said and did, second-guessing yourself? Do you entertain critical thoughts about yourself, your appearance, your performance, or your faults? Are you preoccupied with being in danger?

Pay attention to your habitual behaviors. Do you have the habit of biting your nails, twirling your hair, or tapping your feet? How do you distract yourself: eating, drinking, watching TV, sleeping, playing video games? What do you tend to avoid: social situations, crowds, work challenges, phone calls, or high places? Do you engage in rituals and routines to comfort yourself: counting, washing your hands, checking doors? When you feel threatened, do you act aggressively to protect yourself?

Each day take a personal inventory of your anxious reactions. Over time you will notice a pattern and what triggers the reactions.

Practice: Walk in Nature

Nature heals. When you remain in the confines of your home or stay in the asphalt jungle, it reinforces your anxious, closed-in cave mentality. It leads to isolation and suffocation. Conversely, when you venture into the outdoors, you open yourself to seeing the world from a larger perspective. You can gain a mountaintop, big sky experience that frees your mind, heart, and spirit.

Jesus advised the worried to observe the birds in the sky and the wild flowers in the field. He said to learn from them how they thrive and show beauty without toil or effort. What Jesus suggested was what He Himself did. He often wandered off into the wilderness where He received enlightenment and refreshment. He spent forty days in the desert before beginning his ministry.

In fact, all the founders of the great religions received consolation and inspiration in nature. Moses led his people through the desert for forty years and was given the Law from Yahweh. Buddha fasted and meditated in the forest. Muhammad went off into a desert cave and heard the words of revelation. The wilderness experience can open you to many surprises and help to break out of the confines of your worry.

Make time to spend in the great outdoors. If you are fortunate, you can enjoy the beauty of a walk on the beach, a hike through the mountains, or a stroll through the woods. But your nature walk need not be so dramatic. Simply sit in your garden, walk in a park, or relax by a lake or stream. Just allow yourself to bathe yourself in the experience. Stop your chattering mind and observe with all your senses.

As the Buddha advised: "Whenever you see a form, simply see; whenever you smell an aroma, simply smell; whenever you taste a flavor, simply taste; whenever you feel a sensation, simply feel; whenever a thought arises, let it be just a thought."

Get out of your mind and into your experience in nature. Take in all the sights, the expansive sky, the lush vegetation, the living creatures. Listen carefully to the sounds of nature, the birds singing, the wind rushing through the trees. Smell the freshness of the air, and feel the warmth of the sun. Touch the solid ground. Let the experience liberate you to an awakening of a power and glory that is beyond, around, and within you.

Practice: Follow Your Breath

Caught up in anxiety, your mind jumps around with thoughts of catastrophe. You cannot focus your attention, behaving as if you have attention deficit disorder. You feel even more out of control trying to manage the relentless stream of thoughts and feelings.

An ancient eastern practice to help calm the mind is called "Samadhi," which means "abiding in peace" (1). It is a practice that can help you concentrate, calm yourself, and experience peace. In the process, you experience your own inner power by consciously focusing your attention, which you can control, with practice. You deliberately stand back and observe the passing thoughts, feelings, and sensations without being caught up in the drama. As an observer, you can separate yourself from the psychic parade and not identify with your anxious reactions.

The practice involves the discipline of focusing your attention on one thing, your breath. You exercise your "attention muscle," which, like all muscles, strengthens with use. Why focus on the breath? The breath represents life, freedom, and connection in the present moment, precisely what you miss in your anxious mind. Breathing oxygen, you are alive; when you stop breathing, you die. Your breathing keeps you in the present moment. As a bodily function and immediate experience, you cannot drift into the past or the future as your anxious mind tends to do with its wayward thoughts.

The procedure for this practice is simple:

1) Find a quiet place, away from as many distractions as possible. Sit in a relaxed position with your back erect and your head straight. You may sit in a chair with your feet firmly planted on the ground and hands on your lap, palms facing upward in a position of receiving a gift. You may prefer to sit in the traditional lotus position with your legs crossed, but that is not necessary. Whatever your preferred posture, feel as though you are grounded. Keep your eyes closed to avoid distractions. Begin with the intention to pay full attention only to your breath.

2) Next, breathe deeply from your abdomen. It is important to breathe deeply, from the center of your body, and not in a shallow manner as you do when anxious. Breathe regularly and sense the fresh air filling all parts of your body. Scan your body and notice the areas of tension. Consciously send your breath to those areas and feel the warmth of your breath bring relaxation. Let the frozen tension melt away. Breathe slowly and regularly, not quickly and unsteadily, as when you are fearful. Find comfort in the regularity of your slow, deep breathing.

3) Now focus all your attention on the rising and falling of your breath. You may begin by counting your breaths and noticing the gap between inhaling and exhaling. Follow the sensation of your breathing and the moving of your body from your stomach, through your chest and windpipe, and out your nose. Become body-conscious. Soon you will notice intrusive thoughts and other sensations that distract you from attending fully to your breath. Your racing mind wants to take over, but resist the urge and return to your breath.

4) When you are distracted by thoughts and other sensations, gently let them go. Do not dwell on them as you usually do. Return your attention to your breath. Also, avoid struggling with the thoughts. Do not try to get rid of them as you often do when the thoughts are unpleasant. Simply acknowledge their presence and continue following your breath.

Practice this procedure every day to make it a habit. You can begin with a five-minute practice and gradually extend the time as you become more comfortable with it. You can do this exercise at any time and in any place for brief periods, especially when you are feeling anxious. If you commit yourself to this exercise on a regular basis, you will be surprised at its calming effect. You already know how difficult it is to tame your mind. However, with discipline, you can train your mind to stay in the present moment and find some relief from your anxiety.

One word of caution. If you were traumatized as a child by abuse, being quiet and still may be overwhelming for you. Flashbacks and painful thoughts and feelings may emerge.

Stop the practice if you feel overwhelmed. Learn your zone of tolerance and gradually incorporate quiet in your life.

In the second step, you continue the effort to know yourself. You sense that beneath the painful façade of your anxiety is an unacknowledged strength. That strength comes from a Power greater than your anxious self, a Power that is both within and beyond you. It radiates from your neglected true, sane self.

8

Willful or Willing?
Relaxing with the Unknown

Step 3: "Made a decision to turn our will and
our lives over to the care of God as we understood Him."

"The fear of the Lord is the beginning of wisdom."

—Proverbs 1:9

You experienced so much darkness in your anxious searching. The unknown has been your constant companion, perceived as an enemy. You always sought a sense of security in what you know, understand, and control. But the unpredictability of your life has defeated all your fearful efforts at control. Yet you do not give up.

You continue to wander the dance floor. A light shines in the shadows, giving you a glimpse of a strong, reliable partner. She is attractive and beckoning you to dance, yet she is mysterious in her beauty, somehow foreboding and enchanting.

Because of your naturally cautious nature, you hesitate before stepping forward to ask her to dance. Frightening thoughts arise: "Will she accept my invitation to dance? Will I be an adequate partner? What will she expect of me? What do I risk in asking her to dance with me?" You sense the gravity of the decision. It is not something to rush into. There is a lot at stake.

In your anguished indecision, the band begins to play soul music. The music captivates you, and you start to move with the music, putting aside your anxious thoughts. Then suddenly, you approach that mysterious partner and ask, "Shall we dance?"

"Made a decision…"

The Nike commercial proclaims, "Just do it!" That goes counter to all your natural instincts. Caution rules you. You consider all your decisions from every possible angle, with the specter of defeat nearby. You cannot imagine a good outcome, no matter what you decide. So, you obsess.

Anxiety obsessed, you feel stuck in life. Your obsessive strivings for control fail so often. The familiar does not satisfy you, and the unknown terrifies you. You do not know where to turn to find security. Deep down you sense you will have to sacrifice everything familiar to find a refuge from your fears. No wonder you are caught in the throes of indecision.

Sarah: Obstacles to Making a Decision

"I felt trapped in an unhappy marriage. We rushed into marriage without seriously thinking about it. That was unusual for me because I tend to obsess about everything. But I was obsessed with him and shoved back my fears and commonsense. Now that we have been married for three years, I have no doubt I made the biggest mistake of my life. My husband drinks and carouses with women.

I know I should divorce him but cannot muster the courage. I love him, but I know he isn't good for me. When I think about divorce, my anxiety level becomes intolerable.

I try to imagine life without him. We have moments of great fun. He knows how to make me laugh. I can be so serious. I worry about him finding another woman, changing, and being happy with her. What if I just wait this rough period out, and he changes to become the sober, faithful man of my dreams? I am going crazy trying to make up my mind."

Anxious and fearful, there are many reasons for difficulty in decision-making. Your addictive habits of thinking paralyze you. The following statements reveal your anxious, indecisive mind:

"I don't want to make a mistake." Uncertainty frightens you. If you make a decision, you want some guarantee that it is the right decision. Making a decision also creates change, which requires an adjustment in your thinking and behavior. More uncertainty follows. Instead, you tend to cling to what is familiar and have difficulty imagining that a change could improve your life.

"I can't trust myself to make the right decision." Your inner critic is never silent. The critic monitors all your behavior and thoughts, judging them harshly. You begin to mistrust yourself, your perceptions and judgments. Losing confidence in yourself, you feel inadequate to know what is right for you. Anxiety makes your mental world shrink. You have difficulty tolerating ambiguity because it creates too much uncertainty. For comfort, you reduce your world to clear either-or categories. A situation is either good or bad; actions are either right or wrong. Your black-and-white thinking makes you believe that decisions can only be right or wrong. If the choice is not clear-cut, you feel handicapped to decide.

"No matter what I decide, the outcome will be terrible." Your pessimism makes you imagine the worst. You feel a sense of helplessness that cripples you. No decision to make a change can bring relief. You may seek security in maintaining the status quo, hanging on to the familiar. "Better the devil you know than the devil you do not know," you tell yourself.

"I see dangers everywhere." The core of anxiety is a heightened sensitivity to danger, both real and imagined. Your brain is always on high-alert, which keeps you on-edge. The tension may interfere with your thinking clearly to make a rational decision. Your fear freezes your mind, not allowing you to consider alternatives for decision-making.

"If I ignore it, I won't have to do anything." One way to cope with anxiety is to distract yourself from what disturbs you. You become a master juggler, keeping your mind engaged with constant motion. Plans, projects, and worries occupy your limited mind space. Restlessness prevents you from knowing yourself and what you want to do. You simply keep busy to avoid making a decision.

"What will everybody think?" Your self-centeredness leads you to believe everybody is watching you and cares about what you are doing. Your inner critic imagines that everybody is judging you negatively. As a consequence, you put more energy into worrying about what others think than about what you really want to do.

Scared stiff, you cannot confidently decide and act.

"...to turn our will and our lives over..."

Alcoholics Anonymous identifies in no uncertain terms the root cause of the addict's problems: "Our whole trouble had been the misuse of willpower. We had tried to bombard our problems with it instead of attempting to bring it into agreement with God's intention for us (Steps/Traditions, p. 40)." Not trusting in anyone or anything but themselves, alcoholics try to control their moods, environment, and others with their drug. They become obsessed with power, using it for their own gratification. The pursuit of pleasure and the avoidance of pain direct their lives.

Efforts to Manage Anxiety

Rose commented on her efforts to manage her anxiety:

"When I'm in a crowd, I begin to freak out. My heart pounds, and I can hardly breathe. I can only think, 'I'm suffocating and have to get out of here.' It doesn't matter where I am or who I'm with. The urge to run away is too powerful. I'm not thinking about manners or how my leaving will affect others. I'm only concerned about myself and my safety. I see myself as a polite and generous person, but when I panic, I only think about myself."

The anxiety addiction keeps you stuck on yourself, preoccupied with your own security. Little else matters when you are in the grip of fear. Your only thought is of escape. The pleasure you pursue is really quite basic: security and safety. If you do not feel safe, you lack the psychic freedom to pursue other desires in your life.

To compensate for your sense of helplessness in a threatening world, you obsess about gaining power over your life. Survival strategies fill your mind. You play it safe, not extending yourself into activities that are uncomfortable. You live within the bounds of the familiar, developing daily routines and habits of thinking. Order gives you a sense of security.

The danger, of course, is that you can become a control freak who wants everything to go your way. Everyone must go along with your schedule, your routines, and your rules. Otherwise, your anxiety will overwhelm you.

How can you ever break the bond of fear that enslaves your mind, emotions, and behavior? How can you surrender your will to power and open yourself to a larger reality? You can begin with your mind, paying close attention to your thinking.

The Circus of the Mind

Like all addictions, anxiety is fundamentally a disease of the mind. "Stinking thinking" rules you. Modern psychology affirms the power of the mind to influence feelings and behaviors. It echoes what the Buddha taught in his own commonsense way 2600 years ago: "The mind is everything. What you think you become."

Hooked on anxiety, your own thinking imprisons you. You dwell in an air-tight mental cave, believing the world corresponds exactly to your thoughts about it. Because you think something, you believe it must be true. It never occurs to you how biased you are in your thinking. You fail to realize how your self-centeredness makes you cling to your opinions. Your will to power expresses itself in the following mental attitude: "I want to have power; I will take control; I will always be right; see, I am indeed powerful" (1).

I attempt to nudge my patients out of their thought caves by telling them, "Your thoughts and feelings are like clouds that always pass. They come from you, but are not you. You are the blue sky." I also refer to their thoughts as "thought bubbles," suggesting their lightness and elusiveness. Many of my patients can admit that their feelings come and go, but they experience their thoughts as solid, steady, and reliable. They imagine their thoughts the solid ground on which they stand.

To turn your will and life over, you need to change your mind. I recommend a four step process to help loosen the grip of their cave-like thinking and open you to a view from the mountaintop.

Watch the Parade

First, become an observer of the free flow of your thoughts. Notice how the thoughts arise from nowhere and nothingness, pass through your mind, and return to emptiness. Have you ever asked yourself, "Where do my thoughts come from, and where do they go?" Recognize the almost steady stream of thoughts through your consciousness.

If you pay close attention, you will see gaps in the parade of changing thoughts. You cannot think about more than one thing at once, so your mind is constantly shifting. There is a brief pause as the mind shifts gears. The pause between the steps in the march of thoughts reveals your pure consciousness, which is the source of your thinking. You cannot observe that mindful awareness directly because there is no place to stand to view it. However, you can perceive its products in your thoughts. You can also sense the unbounded depth of the consciousness in experiencing the gaps.

You are probably so accustomed to being anxious, that you do not notice the automatic and repetitive thoughts that run through your mind. Pay close attention to the thoughts that arise from your anxious mind. If you do, over time, you will begin to notice a particular quality of thinking. You will begin to sense that your mind is biased in the following directions:

- engages in "what if" thinking, imagining the worst case scenarios;
- demonstrates pessimistic thinking, biased toward the negative, what can go wrong;
- is sensitive to dangers, narrow-mindedly focused on threats;
- tends to compare, judge, and criticize in a negative direction;
- is preoccupied with its own ideas of how things "should" be;
- engages in rigid, either-or, black-or-white, all-or-none thinking;
- is self-centered, seeing everything in relationship to your safety;
- avoids present experience, regretting the past and worrying about the future;
- does not tolerate uncertainty and ambiguity;
- is unwilling to bear discomfort;
- possesses a will to power, unwilling to give up control; and/or
- dwells in darkness, leading to fear.

As an observer, you will notice another mind beneath your superficial anxious thinking. That mind allows you to be an observer of yourself and others. It is the pure consciousness that dwells in the gaps of the parade of thoughts. I call it the wise mind that emerges from your true self, not your anxious self, and connects you with all of Reality. It enables you a view from the mountaintop, to see things as they are and to see forever. The following are some qualities of the wise mind:

- attends to present experience, not imaginings about it;
- sees both the positive and negative;
- focuses on the totality of experience;
- seeks to know things as they are;
- discriminates the wholeness of things but sees the connection of all things;
- accepts that everything belongs;
- experiences the present moment fully;
- accepts uncertainty, not knowing, as a path to exploration;

- focuses on value and willing to bear discomfort in its pursuit;

- willingly surrenders to the truth; and

- dwells in darkness as the way to the light.

You will also note the constant interplay of the anxious and wise minds. They are in continuous dialogue. Sometimes one mind is louder than the other and in control of your thinking in the moment. Notice who is talking at any particular moment.

Enjoy the Circus

Accept your conflicting minds and thoughts. Enjoy them. Your tendency is to be pre-occupied with your fearful thoughts and engage in a full-tilt battle to eliminate them. You may distract yourself with activities, but the negative buzz persists. You may even attempt to replace the negative thoughts with positive ones. However, the unpleasant thoughts creep back into your mind, and may even grow in intensity.

Instead of fight or flight, I recommend that you embrace the anxious mind with love and attempt to learn its wisdom. Enjoy the circus with the idea jugglers. Remember that anxiety is a natural emotion. It serves a survival purpose. You ignore its warnings at your own peril. However, the anxious noise may become so loud that you cannot hear the wise mind. The wise mind can discriminate real and imagined dangers. It can also unearth the golden nuggets of wisdom contained in the anxious mind, if you are patient and willing to learn. Anxiety, sensitive to darkness, can open you to the mystery of life, beyond control and comprehension.

Appreciate the Show

Investigate and try to understand your anxious mind. In talking about their anxiety, I tell my patients, "That's an interesting way of thinking. How did you learn to think that way?" Then, together we investigate the history of each idea and way of thinking, tracing it back to its roots. Often, my patients echo the fears of their parents. Parents pass on fright-ening messages and styles of thinking to their children, like a contagious disease. I suggest to my patients that their parents' thinking is only one possibility and that there are many alternatives. They learned one version of the truth, the opinion of their parents. Perhaps it was not as accurate or helpful as they imagine.

Investigating the anxious thoughts, you realize their persistence. You likely held the same beliefs that you blindly accepted as the absolute truth for a long time. Your opinions about reality became fixed and automatic, and you willfully hang on to them. Perhaps it never occurred to you how much faith you put into your own ideas of reality. You never questioned your views, assuming their accuracy.

Follow the Ringmaster

Finally, listen to your wise mind. That is the reliable ringmaster that directs the show. See what makes sense to you in the cacophony of your anxious thoughts. Standing back, you can analyze and evaluate your anxious thoughts and beliefs. Do they make sense to you now? Are dangers being exaggerated? Do you want to use those thoughts as a guide for action? What can you learn about yourself and your experience now? Observing and questioning the flow of your thoughts helps you to see their lightness and not give them so much weight. Further, it helps you not to identify with your thoughts, making them the reality of who you are.

Your thoughts flow like a river that cannot be dammed up effectively. As much as you want to eliminate those unpleasant thoughts, all your efforts to do so will fail. However, you do have freedom to choose with your wise mind how much weight you give to those anxious thoughts. You are always free to choose how to behave, whether or not to act on those urges.

"...to the care of God..."

You search desperately for a pillar in your life, someone or something you can rely on for safety and strength. Traditional religion offers a personal God, a Supreme Being, as that pillar. But can you trust that God? Perhaps you have been disillusioned by the religion of your childhood or by the behavior of professed believers. Maybe you trust more in reason and think you have outgrown a religion that calls for blind faith. Many beliefs may not make sense to you, and you cannot accept the God the churches preach.

Where do you find your pillar, your rock of safety?

Jimmy: Growth in Faith

I was raised Catholic and followed all the rules. As a child, I loved all the rituals and devotions. I went to daily Mass and confession every week. I prayed each morning and night and at meals. I had a special love for Mary and prayed the rosary daily. All of these practices matched my obsessive-compulsive temperament. They made me feel safe—unless I missed a prayer and became filled with dread of punishment. The fear of hell was an ever-present danger, held at bay by my devotions. But over time, the fear began taking over my life, and the practices, my worry about doing them right, oppressed me.

My awakening came when I attended a revival and felt Jesus' presence in my heart like never before. He became my personal Savior. Finally, I found some relief for my anxiety by putting my trust in the Lord."

A Friendly or Hostile Universe?

An urgent question confronts you in your powerlessness: "Is there a Power that I can turn my life over to for security?" If you accept the possibility that God exists, you ask yourself if that God is friendly and merciful or hostile and judging. Einstein famously observed: "The most important decision we make is whether we believe in a friendly or hostile universe."

There is no rational proof to help with that decision. There is no guaranteed answer. However, abundant evidence exists to support either choice.

In support of a friendly universe, we observe that it miraculously provides all we need for survival, growth, and prosperity. The earth gives us food, water, and air to sustain our bodies. Minerals, microbes, plants, and animals interact in a great exchange that sustains the circle of life. Humans love and care for each other, squabble, and multiply to fill the earth. They create marvelous works of art that reflect the breathtaking beauty of the universe. They produce literature and works of wisdom that nourish the mind with truth. Saints are born, such as Gandhi, Mother Teresa, and Francis of Assisi, who display the nobility of the human spirit. All this reflects the goodness of God and our own, made in His image and likeness.

In support of a hostile universe, we notice that nature gives and takes back. As majestic as nature can be, it can also be cruel. Storms and earthquakes occur regularly, leaving a path of death and destruction. Changing seasons bring death to plant and animal life. Plants, animals, and humans compete for limited resources, and only the fittest survive. Their competition and struggle create a circle of death. A glance at human history reveals nearly ceaseless conflicts, wars, and violence, with only brief interludes of peace. Nations threaten each other with total nuclear annihilation. Our species has produced monsters, like Hitler, Stalin, and Genghis Kahn, who incarnate evil. How can there be a good God who allows such suffering and evil to exist in our world?

Your anxious mind is drawn to view the universe as hostile, interfering with your willingness to make a leap of faith. However, your wise mind, intimately connected to Ultimate Reality, is open to all possibilities. It acknowledges its ignorance, looks at the evidence, and seeks to know Reality as it is. You can use your wise mind to prepare yourself to make that leap of faith.

With your wise mind you can make a cost/benefit analysis of viewing the universe as either friendly or hostile. You can make your own personal analysis. The following is an example:

What is the benefit of viewing the universe as friendly?

- It encourages optimism about the future.
- You are more attuned to seeing goodness in everything, especially in yourself and others.
- It inspires confidence, openness, and joy.
- It makes you want to be friendly.
- It helps you see everything as connected and belonging.
- You see yourself destined for happiness.

What is the cost of viewing the universe as friendly?

- You can become naïve to the presence of evil in the world and in yourself.
- You may not be motivated to make efforts to protect yourself.

What is the benefit of viewing the universe as hostile?

- It encourages you to stay alert to danger.

- It makes you ready to take steps to protect yourself.

- You recognize clearly that life is difficult and focus on developing coping skills.

What is the cost of viewing the universe as hostile?

- It encourages pessimism about life.

- It can lead to paranoia and despair.

- It reinforces the thinking of the anxious mind.

- It inspires a cautious attitude, playing it safe, and withdrawing from life.

- You see everything as separate, divided, and threatening.

- You see yourself destined for misery.

You cannot reason yourself to give up your willfulness and surrender willingly to a Higher Power, to Ultimate Reality, to God. However, the leap of faith needs to be reasonable to you before you make the wager to turn over your life and will. An honest cost-benefit analysis of the risk of belief can aid in making that life-changing decision.

"...as we understood Him"

All of us create for ourselves an image of our Higher Power, Ultimate Reality, and God. We use familiar material of our daily life to construct that image of an unknown and mysterious Reality. Often, we create God in our own image, using our experience with authority figures in our lives as the background. For example, if we experience our parents as loving and kind, we tend to envision God as a loving Parent. If we experienced harsh judgment as a child, our God emerges in our minds as a Judge.

Our views of God, our Higher Power, and Ultimate Reality are not as substantial as we think. As the Buddhists express it, all our ideas about reality are not the moon but "fingers pointing to the moon." The language we use to talk about God is not as precise as we imagine. As the poet T.S. Elliot expressed it, "Words strain, crack and sometimes break" (Burnt Norton V).

We, nevertheless, strain to talk about God but with a sense of modesty. We are face to face with Mystery, the Great Unknown. The unknown frightens us, especially if we have anxious minds. The Unknown is beyond our comprehension and control.

Turning your will and life over to this Mystery forces you to face your fear. The third step toward recovery invites you to embrace that fear, not run away from it. It invites you to learn wisdom by relaxing with your fear. "The fear of the Lord is the beginning of wisdom." What do you learn? You learn humility and trust that you are part of something bigger than yourself, beyond your control.

When you make the decision to turn your will and life over to God, Ultimate Reality, or your Higher Power, you have a strange, new experience, which is both frightening and liberating. On the one hand, you experience the Ultimate as an awesome Mystery, a great

Emptiness, which frightens you because it is beyond your understanding and control. It also humbles you as you search for its meaning in your life.

On the other hand, you experience your God as the Ground of your being, a Rock, which inspires hope and confidence. It is holy because it is whole, pervading everything, including yourself. The Ultimate, your God, is utterly beyond and totally within you at the same time.

Relief from fear and anxiety comes from learning to relax with the unknown, the Mystery of life. Such rest can come only if you believe the universe friendly.

The Paradox of Surrendering and Winning

"I did it my way," Frank Sinatra famously sang. That is also our natural instinct. Taking charge of your life displays your strength of character, your determination, your will power. The third step may shock you in its recommendation to exchange willfulness for willingness, to turn your life and will over to another. You may protest, "That's submission, allowing another to dominate me. I won't tolerate that!"

The third step proposes a surprising paradox for recovery: "We surrender to win." What do we surrender, and what do we win? When you work the third step, you give up your self-centered ways of thinking that reinforce your anxiety. You gain a sense of freedom to be yourself.

What the steps suggest reflects the wisdom of the ages. For example, the *Tao Te Ching* teaches:

When two great forces oppose each other,
the victory will go
to the one who knows how to yield (69).

Using the image of war, this saying acknowledges that in recovery from anxiety you are waging a life-and-death battle within yourself. You may believe the enemy is your anxiety, the uncomfortable feeling. However, the battle is fought on a deeper level within you. It is between two competing states of mind, your anxious and wise minds. Your anxious mind desperately wants control, certainty, and clarity in a world that does not accommodate your desires. Your wise mind, connected to Ultimate Reality, Your Higher Power, and God, sees and accepts things as they are. Recovery involves surrendering the fanciful wishes of your anxious mind and allowing your wise mind to guide you.

The following practices can help you to become more aware of your wise mind and accept its guidance:

Practice: Journal on the History of Your Anxiety

Anxiety overwhelms you. In moments of panic or when fear possesses you, you cannot think clearly or make rational decisions. The suffering of anxiety is your only reality in those moments. You may come to define yourself as an anxious person and bemoan the fact. You may despair that there is no end to the pain. The pain of anxiety and your desperate efforts to escape it shape your daily life. You believe you are engaged in a life-long battle with anxiety that you will never win.

To help gain a broader perspective on your anxious condition, write in your journal an account of how your anxiety has unfolded over the years. Stop to reflect on the following questions to help you piece together and understand your personal history with the condition:

- When did you first notice feeling anxious and afraid?

- How old were you?

- What signs and symptoms of anxiety did you display: physical, emotional, and mental?

- What were the circumstances in your home, neighborhood, school, or work at the time?

- What seemed to trigger your anxious reaction?

- Was there an ebb and flow to your anxiety?

- Did you seem to be on-edge all the time?

- How did you try to manage your anxiety?

- Did you develop rituals and routines?

- Did you have any recurrent obsessive ideas and compulsive behaviors?

- Did you tell anyone how you were feeling?

- Did anyone understand what you were going through and try to comfort you?

- Did you receive professional help?

- What worked and did not work?

- How much did you restrict your life because of your anxiety?

- What persons, places, things, or activities did you avoid to feel safe?

Hindsight is twenty-twenty. You may not have recognized at a young age that you were anxious. It seemed normal to you. However, you can look back as an adult and recognize what was hidden from you as a child.

You can observe yourself at different periods of your life and ask yourself the same questions. It is not uncommon that anxiety changes forms over time. Different signs and symptoms emerge. One woman told me she counted as a child, cut her hair as a teen, and picked her skin as an adult. Sometimes the fears are in the foreground, then in the background as an annoying hum, and even disappear altogether for periods of time.

When the anxiety disappears, particularly during happy times, I ask my patients, "Where did it go?" I ask this to emphasize the passing nature of anxiety, like a cloud, and the fact that the anxiety does not define them as a person.

This exercise can help you to identify less with your anxious condition. Remember, it is a condition and not your identity. As a condition, it rises and falls, depending on circumstances. It is never constant. All things change, even your anxiety, which is not as solid or enduring as you may think.

Practice: Insight Meditation

When you are anxious, jumbled thoughts of catastrophe keep you on-edge and prevent you from seeing yourself and the world accurately. Lost in your thoughts, you remain on the surface of life. Its richness eludes you.

A traditional Eastern practice called Vipassana, which means "insight meditation," can help you listen to the wondrous depths of your own consciousness. It is sometimes called "choiceless awareness" or "bare awareness" (2). The purpose of the exercise is to help you connect with the vast openness of your consciousness. The procedure for this practice is simple, similar to the exercise of following your breath.

1) Find a quiet place. Assume a relaxed posture, with your back straight and head erect. You may sit on a chair with your feet on the floor or on a cushion in the lotus position. Place your hands on your lap with the palms facing up in a receptive position. Keep your eyes open, focused on a spot in front of you.

2) Breathe deeply from your abdomen and follow your breath, as in the previous exercise. Feel the air filling the various parts of your body, relaxing all the tension in your muscles.

3) Begin with the conscious intention to be open to whatever arises in your consciousness. Welcome everything, the delightful and the unpleasant. Make the intention not to judge or reject whatever you experience.

4) As you quiet your mind and relax your body, notice the various thoughts, feelings, and sensations that arise. Note them and gently let go of them. Returning to your breath can help you hold the contents of your consciousness lightly. Just be an observer of all that comes and goes through your mind. Also, pay attention to your spontaneous emotional reactions to the contents, whether you like, dislike, or are neutral to what you perceive. Notice what persists. Let that go also.

5) As you observe the flow of your consciousness, you can make a mental note of what you experience. Simply label a thought, feeling, or sensation, saying to yourself, "thought," "feeling," or "sensation." Do not ponder what you observe at this time.

6) After the meditation, take a few minutes to reflect on what you experienced. Take note of any powerful and repeating thoughts, feelings, and sensations.

Make this practice a daily habit, alternating it with the practice of following your breath. If the practice raises overwhelming traumatic memories, stop until you are ready. Begin with a 15 minute meditation and extend the time as you become more adept. Remember, practice does not make perfect, but it does make for progress.

Practice: Body Focus

Is your body a friend or an enemy? Can you trust it? When you are in the midst of a panic attack with your racing heart, labored breath, and clammy skin, you think you are going to die. You believe your body is failing you. But are you really in physical danger?

Take a few moments to indulge your imagination before you answer that question. Imagine that you have just run a hundred yard dash. How do you feel after that intense exercise? Your heart is pounding. You bend over trying to catch your breath. You sweat profusely. Your whole body trembles, and you may feel dizzy, lightheaded. Your stomach may be upset. In short, your body is stressed by that intense physical exertion. All the blood rushes to the major muscle groups so that you can run the race. If your body did not automatically mobilize its resources, you would not be able to engage in strenuous exercise. These physical reactions indicate that your body is functioning well.

The physical sensations you experience in a panic attack are exactly the same as what you feel in intense exercise. They indicate that your body is working as it should. A panic attack is merely your body running a test of preparedness for intense physical activity, such as flight or fight. However, there is no immediate danger requiring that protective action at that moment. It is only your automatic, negative interpretation that the physical sensations are harmful, dangerous, or deadly that cause you anxious distress. In reality, you are safe. Your body is testing itself. You are only imagining physical danger during a panic attack.

In the third step, you take action by making a decision to surrender your self-will and open yourself to the guidance of the Power and Wisdom greater than yourself. That Power and Wisdom exist both within and beyond you. Your wise mind, in contrast to your anxious mind, connects you your true self.

9

An Honest Look: Shadow Dancing

Step 4: "Made a searching and fearless moral inventory of ourselves."

"Ultimately, we know that the other side of fear is freedom."

—Dorothy Thompson

You feel insecure and self-conscious in your anxiety. Ironically, even though you are very preoccupied with yourself, with feeling safe and protecting yourself, you really do not know yourself well. A stranger lives in your body. If someone praises you, you do not believe that compliment. If another criticizes you, you become defensive and demoralized. Yet, something deep within cries out to be recognized, loved, and accepted.

Those urgent longings to be known and loved motivate you to keep searching. You walk around the dance floor, searching for a partner. Having danced with the mysterious, attractive one, your step is lighter. Some of the heaviness has lifted from your heart. Walking about, you notice a homely, unattractive person sitting in the shadows at the edge of the dance floor. Looking forlorn, she is watching you closely while pretending not to be looking. You sense her yearning to be noticed by you. Your cautious mind entertains many questions: "Shall I ask her to dance? She's so ugly. What will people think?" In a burst of courage, you approach her and extend your hand.

In the fourth step, you begin the process of cleaning house. The process involves taking an honest look at yourself. To undertake such an investigation requires courage and humility. Unless you have taken the three previous steps, you will not be able to muster the courage to see yourself clearly. Unless you have some faith in God, a Higher Power, or Ultimate Reality and see your life from a larger perspective, your self-searching will hit a wall. What you glimpse may discourage you.

When you approach this self-examination with faith, you have a hopeful perspective. Aware of your basic goodness, you tell yourself, "Yes, I have many faults, but I'm better than that." The contradiction stares you in the face.

The *Tao Te Ching*, referring to qualities of a great nation and great person, expresses clearly and concisely the steps of housecleaning:

When he makes a mistake he realizes it.
Having realized it, he admits it.
Having admitted it, he corrects it (61).

Obstacles to Soul-Searching

Commonsense and all the great philosophies underline the importance of knowing yourself. However, if you are anxious, you face several obstacles to this honest self-appraisal. You avoid the search. These include

- a preoccupied mind;

- becoming distracted by busyness;

- blaming yourself;

- correcting others;

- blaming others; and

- worrying about what others think.

Preoccupied Mind

The anxious mind is a preoccupied mind. There is no room for anything else. Like a pot that is already full, you cannot put more into it. Your many and varied fears occupy your mind and drain your energy. In an anxious state you cannot undertake the work of an honest self-examination. You lack the mental capacity and energy.

Monica: Anxiety Attack

"When I have an anxiety attack, the only thing I can think about is running away to find some relief. 'Make it stop!' I say again and again in my head.

Even when I'm not in the panic mode, just normally on-edge, my mind is buzzing with worries of one sort or another. My brain is never at rest. Sometimes I'm amazed that I can function at all because so many thoughts bounce around in my head."

Distracted by Busyness

Your anxious mind keeps you busy, mentally and physically. It is as if you have attention deficit disorder. You hyper-focus on your fears and overlook what is going on around and within you. You are also hyper-active, always moving to calm your fears and find some measure of relief. Rituals, routines, and rules keep you busy. A restless mind lives in a restless body. Lacking the capacity for peace and quiet inhibits you from taking a good look at yourself.

Larry: Distraction

"I was diagnosed with obsessive-compulsive disorder as a child. That describes me well. I'm an OCD guy. My mind and body are always busy. I don't know how to relax. Once I get a thought in my head, I turn it over and over in my mind. It might be some crazy thought, like the number of spots on the ceiling tile. Then, I have so many rituals and routines that keep me busy. I check things over and over, like the doors and windows being locked. Even when I do something simple like walking, I count my steps and avoid stepping on cracks."

Blaming Yourself

When anxious, your mind drifts toward the negative. You have a mental bias. You are especially critical of yourself and focus on your negative qualities, feeling inferior. You are acutely aware of any mistakes you make. However, your harsh inner critic is neither rational nor reasonable. Your fault-finding is selective, preoccupied with what you fear. These faults then become exaggerated. Such unbalanced self-criticism interferes with an honest, realistic self-appraisal, which recognizes both strengths and weaknesses.

Lori: Self-Blame

"I'm a wall flower at a party. I never feel like I belong in a crowd of people. I don't know how to make small talk. When people approach me at a party, I'm afraid I won't be able to carry on a conversation, won't know what to say. So, I freeze up.

After the party, I rehash all my conversations in my mind. 'Why did I say that? I sounded so stupid.' I rehearse what I could have done and said differently."

Correcting Others

Living in your mind with fixed ideas of how the world should be, you are often disappointed. You instinctively turn your critical eye toward those around you as if you are superior. What do you notice? How much they are not living up to your standards. Even though you may realize how unrealistic those standards may be, that no one can be perfect, you cannot let them go. Focusing on the faults of others clearly interferes with you honestly looking at yourself.

Ben: Perfectionism

"I'm a foreman at a factory, working in quality control. Because I'm a perfectionist, my desire to make everything perfect helps on my job. I have high standards. I notice immediately when someone is not doing his job. I pick up when a part is off even in

the slightest way. When there is a problem in the flow of work, I can spot it quickly and figure out a solution.

My perfectionism serves me well at work, but not so well in my relationships. My wife accuses me of being a nitpicker around the house and overdoing my corrections of the children."

Blaming Others

You may notice in yourself a habit of complaining, especially when you are feeling anxious. You imagine that people or situations cause you to feel what you feel. However, no one causes you to be anxious or unhappy. When you blame others for your reactions, you make yourself helpless, increasing your anxiety. You imagine that you cannot change unless the other person changes. That makes you dependent on others for your own wellbeing. Blaming others also distracts you from looking honestly at yourself and taking charge of your own life.

Kimberly: Unable to Relax

"My husband makes me miserable. He has a terrible temper. I know he would never hit me, but when he even raises his voice, I tremble. I walk on egg shells around him. I feel like a scared child and want to run and hide. If only he could be less angry. Then I could learn to relax."

Worrying about What Others Think

Worrying about what others might be thinking about you drains you. Somehow you believe that you must please everyone and live up to their expectations. You spend so much energy trying to figure out what others expect of you that you ignore what you want for yourself. How do you measure your own behavior? An honest self-appraisal requires that you work out a clear sense of your own standards for yourself.

Marilyn: Self-Consciousness

"I've always been self-conscious about how I look and what people are thinking about me. I know it's absurd to think everybody is paying attention to me. Or even that they are judging me critically. That's so self-centered and negative, but I can't help myself.

I worry about being neat and my clothes looking good. My hair and makeup have to be just so. I have to watch my weight and keep myself fit. I'm afraid people will notice any flaws and even talk about me."

"...a fearless..."

You feel anything but fearless and heroic in the grip of anxiety. You feel like a coward. Perhaps you do not give yourself enough credit. You took the risk in the first three steps of looking deeply inside yourself. You began a journey of faith, surrendering your obsession with power and control. You tasted being loved by God, embraced by a friendly universe. In the process, you glimpsed your basic goodness, innate bravery, and brilliant sanity.

A Hero's Journey

Now you are on the verge of taking a second look inward, a moral inventory. What do you expect to discover?

Homer's *The Odyssey* provides a clue. The book follows the adventures of the Greek hero Odysseus in his ten-year journey from Troy to his home and family on the island of Ithaca. Odysseus had shown his bravery on the battlefield, but he could not rest on his laurels. Other trials awaited him on his way home. His struggles, played out on a sea voyage, reveal his inner conflicts to find his true identity. The battlefield shifts to his inner world. No less courage than that required for the Trojan War was needed for this personal confrontation.

Odysseus, a "man of twists and turns," faced many trials and temptations on his journey home that revealed and shaped his real identity. Temptations came in the form of many seductresses: Circe, the Sirens, and Calyspo. He resisted them all, learned about his vulnerabilities, and grew in strength. Reaching his homeland, he had to find his way through treachery and confusion to his family. Enduring his trials, he finally came to know and reveal himself.

Taking your moral inventory in the fourth step, you come to realize the obstacles to your recovery of your true self. You can say, "We have met the enemy, and he is us."

In meeting the enemy within, your personal demons, you are travelling a well-worn path. You follow in the footsteps of all the great spiritual and religious leaders of the past. Moses led the chosen people into the desert for forty years before entering the Promised Land. The desire to return to idol worship and forsake faith in Yahweh never left the people. The shadow of discouragement followed them throughout their journey.

Siddhartha Gautama, a prince in a small kingdom, sought the means to relieve suffering. He meditated, fasted, and studied the religious traditions but found no satisfactory answer. Then, he decided to sit in silence under a Bodhi tree until he achieved enlightenment. It was not a quiet rest. Mara, the Deceiver, assaulted him with temptations of sensual pleasure, terrifying battles, and self-doubt. Siddhartha embraced his demons, appealed to the earth as his witness, and rose up an enlightened man, the Buddha.

Jesus, raised a carpenter's son, went off into the desert after being baptized by His cousin John. For forty days, He fasted and was tempted by Satan to seek wealth, power, and prestige. But He refused, answering each temptation with God's words. He left the trials of the wilderness with a clear idea of His identity and mission. He began preaching, "Reform your lives; the kingdom of God is at hand."

Muhammad, a successful businessman, found little solace in the idol worship of Mecca. He often went off into the desert to fast and pray. There, he experienced a personal jihad, a holy war. Later, a combatant, after a battle, asked the Prophet, "What is the greater jihad?" He responded, "It is the fight against the desires of the self." Only after engaging in this personal struggle could he become the prophet, with a clear identity and mission.

There are no shortcuts. Recovery demands an acquaintance with your demons. You may think your anxiety itself is demonic. However, the truth is that your anxiety disguises many other hidden demons.

"...moral inventory of yourself"

You may wonder why you need a moral inventory if you are addicted to anxiety. Unlike someone addicted to alcohol or drugs who appears to choose to use, you had no choice about being anxious. You believe you were born with this condition and wish you were not.

Behind your anxious reaction, however, lurk many unacknowledged attachments and hidden desires. You fear losing something that is important to you. If you did not care about something, you would not be anxious about living without it. Your anxiety expresses hidden desires, which are unconscious choices regarding value for you.

Ron: Fear and Faults

Ron talked about getting to know himself through his anxiety: "I've been anxious my whole life and became resigned to the fact that I'm just an anxious person. I'll learn to deal with it. I had a breakdown after being fired from my job, was hospitalized, and began intensive therapy. I'd never examined closely my anxiety and specifically what I was anxious about. What I learned through a long, grueling process of investigation was astounding. What bothered me most about being fired was the shattering of my self-image as a successful person. I never realized how much I was driven by success and all the recognition that came with it."

Alcoholics Anonymous, in its clear-sighted understanding of addiction, acknowledged the distorting power of fear: "The chief activator of our defects has been self-centered fear—primarily fear that we would lose something we already possessed or would fail to get something we demanded" (Steps/Traditions, p. 76). The wisdom of AA observes that all our failings generate fear, not contentment. "Then fear, in turn, generates more character defects" (p. 49).

No one lives without fear and anxiety, even the most courageous among us. Fear and anxiety are natural reactions to threat and potential loss. Since we are not all-powerful and all-knowing, we are always at risk of losing what is important to us.

If you pay close attention to your fears and anxiety, you can learn much about yourself. That entails resisting your natural urges to run away from, control, or suppress the uncomfortable feeling. By directly experiencing, watching, and investigating your anxiety, you can learn about your defects and strengths.

How to Clean House

There are several ways to learn the wisdom of your fear, get to know your personal demons, and clean house. Some suggestions are to

- spend quiet time with yourself;

- welcome criticism;

- learn from your enemies; and

- make friends with your demons.

Spend Time in Quiet Personal Reflection

Get to know yourself. That requires time alone with yourself. Many people say they avoid being alone and doing nothing because they feel bored. What I observe is that when they become quiet and undistracted, uncomfortable feelings and thoughts emerge.

Instead of running to entertain yourself, stay with the silence and pay close attention to whatever thoughts, feelings, and sensations arise. Especially when you are feeling anxious, this is a valuable time to be quiet and reflective. Ponder the questions: What am I really afraid of? What do I fear losing? What will happen if I lose it? Let your mind and imagination float around these questions.

Welcome Criticism

See your critics as teachers. The *Tao Te Ching* states, "[A great man] considers those who point out his faults as his most benevolent teachers" (61). You have blind spots, like everybody else. Your anxiety makes you fearful to take off your blinders because you imagine you will see terrible things and feel worse about yourself. Both your friends and your enemies can give you valuable feedback. They can give you a different perspective on yourself, letting you know how you come across to others. You might be surprised at what you hear, if you are open. Further, how can criticism and correction really hurt you? Always evaluate what others say about you, weighing its truthfulness. Take what helps, and discard the rest.

No one likes criticism. You may secretly yearn to be perfect. The criticism of others has power to disturb you to the extent that it echoes what you are already telling yourself. Your own inner critic is harsher than anything anyone else could tell you.

See Your Enemy As Your Shadow

"(A great man) thinks of his enemy as the shadow that he himself casts," the *Tao Te Ching* (61) observes. To avoid looking honestly at yourself, you may turn your attention to the faults of others. You see the splinter in their eye, not the plank in your own. I encourage you to pay close attention to what you dislike in others, to what drives you crazy about them. Notice their annoying habits. However, instead of condemning them, ask yourself honestly if you can identify with any of those irritating behaviors.

If you are honest with yourself, you will discover that what you hate in others you despise and disown in yourself. In other words, if you spot it, you got it.

Make Friends with Your Demons

As the Arabic proverb goes, "Keep your friends close and your enemies closer." Jesus advised getting to know your demons by name. Buddha suggested having tea with your demons. Do not try to get rid of them too quickly. They will only sneak back in without you knowing it.

Accept the reality that you are not perfect and will have a lifelong struggle with your faults. Do not imagine you will ever be perfect. That will only open the door to pride, and more devils taking residence. Instead, accept that you are imperfect, have faults, and learn from them. Your weaknesses are really exaggerations of your strengths.

An Inventory: Sermon on the Mount

Anxious people are often scrupulous about themselves and their behavior. Steve, below, relates the ways in which scrupulosity took over his life.

Steve: Scrupulosity

"I was raised Catholic. The nuns taught me to examine my conscience daily using the Ten Commandments as a guide. They also told us to go to confession regularly to cleanse our souls of sin and avoid going to hell. I was an obedient child, easily frightened, and took everything they told me literally. I lived in fear of committing a mortal sin and going to hell. So, I watched myself like a hawk and pounced on any imperfections. I went to confession every week, making a laundry list of everything I did wrong, but the continual scrutinizing and confessing never relieved my sense of guilt. God was a harsh Judge for me, not a loving Father. The breakthrough came for me when I took a Scripture class and took the Bible seriously."

Alcoholics Anonymous recommends, "Fake it until you make it." Just do the right thing, and your attitude will follow. That means to stop drinking even though you have powerful urges to drink. It also means coming to meetings and following the program even though you do not feel like it. Change occurs from the outside-in by modifying your behavior and living the sober life.

In His Sermon on the Mount, Jesus takes another tack (Matthew 5:1-7:29). He recommends, "Change your heart." Conversion involves a new consciousness, "putting on the mind and heart of Jesus." Instead of focusing only on the right behaviors, you must also pay attention to your motivations, desires, and intentions. Transformation is an inside-out job.

Both perspectives, of course, are true. Recovery from addiction involves changing both your behavior and your attitude. What does Jesus recommend as a moral inventory for those addicted to anxiety? What self-questions does He confront you with? "Do not *worry* about your livelihood, what you are to eat or drink or use for clothing."

That sounds simple, but it is enormously complex. Your anxiety disguises many attachments that you resist letting go. What you worry about reveals what you deem important for your wellbeing. You do not worry about what you do not care about. The problem is that you care too much about the things you fear losing. You become addicted to things without realizing it, looking for happiness in the wrong places. "Remember, where your treasure is, there your heart is also," Jesus says. Pay close attention to your anxiety and ask yourself:

- Do I worry excessively about money and material possessions?

- Am I envious of what others have?

- Am I preoccupied with having a comfortable life?

"Everyone who grows angry with his brother shall be liable to judgment."

"Resentment is the 'number one' offender," observes Alcoholics Anonymous (p. 64). Those who are addicted become easily angered when they do not get what they want, or when they get what they do not want. Anxiety reveals what you love, but also what you hate. Anger is the handmaid of your anxiety. Sensitive to loss, you may quickly become angry when what you hold precious is threatened. You defend yourself by becoming angry. Feeling powerless, the anger gives you the illusion of power and control over your life and others. Ask yourself:

- Do I have a temper?
- Do I become quickly angered when I do not get my way?
- Do I react with anger when others do not behave in ways I expect?

"Go first to be reconciled with your brother."

To cope with your anxiety, you may become obsessed with *power* and *control*. Hooked on anxiety, you lack a sense of freedom. Feeling unfree, you have difficulty understanding, tolerating, and accepting the freedom of those around you. Feeling powerless, you attempt to reclaim mastery by manipulating others. The result is that relationships become power struggles, competitions for having your needs met, often at others' expense. Ask yourself:

- Do I need to control situations and people to feel secure?
- Am I a "control freak?"
- Do I insist that things be done my way?

"Anyone who looks lustfully at a woman has already committed adultery with her in his thoughts."

As much as we want to convince ourselves otherwise, we live a short distance from our Puritanical roots. *Sex* preoccupies us and is a great source of anxiety. Sexually satisfied, you feel calm. Dissatisfied, you become frustrated. You may also seek safety and security in your sexual relationships, becoming jealous and possessive. You may believe that your relationship with a significant other will make you happy. Your fear centers on losing that relationship. Your life revolves around keeping that person close and under control. Ask yourself:

- Am I obsessed with having my sexual desires met?
- Do I cling to anyone to feel secure with myself?
- Do I tend to become overly-dependent in relationships?

"Be on guard against performing religious acts for people to see."

Your anxiety may make you extremely self-conscious about what others think about you. You imagine others watching you closely and judging you critically. However, you desperately want others to like you. Your self-esteem depends on their *approval*. So, you always try to make a good impression. You become an actor who wears many disguises, adjusting your behavior to what you imagine others expect of you. In the process, you become a master at deceit, leading a double life. Ask yourself:

- Do I have an insatiable desire for reassurance from others?
- Do I crave praise from others?
- Am I overly sensitive to criticism?
- Am I driven by the pursuit of success?
- Am I intolerant of failure?

"If you want to avoid judgment, stop passing judgment."

Your inner critic never rests. You entertain high, even impossible, expectations for yourself and others. Many "shoulds" dominate your thinking. You have many fixed ideas about how you, others, and the world should behave. Some may call you a "perfectionist" because of your high ideals. You may even take pride in your ambition to be perfect and in your occasional successes, but mostly, you focus on imperfections, on the gap between your own and others' performance and your ideals. Your searchlight of judgment spares no one, including yourself. Ask yourself:

- Am I a perfectionist with unreasonably high standards?
- Do I always need to be right?
- Am I intolerant of disagreement, criticism, or correction?

"Offer no resistance to injury."

This command may shock you. With your anxious mind, you live in a hostile world, constantly feeling threatened. To survive, you build strong *defensive* walls around yourself. You imagine it would be too overwhelming to offer no resistance to your attackers. Stop to consider for a moment the dangers you perceive. How much are you exaggerating them with your anxious mind? Are those threats more real or imagined? Are people really so against you, trying to hurt you? Your fears may be a justification for your aggressive defensiveness that invites others to be unkind and guarded with you. Ask yourself:

- Do I always hold myself back in relationships, afraid of being hurt?
- Do I see myself as helpless and weak?
- Do I tend to become aggressive when I feel threatened?

"Love your enemies, pray for your persecutors."

Your inner critic convinces you that enemies abound and surround you. Of course, the one who attacks you most is yourself. You are your own worst enemy. You persecute yourself. At the core of your anxiety is the belief that you are not good enough and must prove your worth. Your aggression has many faces. It reveals itself most clearly in the harsh judgments you direct toward yourself and imagine others are aiming at you. Ask yourself:

- Do I demand perfection from myself and others?

- Can I be forgiving of my faults, of others' faults?

- Am I impatient with myself and others?

"Treat others the way you would have them treat you."

Your anxiety makes you preoccupied with finding *safety* and *security* in an uncertain world. In the hierarchy of needs, safety and security are the most basic. If you do not feel safe, you are not free to pursue other wants and desires. However, you can become self-obsessed in that pursuit. When threatened, you only think about escaping. What others may need from you in the moment of fear does not concern you. Ask yourself:

- Do I indulge my sense of helplessness and avoid engaging in life?

- Am I attuned to the needs of others as much as I am to my own?

- Do I tend to withdraw into my own world to feel secure and ignore others?

"Be compassionate as your Father is compassionate."

You suffer a great deal from your anxiety. It is an indescribably painful experience. Although you did not choose your condition, you can choose how you relate to it, what attitude to assume. You can become bitter about your lot in life, the unfairness that you have been afflicted with a mental/emotional disturbance. You can *feel sorry for yourself*. Or you can let the suffering open your heart to become compassionate toward others who suffer. Ask yourself:

- Do I often feel sorry for myself because of my condition?

- Am I sensitive to the suffering of those around me and try to offer relief?

- Do I try to numb myself to my own and others' suffering?

Paradox of Weakness and Strength

Fixated on anxiety, you are overwhelmed by your sense of powerlessness in a dangerous world. Your natural instinct is to defend yourself. You want to be strong. To compensate for your weakness, you try to exert control over your environment and over others. In the process, without realizing it, you can become quite aggressive. Your anger comes out, which gives you a feeling of power and control. It is, however, only an illusion of real power.

Step 4 may surprise you because it invites you to acknowledge and embrace your weaknesses, not ignore them. Already feeling bad about yourself, the step encourages you to see clearly what you do not like about yourself. The purpose is not to increase your self-loathing or give you more material for condemning yourself. Instead, by acknowledging your faults you can begin freeing yourself from their power over you.

Alcoholics Anonymous suggests a fourth step paradox for recovery: "From weakness comes strength." This slogan echoes the insight of St. Paul who had become discouraged in his fight against his faults: "(The Lord) said to me, 'My grace is enough for you, for in weakness power reaches perfection.' And so I willingly boast of my weaknesses instead, that the power of Christ may rest upon me (II Cor. 12: 9)."

Recovery comes from letting go of your futile efforts to eliminate the anxiety you dread. Instead, your relief will come from knowing yourself intimately, including the character defects that underlie your anxious reactions. You exercise inner strength in making the moral inventory. It takes courage to face your faults. It takes honesty to acknowledge them. What is the hidden source of that courage and honesty? In the process of examining yourself, you experience a power both within and beyond you that heals you.

The following practice can aid you in your personal examination of conscience.

Practice: Peeling the Onion

Continue to write in your journal. Take quiet time to reflect on the "Sermon on the Mount" in Matthew's *Gospel*, Chapters 5-7. Imagine yourself in the crowd listening to the words of Jesus. Let his words penetrate your heart. Read the text slowly, pausing when a thought captivates you. Let the words question your life. Let the words challenge the way you are living. Look at your thoughts, words, and behaviors. Look more deeply at your more hidden motivations, desires, and intentions. You can use the questions above to stimulate your self-exploration. Do not limit yourself to those questions. Let your own concerns about yourself emerge.

If you look deeply at your anxious reaction, you notice many competing thoughts and desires, which the "Sermon on the Mount" may help you identify. Paying close attention, you observe many layers to your reaction, a variety of fears. It is like an onion with many layers of skin. Peel the onion to see what you discover. Use the question to explore, "What would happen if...?"

For example, you may notice that you worry about not having enough money. Ask yourself, "What would happen if I didn't have enough money?" Of course, you are concerned about not being able to provide for yourself and your family. However, there may be deeper concerns. Perhaps you worry about being perceived by others as a failure. Then, ask yourself, "What would happen if others thought of me as a failure?" You might think others would not like you. Ask yourself, "What would happen if others did not like me?" You may then feel alone and isolated. Then, ask, "What would happen if I felt alone and isolated?" You might imagine then that you could not survive emotionally or that you would always be alone. But is that really true? Allow yourself to challenge your fears in the process.

As you reflect on the thoughts, feelings, and desires that underlie your anxiety, peel the onion with "What if" questions. Then, write in your journal what you discover about yourself.

Fortified by confidence in God, a Higher Power, or Ultimate Reality, Step 4 encourages you to look honestly at the character defects that give rise to your anxiety. You imagine that anxiety is your problem. In reality, it is a symptom of a deeper dilemma, a knot you will unravel through recovery.

Dennis Ortman, Ph.D.

10

Out of Hiding: Facing the Shame

*Step 5: "Admitted to God, to ourselves, and to another
human being the exact nature of our wrongs."*

*"To share your weakness is to make yourself vulnerable:
To make yourself vulnerable is to show your strength."*

—Criss Jami

Suffering from an anxiety disorder, you wear a mask. Few people, if any, know the depth of your pain and insecurities. It is not because they are unobservant. You hide your insecurities because you are ashamed of your weakness. You also fear others will think you are crazy, especially if they were to know the bizarre ways you manage your fears. You hesitate to let anyone really know you. Maintaining a calm exterior while churning inside, you live a double life, hiding your real self.

Your courage gathers as you wander the dance floor. You took the risk to dance with many partners. You introduced yourself, asked their names, and made small talk while you danced. Some of your partners were quite talkative and let you know quite a bit about themselves, but you held your reserve, not ready to tell them about yourself. The music and the dancing help you to relax with yourself and gain some confidence. Now you consider the next step. Will you sit down after the dance with your partner simply to talk and let that person know you? Will you risk an intimate moment? Will you risk making yourself vulnerable to being misunderstood and rejected?

In Step 5, your recovery takes an interpersonal turn. You are more self-aware. You spent time and effort getting to know your painful self, your higher self, and your shadow self. Intimacy, of course, begins with yourself getting acquainted with yourself. That intimacy deepens when you share yourself with another. You get a response, feedback, and you see yourself through the mirror of another's reactions.

Step 5 encourages forming an intimate relationship, not simply admitting faults to another person. Many think of intimacy in romantic or sexual terms. They think of it as "hearts and flowers" or "sexual fireworks." However, intimacy is much more and much less. It is simply knowing another and allowing another to know you at ever deeper levels. Such intimacy requires an emotional risk of exposing yourself. Yet, the revelations are simply letting the other know what really matters to you in the moment. Nothing really dramatic.

Commenting on Step 5, the Steps/Traditions book states: "All of A.A.'s Twelve Steps ask us to go contrary to our natural desires...they all deflate our egos. When it comes to ego deflation, few Steps are harder to take than Five" (p. 55). All the addicted have inflated egos, believing they can do whatever they want, without counting the cost. They live secret lives, avoiding accountability for their actions. Confessing their faults to another is a humbling, ego-shattering experience.

Anxiety addicted, you also live a secret life, ruled by fear. You withdraw into a mental cave for safety and attempt to exert power and control over your daily life, your environment, and others. What can ever free you from your self-created prison? You liberate yourself by facing your greatest fear, the fear of being exposed and rejected.

You may imagine that being intimate, letting another know you thoroughly, is only difficult for you because you suffer anxiety. You worry about what others think about you and expect negative judgment. However, intimacy, with the risk of self-disclosure, is challenging for everyone.

When you reveal yourself to another, you take an enormous risk. You never know for sure how the other person will respond to your personal revelation. Will they respect you, judge you, laugh at you, run away, or gossip about you with others? You have no control over their reaction. You must be prepared for rejection and can only hope for understanding and acceptance. If you have been betrayed after a shared intimacy, you may struggle for a long time to trust again.

Step 5 asks you to face your greatest fear, which arises from your ego. Having taken your own moral inventory, realizing your faults, you need to share with another person what you discovered about yourself. That is the only way to achieve peace of mind, to have "admitted to God, to ourselves, and to another human being..."

Obstacles to Admitting: Hiding in the Cave

We are social animals. Our natural instincts to connect with others motivate us to form relationships. However, fear interrupts this natural process. Acknowledging those fears can be an important step to overcoming them and allowing our true selves to emerge.

Roy: Sense of Privacy

"I've always been a shy person and had very few friends. I value my privacy and don't tell people about my business. It's not that I'm afraid to tell them or worry about what they might think. I simply prefer to keep things to myself. Even among my friends, I never gossip and am always the last to know the latest rumors about people. I suppose I learned about the value of privacy from my family. Over and over I heard my parents talk about keeping what happens in the family in the family. They cautioned about airing dirty laundry in public."

Your temperament, and not necessarily your fears, may make you a private person. Many anxious people tend to be shy and introverted, preferring to keep to themselves. They put more energy into pursuing their personal interests than spending time in conversation. They can be sociable when they want but become easily bored with small talk, gossip, and sharing secrets. If you are a private person, you may need much convincing of the value of revealing yourself, especially your faults, to another person.

Randy: Distrust of People

"I don't trust anyone, or more accurately, very few people. I never assume somebody can be trusted until they show me they are trustworthy. It can take a long time for them to prove it to me. And then I test them with a little information about myself. I have been betrayed too many times by family and friends. It takes a while to get over the hurt. I don't know if I'll ever get over some of the betrayals. So, I'm very cautious in opening myself up to someone."

Your distrust may be born of painful experiences of betrayal. It keeps you from being hurt again. Particularly if you have been traumatized as a child by physical or sexual abuse, you withdraw from relationships to protect yourself. Anxiety and hyper-vigilance keep you alert to signs of threat from others. You need to feel safe before you will take the risk to disclose your faults to another. That may take time and patience with yourself.

Raymond: Pride

"I worked hard to become a physician and am proud of my success. I admit that I am a perfectionist in my work. That has helped me gain a good reputation. When I was arrested for a drunk driving, my world fell apart. I died a thousand deaths preparing to tell my colleagues about my arrest and drinking problem. I went back-and-forth in my mind about what I would say. I knew I had to tell them because they would find out, anyway. I wondered what they would think of me. Would they still value me as a doctor? Would they still respect me?"

You may hold yourself and others up to extremely high standards of performance. You may consider that a strength because you are not satisfied with being ordinary. You want to be special. Your ambition to excel may lead to extraordinary accomplishments. Your successes and the approval of others may contribute to you developing a proud self-image, which you cherish. Admitting your faults to another may feel like a personal insult, tarnishing your carefully constructed image.

Becky: Shame

"My doctor diagnosed me with obsessive-compulsive disorder. I knew something was wrong with my thinking and bizarre behavior. His giving it a label made it too real for me. I'm ashamed that I have a mental illness. I'm embarrassed that I can't control myself and that I need medication. I don't want any of my friends to know. They would think I'm crazy."

Your internal critic has two faces. One face presents itself with high standards, successes, and a proud self-image. The other face judges you harshly for not meeting those standards, focuses on failures, and provokes a sense of shame. Deep down you believe you are not good enough. In reality, you could never measure up to the impossible ideals of your inner critic. So, you are doomed to fail. Your shame makes you want to hide your faults for fear of further judgment.

To overcome your resistance to admitting your faults to another person, you must be convinced of the value of confessing. How will it contribute to your recovery? The following are some of its benefits:

Benefits of Admitting: The Truth Will Set You Free

There are a number of benefits to admitting your weaknesses. Admitting them will help you to

- overcome isolation;

- receive acceptance;

- experience humility;

- confront self-deception; and

- sense God's presence.

Overcome Isolation

The Steps/Traditions Book observes: "Almost without exception, alcoholics are tortured by loneliness. Even before our drinking got bad and people began to cut us off, nearly all of us suffered the feeling that we didn't quite belong (p. 57)." The loneliness of those addicted to anxiety matches that of the alcoholic. However, unlike with alcoholics, others do not cut you off because of your intolerable behavior. You isolate yourself. Feeling unworthy or odd, you withdraw from the social arena to feel safe. Your anxiety does not cause you the greatest suffering. Your attempts to cope with it do. Withdrawing from others makes you lonely.

The fifth step encourages you to move out of your isolation, not bearing the burden of your faults alone. As the AA saying goes, "If you share your pain, you cut it in half; if you don't, you double it." In taking the risk to disclose yourself, you confront directly your fear of being judged and rejected. Acting against the fear, you gain a sense of control over your life, which lessens your fear. Remember, fear is in the mind and imagination. You always have control over your behavior and can choose not to act on every anxious urge to withdraw.

The benefit of intimacy is a life of joy. The cost of staying isolated is loneliness.

Receive Acceptance

Your anxious mind expects to be judged and rejected by others. You imagine others watch you critically. So, you hold yourself back. Why place yourself in danger by letting people know you by exposing your faults? It only gives them ammunition for attacking you.

Others, though, are not really the enemy who attacks you. You wage war against yourself. You measure yourself by impossible standards and constantly feel like a failure. Your inner critic, which focuses on the negative, keeps you down. It exaggerates your faults and minimizes your virtues, making you reluctant to share your inventory.

How can you free yourself from your fear of judgment and rejection? Telling another about your wrongdoing brings you face-to-face with your fear. It presents an opportunity to unmask it. Your humble, honest, courageous self-exposure inevitably invites a favorable response from your listener, whomever you choose. Instead of the expected rejection, you receive an open-arms acceptance. The surprise may shock you into awareness that forgiveness is available for even the most grievous faults. As if by some miracle, feeling forgiven opens your heart to forgive yourself.

The benefit of risking rejection is a surprising acceptance. The cost of holding back is you remain the whipping boy of your inner critic.

Experience Humility

The Steps/Traditions book astutely comments: "So false pride became the reverse side of the ruinous coin marked 'Fear.' We simply had to be number one people to cover up our deep-lying inferiorities (p. 123)." Stuck on anxiety, you judge yourself inferior because of your condition. However, fear wants to hide behind a mask of superiority. To overcome your low self-esteem, you work hard to create an ideal image of yourself. You push yourself to climb the ladder of success. Ambitious to be the best, you compete with everyone around you. The judge in your mind never rests, putting yourself and others on trial. In the process of proving that you are not worthless, you exhaust yourself.

How can you find rest from the endless climbing, competing, and correcting? Peace comes from accepting yourself as you are, not as you wish you would be. That is true humility. Humility is accepting the truth of who you really are. Actually, you are more and less than you think. You are more than the sum total of all the faults you realized in the moral inventory, which leads to shame. You are less than the idealized image you portray, which feeds your pride.

In reality, you are an ordinary human being, like everyone else, with strengths and weaknesses. Therein lies your true dignity. Simply being yourself means you have nothing to prove, nothing to defend, and nothing to live up to. As the *Tao Te Ching* puts it:

When you are content to be simply yourself
And don't compare or compete,
Everybody will respect you (8).

Most important, you will respect yourself.

You take a major step toward humbly accepting yourself by admitting your faults to another. You come out of hiding behind the mask. You no longer have to be an actor in the drama of your life. What a relief in giving up the burden of maintaining the pretense of a false self!

The benefit of risking humiliation is the letting go of your pride. The cost of not taking the chance is the relentless drive to continue proving how good you are.

Confront Self-Deception

After taking a good look at yourself in the fourth step, the first thing that might strike you is how blind you have been to your faults. Much of your life has been lived on automatic pilot: not only your anxiety but also all the distorted desires that gave rise your fear and controlled your choices. Fear dominated you in many disguises. You did not see clearly those disguises and their influence on your living. With the moral inventory, you began to unmask yourself. You glimpsed the wisdom of AA which calls any addiction "a disease of perception." You may wonder to yourself, "If I have fooled myself for so long, how can I be sure I am not continuing my ignorance?"

The fifth step offers a check on self-deception. When you tell someone else about your wrongdoing, it becomes more real for you just by saying and hearing it. The truth is out and cannot be denied. Further, your honest self-disclosure also invites honest feedback from your listener. You gain another perspective on your behavior. Perhaps you exaggerated or minimized your faults, or did not look deeply enough into them. You may even ask your listener for advice and counsel, which can give you helpful direction on the perilous road of recovery. You do not have to travel alone. Taking the fifth step commits you to work with others on the path to healing and growth.

The benefit of letting another know you is the gift of honesty. The cost of keeping yourself hidden is a life of illusion.

Sensing God's Presence

Caroline experienced a life-long struggle with anxiety. Then, she risked sharing, and in the sharing felt the presence of a Higher Power.

Caroline: Life-Long Struggle

"I battled anxiety my whole life and tried everything. But nothing helped, and I resigned myself to be the victim of my fears for the rest of my life. My therapists encouraged me to join support groups. I always resisted because I'm just too uncomfortable in groups of people. It's hard enough to meet with my therapist whom I know well.

One day I suddenly decided to take the plunge, more out of desperation than anything. I saw that an anxiety support group met at a local church and decided to go. The people in the group were so kind and welcoming, but I was still terrified. I didn't speak for the longest time in the group. I came to meetings and listened. Going week after week to the meetings, I felt something frozen inside me begin to melt. The warmth, honesty, and courage of the people seeped into me. I found the courage to talk about my fears at long last. I've never been a religious person, but I sensed in the group a Power greater than myself that helped overcome my fears."

Possessed by anxiety, you feel powerless not only over your emotional reactions but also in relationships. You are acutely aware of your vulnerability. When you open up to another, you risk losing yourself. The possible benefits of intimacy—being accepted and validated by another—recede into the background of your consciousness.

Preoccupied with the dangers of closeness, you devise evasive maneuvers to protect yourself so you can feel in control. You may avoid intimacy altogether, living in isolation. You may cling to a particular person, depending on him or her for your security. Or you may exert power over others, manipulating them to satisfy your needs. The result of these fear-driven tactics is emotional distance and loneliness.

Relationships generate energy, greater than the energy of each individual separately. To tap into that energy, you need to give up your attempts to control the other person. Genuine intimacy requires that you allow the other person and yourself to be free, free to think, feel, and behave however you or they want. That can be frightening. You experience a power in the relating that is beyond your control. It is a power that heals.

Imagine two individuals in a relationship as two intersecting circles. Part of each circle is separate, while another area is shared. The meeting of the two circles creates a third oblong shape. The shared area has a relational energy, created by the contribution of each individual. That energy is greater than the sum total of the energy of each individual. You experience in heart-felt intimacy a Power greater than yourself that comes from you, but is beyond you. That Power is life-giving.

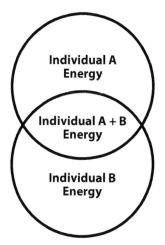

Those of a religious temperament experience it as a sacred presence. As Jesus teaches, "Where two or three are gathered in My name, I am in their midst."

The benefit of meeting with others is the opportunity to encounter a Power greater than yourself comforting you. The cost of staying alone is a magnified feeling of powerlessness.

Your Dialogue Partner

Once you have committed to admit your faults to another, you must choose your dialogue partner. The fifth step suggests three: God, yourself, and another.

"Admitted to God..."

If you believe in God, you can pray to Him. You do not have to pray with a formulaic prayer, such as the *Our Father* but in your own words. You can have a conversation with God as with a friend about your wrongdoings. God already knows your heart. There is nothing to hide from Him. You can be honest in admitting your failings and ask for His mercy. What is important in feeling free to admit your faults to God is the renewed confidence that He is all-loving and merciful, not a harsh judge. You judge yourself harshly enough.

If you do not believe in a Supreme Being, admitting your faults to God makes no sense. However, you can still listen to the deep longings of your heart for an "other" to listen attentively, accept unconditionally, and forgive without limit. The yearnings come as a still quiet voice that is easily unheard in the loud noise of everyday life. Your anxiety, with its racing thoughts, interferes with your attentive listening. Stillness and silence are required to hear the longings for an accepting "other."

"Admitted to yourself..."

After realizing the faults that underlie your anxiety, the next step is to acknowledge them to yourself. That means taking full personal responsibility for your behavior. There are many ways to avoid taking responsibility.

First, you may ignore your vices, pretending they do not exist. In ignoring them, you entertain the fantasy that they will disappear on their own, without any effort on your part.

Second, you may wallow in self-loathing for not being perfect. Indulging your inner critic, you berate yourself, imagining that hating yourself for your wrongdoings will eliminate them. You wage an inner war against yourself which you cannot win. There are no survivors in such a war.

The third approach, which this step recommends, is to acknowledge your faults. That places you on a path to accept, work with, and learn from them. The attitude of acceptance that can lead to fruitful change is beautifully expressed in a poem by Rumi, a Sufi poet, entitled "The Guest House." (1)

> This being human is a guest house.
> Every morning a new arrival.
> A joy, a depression, a meanness,
> Some momentary awareness comes
> As an unexpected visitor.
>
> Welcome and entertain them all!
> Even if they're a crowd of sorrows,
> Who violently sweep your house
> Empty of its furniture.
>
> Still, treat each guest honorably.
> He may be clearing you out
> For some new delight.
>
> The dark thought, the shame, the malice.
> Meet them at the door laughing,
> And invite them in.

Be grateful for whoever comes,
Because each has been sent
As a guide from beyond.

"Admitted to another human being..."

Your fear of being judged interferes with you taking the step to be honest with another human being. You stand at a crossroads. Will you give in to your fear and let it continue to dominate your life? Or will you act in spite of your anxiety, asserting your will? Will you let fear control you, or will you take charge of it? The commitment to reveal yourself to another signifies a major step in freeing yourself from your addiction to fear, shame, and pride. With the admission you begin to take control of your life.

Time to Confide

The question arises, "To whom should I make this confession?" Because of the sensitive nature of your self-revelation, you will look for an individual with qualities that would benefit you. Above all, you need a person with whom you can feel safe, in whom you can have confidence. That person must be trustworthy, someone you know will keep your secrets safe and not gossip about you. You also want your confidant to be open-minded and not judgmental, someone who will really listen to you. What you fear most is being judged. Avoid anyone who tells you that you are special, the greatest. Such comments only inflate your ego, increasing your pride and shame. What you need most is sincere, whole-hearted acceptance. You may also seek a wise, prudent person who can give you valuable feedback.

Where can you find such a person? You may look among the ranks of the professionals: a counselor, physician, or clergyman. Admittedly, not all professionals possess the qualities you want in the person who will listen to your confession. You must choose carefully and wisely. You may also consider a close friend or a spouse who may already be aware of your defects of character. Or you may choose a relative stranger from a support group who has impressed you with their trustworthiness, openness, and wisdom.

"...the exact nature of our wrongs"

I recommended that you journal about your defects of character. When you meet with your dialogue partner, you may read from your journal or refer to it to keep you on track. It is important that you not stay general and abstract in talking about your faults. Do not simply say, "I fail like everyone else." That is not true. You fail in your own unique way, according to your personality and life experience. Take the risk to reveal the unpleasant details, the exact nature of your wrongs, so that your partner can know you as a person.

Your self-consciousness and shame may lead you to think that you are embarrassing yourself in exposing your vices. However, in admitting the exact nature of your wrong-doings you are saying much more about yourself without saying it. You reveal yourself a person with a conscience. In telling another about your faults, you demonstrate your strengths, particularly your honesty, humility, and courage. By confessing, you exercise and strengthen these virtues, which replace your bad habits.

Dennis Ortman, Ph.D.

The Paradox of the Humbled and the Exalted

Our culture promotes the glorification of the self, which breeds personal ambition. We feel constant pressure to keep climbing the ladder of success. We strive to make a better life for ourselves. The desire for progress drives us. That pursuit encourages us to compare ourselves and compete with others for the prize of being number one. That prize promises, we hope, a genuine and lasting happiness.

Step 5 turns our culture's penchant for happiness upside down. Instead of ego inflation, it suggests that ego deflation, a giving up of your false, meticulously constructed, ideal self-image, is the path to peace and contentment. Peace comes from accepting yourself as you truly are, with all your strengths and weaknesses. That is humility.

The paradox is expressed in the Gospel mandate (Matt 23: 12): "Whoever exalts himself shall be humbled; and whoever humbles himself shall be exalted." It is also echoed in the *Tao Te Ching*:

> If you want to be whole,
> let yourself be partial.
> If you want to be become straight,
> let yourself be crooked.
> If you want yourself to be full,
> let yourself be empty. (22)

Consider for a moment the relief you feel when you are simply yourself, giving up all the pretenses of being better, or worse, than you are. Instead of exhausting yourself in the relentless and impossible climb to perfection, you can relax with being who you are. You can find dignity in being human, with all its flaws and glories. The power of acceptance of yourself with the aid of another's love sets you free from the treadmill of having to prove yourself.

Practice: Loving-Kindness

A traditional Eastern practice to uproot fear is called *metta*, or loving-kindness (2). According to legend, it originated when a group of frightened monks approached the Buddha for help. They were being sent into the forest to meditate, but their fear stopped them. They had heard stories about rampaging elephants, poisonous snakes, and ferocious tigers attacking people. As an antidote to their fear, the Buddha taught them the following practice of loving-kindness. It is noteworthy that he did not tell them to stay out of the forest or offer them physical protection. He approached their fear as an affair of the mind and proposed a practice of mind training.

The practice is deceptively simple and powerful, engaging an unseen power within you:

1) Sit comfortably in a quiet place. Close your eyes and focus on the rhythm of your breath. Breathe deeply from your abdomen, and allow the muscles of your body to relax. Sense the warmth of your breath radiating into your tense muscles, loosening the knots.

2) Once relaxed, consider for a moment where you are in life. Allow yourself to feel the stress, turmoil, and confusion. If you are preoccupied with your fault-finding expedition, feel deeply the guilt, shame, and disappointment in yourself.

3) Then, select and focus your attention on phrases that address the pain and turmoil you feel at the moment. Express them as heart-felt wishes for yourself. For example, say to yourself: "May I be happy." "May I be free from fear and anxiety." "May I feel content with my life." "May I be kind and loving." "May I be patient with myself." "May I forgive myself." Add whatever wishes best express your deepest desires in the moment.

4) Repeat three or four phrases to yourself for a period of time. Repeat the phrases slowly and thoughtfully for about ten minutes. Coordinate the repetition of the phrases with the rise and fall of your breathing. Allow the words to sink into your mind and body.

This exercise fosters an attitude of loving-kindness toward yourself. It is the perfect antidote to fear because fear and love are opposites that cannot coexist in the mind at the same time. In reality, you can only have one thought at a time, although the thoughts may come in rapid succession, negative and jumbled. Your mind heals as your thoughts become more wholesome and positive, shaping your behavior. You can extend loving-kindness wishes to others in your life, radiating out toward your loved ones, toward anyone you encounter, toward those who harmed you, and toward the entire world.

Practice: Comfort Meditation

Another practice to help you on the path toward self-acceptance is meditating on select passages from the *Bible*. I suggest that you meditate on the following verses from the *Gospel of Matthew* (11:29-30). Jesus is addressing the crowd and you personally. Consider the words a personal message from Jesus to you:

"Come to Me, all you who are weary and find life burdensome, and I will refresh you. Take my yoke upon your shoulders and learn from Me, for I am gentle and humble of heart. Your souls will find rest, for My yoke is easy, My burden light."

The following steps summarize a meditation practice called *lectio divina* (3) (a divine reading):

1) Sit comfortably in a quiet place with your *Bible*. Take a few moments to quiet yourself and focus on being present in the moment. Be aware of God's presence and love for you. Ask Him to open your mind and heart to His words.

2) Read the words of the passage slowly. Allow the words to penetrate your soul. Consider them to be Jesus addressing you in your here-and-now situation with all your fears and anxieties. If a phrase jumps out at you, allow yourself to linger over it. Savor the phrase, tasting its truth. Repeat it to yourself, allowing its truth to reach a deeper level within you.

3) Next, respond spontaneously to the words. Let the feelings of gratitude, consolation, and even discouragement emerge without hindering them. Reflect for a moment on your reactions to the words and what they reveal about you. Let your concerns show themselves.

4) After a time of reflection on the word and your reactions, rest in silence. Let all the chattering thoughts pass and do not dwell on them. Be still and sense God's loving presence. Enjoy the stillness and peace, which may be unfamiliar to you. The silence may be uncomfortable for you at the beginning. Stay with it. Extend the quiet time from just a few minutes to as long as you like as you become more familiar with this practice.

5) Finally, end the session with a spontaneous prayer of thanksgiving. Carry a meaningful phrase with you throughout the day.

The Twelve Steps flow in an alternating rhythm of contemplation and action. After taking your moral inventory, it is time to act by admitting your faults to another. Such action, which goes against your fearful and shameful instincts, requires humility, honesty, and courage. Practicing those virtues transforms your fear-filled pride and prepares you for the next step.

11

Root Causes: Digging Deeper

Step 6: "Were entirely ready to have God remove all these defects of character."

"Change only happens when the pain of holding on
is greater than the fear of letting go."

—AA saying

Addicted to anxiety, what you fear most is change. You face a seemingly impossible dilemma. While hating the discomfort of your anxiety, you fear making changes in your life that may help. Consequently, you hang on to thoughts and behaviors that maintain your anxious condition. Predictable pain is better than uncertain relief.

Yet, being honest with yourself, you know your automatic reacting imprisons you. Your sense of powerlessness deepens as you keep doing the same things over and over. So, you surprise yourself at how much you enjoy the dance. You took a big risk. The soft light on the dance floor, the lively music, and the energy of the dancers thrills you. For once in your life you feel like you belong and have found yourself.

Now, as you look out from the dance floor into the shadows on the sidelines, you see many strange faces. Who are those people? Do you want to get to know them? Or do you remain satisfied with what you are currently enjoying?

That stranger in the shadows is the part of you that remains unconscious. It always lurks in the background, influencing your thinking, feeling, and behaving in ways beyond your awareness and control. Step 6 invites you to recognize the unconscious roots of your anxious addiction.

A Giant Leaning Tree

You experience anxiety like a giant tree planted in the middle of your life. Its shade blocks out the sunlight, providing relief from its searing heat while keeping you in partial darkness. It obstructs your view of the world around you. You may try to trim the branches of that tree, using various strategies. You can distract yourself from negative thoughts and even replace them with positive ones. You can engage in relaxation techniques, challenge your irrational thinking, and act despite your discomfort. Such procedures allow some sunlight to enter your life.

The fourth and fifth steps suggest looking closely at the trunk of the tree which supports and nourishes the branches. Your anxious reactions are really flowerings of character defects. What you fear losing reveals deeper attachments of your ego. Conditioned by your childhood and later life experiences, you come to believe that you cannot survive without certain things. You believe you need physical comfort, financial security, power and control, attention and affection to really be happy. So, you organize your life around the pursuit of these desires and become terrified when they are threatened. By coming to know your weaknesses, accepting and working with them, you gain a measure of freedom.

The sixth step invites you to dig more deeply and uncover the roots of these character defects. They lay buried deep in the ground of your unconscious mind, shaped by early life experiences beyond your conscious awareness. The roots of your weaknesses need to be explored, acknowledged, and removed before you can be truly free to be yourself.

The sixth step also reminds you of your powerlessness. You cannot uproot your unconscious conflicts with sheer will power or rational digging. You must learn to let go at a deeper level, which can be frightening. You must make yourself ready to surrender control to a higher Power.

Then, wait for healing as you focus on the nature of this step: "we're entirely ready..."

Obstacles to Readiness

Step 6 suggests that to advance in your recovery you must be "entirely ready" to surrender the character defects that cause your anxiety. Certainly, there are degrees of readiness before you make the commitment to take the leap and let go of your fears. Always realistic, the Steps/Traditions book admonishes: "Even then the best of us will discover to our dismay that there is always a sticking point, a point at which we say, 'No, I can't give this up yet.' And we shall often tread on even more dangerous ground when we cry, 'This I will never give up' (p. 66)."

What are your sticking points that make you hesitate to give up your fears? Maureen's is an irrational fear of flying.

Maureen: Fear of Flying

"I'm terrified of flying and avoid it like the plague. I know my reaction is irrational. I've studied all the facts about traveling: the rarity of plane crashes, its relative safety of flying compared to other forms of transportation. I know I have less chance of being hurt flying than driving a car, but I still panic even thinking about getting on an airplane. My doctor offered to give me a tranquilizer for the flight, but

I'd have to be tranquilized for the whole trip because I'd be so worried about getting back on the plane for the return flight. I'm a rational person. This fear of flying seems so crazy to me."

Your fears and the personal weaknesses they represent defy rational examination. When someone asks you why you are so afraid of something or why you worry so much, you can only shrug your shoulders. You may venture an explanation, but you know it is only an absurd rationalization. The truth is you do not know the reasons for your fears. However, you sense that some unconscious force is taking possession of you. Your fear protects something important to you that you do not fully understand. So, you hesitate to surrender your anxiety.

Bertha: An Elderly Woman with Lifelong Anxiety

"I've been a worrier like my mother since childhood. My mother always worried about her health and about dying. I was infected with her preoccupation and became a hypochondriac. I monitored every ache and pain in my body, imagined something terrible happening, and ran to the doctor often. The doctors must have been tired of seeing me. When I was pregnant with my son, I worried about a miscarriage or him being born with some defect. As he grew up, I watched closely for any signs of illness and quickly took him to the doctor. Worry has been my constant companion and my job in life. If I didn't worry, I don't know what I would do or who I would be."

As much as you hate your anxious reactions, they are familiar to you. You find comfort in the familiar. You fear the unknown more than anything else. If you give up your anxiety, you venture into unknown territory, which arouses an even greater anxiety. Your normal is to be anxious. Even though painful, it is predictable. It would be too frightening to give up your fears and not know the outcome.

Jeremy: A Perfectionist with a Sense of Helplessness

"I've been a perfectionist my whole life. I know the standards I judge myself and others by are unrealistic, but I can't change them. People tell me I'm too hard on myself, and I agree. If I were to settle for lower standards of success, I would feel like a failure. It would be like giving up, admitting defeat. So, I keep pushing myself to be the best I can be even if it kills me. I don't know any other way to live. It's who I am. I can't change that."

The anxious mind entertains many fixed ideas about how life should be. Many *shoulds* float around in your head. You may notice how much your daily life and interactions are governed by expectations. You expect your spouse, your children, and your friends to act in certain ways. Ideals of excellent performance guide your work. The world becomes predictable and safe if events unfold according to your expectations. Without realizing it, you can become a prisoner of your own rigid, fixed ideas, and close yourself off from experiencing the fullness of life.

Allan: Hopelessness

"Anxiety has crippled me my entire life. I'm a deeply wounded person. I've tried every therapy and self-help imaginable to find relief. I felt better for a while, but the anxiety always came back with a vengeance. I don't believe there is a cure for my ailment. I'm at the point of giving up in despair."

You cannot cure your anxiety on your own, with your own power. When you reach the point of despair, you face a crisis. A crisis is both an opportunity and a danger. You can give up entirely and wallow in self-pity. Or you can give up all your futile efforts to control your life and begin to let go, as Step 6 suggests. Indulging a sense of hopelessness will only keep you stuck where you are.

Madeline came to me for therapy because she was so anxious and depressed after cancer surgery. The doctors told her the cancer was in complete remission, but the news offered her no consolation. She remained paralyzed with worry about dying. Madeline had always sacrificed herself caring for the family. Now she berated herself that she lacked the energy and motivation to resume her daily chores around the house. All she wanted to do was sleep.

When I asked her how she felt about being the caretaker for the family for all those years, she honestly told me, "I hated it, but I accepted it as my lot in life."

I suggested, "Perhaps your cancer and now your anxiety give you permission to take a break from being a caretaker. Now you can be taken care of for a change." Madeline shook her head and insisted she still wanted to get back to usual role. It was only her anxiety and depression that kept her from returning to her normal life.

Although you hate the discomfort of your anxiety, you may secretly love your condition. It works for you! That may come as a shock. Naturally, you want to get rid of the painful feelings. But character defects accompany your anxious reactions, and you are more reluctant to let them go. In fact, being anxious and withdrawing from life may provide unacknowledged benefits. The Steps/Tradition book states: "What we must recognize now is that we exult in some of our defects. We really love them (p. 66)."

Loving your illness keeps you stuck. Victims have status.

Surrendering Your Faults

If someone were to ask you if you wanted to get rid of your anxiety, you would respond, "Of course, in a heartbeat." Yet, you feel powerless to stop your anxious reactions, suggesting an underlying addiction of which you are not fully aware. Your anxious reactions are entangled with your character defects, which are deeply engrained through many years of practice. Your failings generate fear. Then fear, in a vicious circle, generates more character defects.

What does it mean to be entirely ready? It means making a whole-hearted response to do something. Such a response involves an intentional commitment to take decisive action. Of course, being entirely ready to let go of your both your anxiety and faults does not occur all at once. It takes time and effort. The process unfolds in stages of being ready, willing, and able.

Ready?

Your work on the fourth step may have surprised you in several ways. You did not see clearly before the connection between your anxiety and your character defects. Further, you did not realize how entrenched were your vices. These personality traits have deep roots in your emotional programming from childhood. You mistakenly thought anxiety was your problem.

Anxiety is only a symptom of the problem. Your anxiety reveals and expresses what you hold dear and fear losing. The intensity of your anxiety shows the degree to which you are attached to your desires, how desperately you cling to them.

You are born with natural instincts for security and safety, power and control, affection and self-esteem. However, if you felt deprived in some way, the pursuit of some desire may take on an exaggerated importance. Supported by the culture, you develop emotional programs for happiness, believing that the satisfaction of these needs is essential for your wellbeing. Anxiety arises when any of these desires, perceived as necessary for your happiness, are threatened. For example, you may come to believe that performing well and achieving success in life are absolutely essential for you to be happy. You may then develop an excessive fear of failing and performance anxiety. You crave the glory of success. Addicted to succeeding, anxiety about failing creeps in.

As you discovered working through the first step, failure, defeat, and despair launch you on the path to recovery. There is no other way. Healing comes by walking through the pain, not around it. You continue to acknowledge your powerlessness over your anxiety and bad habits. You admit that your excessive concerns have made your life unmanageable. The absolute security you seek by indulging your desires is not possible. You realize the truth expressed in the *Tao Te Ching*:

> Chase after money and security
> and your heart will never unclench.
> Care about people's approval
> and you will be their prisoner (9).

Assess your own level of readiness, using a scale from one to ten. A one says, "I don't see any problem." A ten exclaims, "I'm so miserable I'll do whatever it takes to resolve this problem." Acknowledging honestly the trouble your anxious reactions and bad habits cause you increases your readiness.

Willing?

In addition to being ready, you must be willing to take the next step. Julia, who discusses her health worries below, appears not to be completely willing. There is something holding her back from taking the next step.

Julia: Health Worries

"I'm anxious about my health, but believe I have reason to be so concerned. My parents died at young ages. My husband tells me I'm a hypochondriac because I worry so much and go to the doctor so often. I don't see the problem. I'm just being

cautious and alert to any changes in my body. Perhaps, though, I imagine the worst at times and jump to conclusions that something minor, like an upset stomach, is a major health problem. I spend a lot of time and energy worrying, but I'd rather be safe than sorry."

When you dig deeper into your anxious reactions, you discover your natural concerns, i.e. what you want to protect. Who is not concerned about safety, security, health, control over their lives, affection, approval, and many other natural desires? Pursuing these desires in a balanced way is virtuous living.

These normal instincts, however, become faults when their satisfaction becomes an obsessive preoccupation. You believe that your happiness depends entirely on their fulfillment. You believe that your survival as a person depends on getting what you think you need. You cling to what you fear losing. Your obsession has become a vice. Vices are exaggerated virtues, compulsively lived out in a self-centered way.

You hesitate to change because you have mixed feelings about it. You feel the pain of your anxiety and the obsessive pursuit of your desires. You want a different life. However, change arouses anxiety because it involves a leap into the unknown. Your anxious mind craves certainty, clarity, and control. Making changes you break away from familiar, habitual patterns. That introduces an element of unpredictability. Consequently, you seesaw between finding reasons to change and reasons to stay the same.

You are willing to take the risk of change if you believe that the trouble your attitudes and behaviors cause outweighs the benefits. However, because your attitudes and behaviors have become so engrained, so automatic, it takes effort to assess their true impact on your life and relationships. The assessment requires the effort and honesty of clear thinking.

Getting off the Teeter-Totter

What can help you to get off that teeter-totter of indecision? The following four-step process can aid in your discerning and deciding.

(1) First, be aware of your shortcomings and sense the darkness from which they emerge. Caught up in the emotional storm of your anxious reaction, you cannot think clearly. You are tossed about on the waves of emotion, unable to plumb the depths.

When I ask my patients what they are afraid of (where is the danger), they often respond, "I don't know. I'm just scared." I invite them to pay attention to the rush of thoughts through their minds. When they insist that their mind is blank, I encourage them to persist in observing the thoughts and beliefs that arise from their depths.

If you pay close attention, you will recognize that your fears and anxiety reveal something important about yourself. They show your sensitivities, which need to be respected. They also display the black hole in your heart, the fearful emptiness from which all your insecurities arise. Have the courage to look into the darkness and the many ways you try to create the illusion of security for yourself.

(2) Next, accept your shortcomings without judging yourself. When you admit to yourself that you are not perfect, you naturally react with shame. "How can I be so flawed?" you ask yourself. Your anxious mind holds high standards of perfection which activate your

inner critic. You then hate your vices. The self-hatred, though, does not release you from the bondage to your unwholesome habits. It only increases your sense of hopelessness and despair. Your eventual healing will come through the power of forgiveness, which is a whole-hearted self-acceptance, warts and all.

(3) Third, investigate closely the nature of your anxiety and the attachments it reveals. Recognize honestly how you both love and hate your flaws. Your habitual attitudes and behaviors serve a purpose. They provide benefits for your perceived wellbeing, but at a price. They both help and harm you and those you care about. Face squarely your mixed feelings toward the following habitual reactions:

- fear and anxiety;
- pride;
- greed;
- anger;
- gluttony;
- vanity;
- lust;
- envy; and
- laziness.

You experience your *fear* and *anxiety* as both a blessing and a curse. These reactions alert you to danger, motivating you to protect yourself. They also give you the opportunity to withdraw from situations and activities that are uncomfortable for you. However, when these emotional reactions become excessive, you suffer. In an effort to find relief, you shrink your life, avoiding valued activities. You become preoccupied with your own safety, ignoring everyone and everything else. Ask yourself:

- How preoccupied am I with my safety and health?

Pride inflates you with a sense of self-importance. Healthy pride fosters self-esteem, self-confidence, and the desire to care for yourself. You relish your own goodness and value. When your pride takes a self-obsessed turn, you exaggerate your worth and power, considering yourself superior to others. Such a pride is fragile, easily wounded, and afraid of being humiliated. Ask yourself:

- How much do I need to be right?
- How much do I need to be perfect in my own and others' eyes?

Greed, the love of money and material possessions, fuels our consumer culture. It also feeds your ambition to work hard and accumulate wealth. Why not enjoy the good things of this earth? At some point, seeking wealth and desperately holding onto it can become an obsession. Like King Midas, you sense yourself becoming possessed by your single-minded pursuit of more, a quest that never satisfies. The more you have and the more you want, the more you worry about losing. Ask yourself:

- How driven am I in accumulating money and material possessions?

Anger is a close companion of fear. Both arise from the same survival instinct. Whenever you perceive an injury or obstacle to what you want to achieve, anger is aroused. It energizes you to fight for yourself, making you feel powerful. Threat can lead either to anxious flight or angry fight. Your survival depends on these reactions. Anger becomes harmful when it begins to consume you and you express it destructively. You perceive injury and threat everywhere. You react with an angry protest when the world, others, and you do not behave the way you think they should. You begin to live your life in a tense watchfulness, ready to pounce, and react with hostility. Ask yourself:

- How much do I cling to my fixed ideas about how my life should be?
- How much does anger possess me?

"Eat, drink, and be merry; for tomorrow we die," the saying goes. *Gluttony* moves you to seek pleasure and avoid pain, a natural instinct. It also motivates you to seek more in life: more experiences and more satisfactions. At what point, though, is more of whatever you want not enough? Then, pleasure-seeking, like any addiction, becomes painful. Your passion for pleasure-seeking begins to interfere with your pursuit of higher values. You worry about not getting enough because you believe your happiness depends on it. Ask yourself:

- How much am I motivated by the pursuit of comfort and stimulation?

Vanity calls attention to itself. You take pride in your appearance, seeking approval and admiration from others. Vanity can motivate you to be successful in life. The desire for recognition is a powerful motivator. However, when the desire for approval from others becomes excessive, you risk losing yourself. You become an actor in a play, wearing a mask that disguises your true self. In your desire to please others, you become a slave to their expectations about you. You live in constant fear of being exposed. Ask yourself:

- How much do I seek approval from others?
- How much do I crave recognition, status, and prestige?

Lust involves not only the desire for sexual pleasure but also for power and control. It is the passion for living large, knowing no limits. When your life is constricted by anxiety, you long for power and control, the freedom to expand your life. In your quest for control, you may try to manipulate and dominate others for your own self-interest. Relationships then become power struggles that lead to hostility, estrangement, and eventual loneliness. Ask yourself:

- How much do I crave power and control over my world?

- How dependent am I on my relationships for happiness?

Shakespeare called *envy* "that green-eyed monster that mocks the meat it feeds on." Envy longs for what others have and you feel missing in your life. Comparing yourself with others and wishing for what they have may motivate you to work hard. Our culture breeds envy through competition, believing that it brings out the best in the competitors. On the negative side, indulging your envy may deepen your discontent. You are never satisfied. You focus on what is missing in your life and overlook its fullness. Ask yourself:

- How much do I compare myself with others?

- How much do I focus on what is missing in my life?

Laziness serves a purpose when you are anxious. You withdraw from any situations you perceive as threatening to protect yourself. Your mind is so agitated with worrisome thoughts that you wish you could fall asleep to your life. Laziness means peaceful relaxation for you. However, when your means of coping becomes a way of life, your world becomes very small. You avoid full engagement in life and deep contact with your inner wellspring of joy and strength. Apathy eventually leads to hopelessness and despair. Ask yourself:

- How much am I caught up in a sense of helplessness about my life?

Reflect deeply on the faults you discovered in your moral inventory. Without realizing it, you embraced those unwholesome habits because they benefited you in some way. Acknowledge the benefit. However, when these habitual reactions became excessive, their usefulness diminished. They began to cause you pain. Acknowledge the cost to your well-being.

Finally, make the conscious intention to let go of your shortcomings. The faults, the bad habits, you so desperately want to get rid of are not as solid as you think. They arise from your futile attempts to be complete masters of our life. They are your own creations, not reflecting who you really are as a person. As your creations, they are really illusions of the reality of your person. Because you made them, you can unmake them. The process begins with your intention to let them go and allow your true self to shine forth.

Able to Move On

Assess your own level of willingness, using a scale from one to ten. A one says, "I am unwilling to put forth any effort to change." A ten affirms, "I will do whatever it takes to improve my life." An honest analysis of the cost and benefits of your unwholesome habits can open your mind to the desirability of change.

Amy: The Value of Perseverance

"I have a lot of insecurities from my childhood, from being abused. I became a fighter just to survive. I can be very stubborn when I want something and have learned to battle my many fears. I refuse to give in to them. From an early age, I developed a motto for myself: "POR," which means, "Press on regardless." I'm very self-conscious around groups of people, especially strangers. When I'm invited to a party, I debate

with myself and don't let the fear get the best of me. I repeat the motto to myself over and over. I force myself to go to the party. Almost invariably, I end up enjoying myself.''

Who is in control of your life? You or your anxiety? When you are in the grip of anxiety, you feel helpless, out of control. Your fear generates many expectations and false beliefs about life. For example, you believe that following routines, worrying, or avoiding people and uncomfortable situations will keep you safe. You believe that anxiety harms you and will overwhelm you. You also believe that you are helpless to overcome it. Scared stiff, your fear paralyzes you.

Like a self-fulfilling prophesy, if you do not challenge your anxiety, it will take over your life. It will rob you of your self-esteem and self-confidence. However, you can confront with your wise mind the negative thoughts of your addictive, anxious mind. You can act against your fears, not letting the feeling dictate your behavior. You can make choices to act based on what is important to you. Your chosen values, not your passing emotional states, can be the guides for your life.

When you act in accordance with your chosen values, you empower yourself. You begin the process of freeing yourself from your addictive mind. Of course, you also begin to liberate yourself from your slavery to your passions, such as anger, greed, laziness, and so forth when you choose to behave in a virtuous manner.

Assess your own level of ability, using a scale from one to ten. A one says, "I am completely helpless and can do nothing on my own." A ten affirms, "I am confident I can be the person I want to be." Challenging your false beliefs and acting against your fears empower you.

"…to have God remove all these character defects"

Digging deeper, you discover the unconscious roots of your character defects. You become more aware of the purpose they serve in supporting your self-centeredness. While embarking on that exploration, you also uncover a hidden treasure. You gain a glimpse of your true self.

Before getting on the path to recovery, you imagined that your anxiety and character defects were unmovable. "That's just who I am," you rationalized. Through taking the steps, you begin to realize that your faults really operate on the surface of your life. They are fleeting shadows that obscure a persistent light. Your authentic self is the light hidden in the darkness, the core of who you are as a person. Further, as a person, you are infinitely more than your unwholesome habits.

That hidden true self is intimately connected with a Power Greater that is both within and beyond you. You may call that Power, God, Ultimate Reality, or Life itself. In making yourself entirely ready to surrender your shortcomings, you remove the obstacles that prevent you from being yourself. You consciously seek to release that Power to set you free. Removing your character defects is really transforming them through that released Power to become virtues, reflections of your true nature. Never forget your basic goodness, sanity, and beauty obscured by your shadow-faults.

Perfection is an idea in the mind, an ideal. It does not exist in reality. In becoming ready to remove all your character defects, you are really committing to "make a beginning and keep trying." As the Step/Tradition Book states, "we ought to become entirely willing to aim toward perfection...to make a beginning on this lifetime job (p. 65, 66)." This task can only be accomplished through patient effort and openness to change.

Paradox of Perfection and Improvement

"We are already perfect but need some improvement." This slogan expresses the paradoxical reality of change. You are already perfect, complete, in yourself but do not fully realize it. The second step invited you to look inward and appreciate your basic goodness, which you share with the Divine and All Reality.

At the same time, you are not yet perfect. More work needs to be done to allow your true self to shine. Habitual negative patterns of thinking, feeling, and behaving need to be dismantled. Your work on the fourth step alerted you to what needs improvement in your life, to the darkness that obscures the light.

Recovery from your addiction to anxiety and your character defects involves a journey back to yourself, a homecoming. It is a remembering of what you forgot. Caught up in your addictions, you forgot who you really are. You wandered away from yourself without realizing it until the pain awakened you. Below are two practices to assist you on that homecoming journey.

Practice: Weighing the Costs and Benefits

From your moral inventory and the list of faults in this chapter, choose one to concentrate on. Be honest with yourself. Focus on the shortcoming that causes you the most trouble. Often, we do not see that weakness as clearly as those around us, particularly our loved ones. Ask someone closest to you to help identify the fault that underlies your anxiety. When you have made the selection, begin a cost/benefit analysis of it. Pay attention to what purpose the behavior may serve in your life. Recognize clearly how you both love and hate that character defect.

For example, you may choose vanity as a core fault. Vanity takes pride in appearance and seeks approval and admiration from others. Ask yourself the benefits of being a vane person. You might consider the following benefits:

- You work hard at looking good.
- You are motivated to be competent and to succeed.
- You value others' opinions about you.
- You know how to make a good impression.
- You seek to connect with people.

You might consider the following costs:

- You are not true to yourself in trying to please people.
- You become manipulative in getting people to like you.

- You chase after approval from others and become terrified of disapproval.

- You lose a sense of who you are in playing roles.

- You worry excessively about failing.

Write in your journal what you discover about yourself. Make two columns, one for benefits and another for costs. Write down the gains and losses of the trait you are considering. Do the costs outweigh the benefits? How does the fault increase your anxiety?

Practice: Remaining Like a Log

Mired in anxiety, you cannot sit still. Your anxiety propels you to keep in restless motion. Moving about, with racing fearful thoughts, you feel out of control. You lack a firm foundation from which to observe yourself closely and make a change.

An ancient Eastern text, *The Way of the Bodhisattva* (1), suggests a practice to stop, look, and listen to yourself before acting. The practice is called "Remaining Like a Log." Self-control begins by learning to take a pause between an arising urge and the automatic behavior. Shantideva, the author, advises:

When the urge arises in the mind
to feelings of desire or wrathful hate,
do not act! Be silent, do not speak!
And like a log of wood be sure to stay.

When an urge arises, such as fear, anger, or any other emotional reaction, there are four moments to intervene and gain control of yourself:

1) Before a thought is formed in the mind, the reaction begins with an initial perception. Some sight, sound, physical sensation, or memory causes discomfort. Awareness of this initial discomfort can prevent an emotional avalanche from gaining momentum.

2) Next, be aware of the spontaneous thoughts that accompany the discomfort. You may be unaware of these emerging thoughts which express some negative interpretation of the perception. Simply observing these thoughts keeps them from gaining power over your mind.

3) If you ignore the subtle thoughts that accompany your emotional reaction, your emotions will intensify and be prolonged. It is still not too late to catch with your mind's eye these arising thoughts and stop the avalanche of emotion. You can observe the pattern of these gathering thoughts and recognize the negative bias they express.

4) Finally, there is a moment when the urge leads to action: fight, flight, fainting, or freezing. You can train yourself to stop and think before taking action. You can interrupt the automatic chain reaction that has formed into an addictive habit. You can stop to consider what you value and how you want to act, making a free choice. Even in the face of intense emotion that seems overwhelming, you are not as helpless as you think.

In Step 6, you again become an observer of yourself. You look closely at what prevents you from surrendering your faults. Becoming ready, willing, and able, you make a committed decision to allow yourself to be transformed into the image of your true self.

Dennis Ortman, Ph.D.

12

Please Release Me: Asking From The Heart

Step 7: "Humbly asked Him (God) to remove our shortcomings."

"...we all have reservoirs of life to draw upon of which we do not dream."

—William James

You felt powerless and defeated by your anxiety. Your best efforts at relief failed. In working the steps, you have realized that you are engaged in a more serious struggle. Your anxiety, which you considered your foe, disguised another more daunting enemy, your character defects. Fighting your fears distracted you from a more intense, protracted battle against your inner demons. Aware now of the many faces of your faults, you again feel powerless and defeated to overcome them. Will you give up in despair, or choose to fight on? What weapons can you use?

You danced with many different partners, and your fear of dancing noticeably decreased. You feel more confident in yourself. When you look out from the bright dance floor into the shadows on the sidelines, you see many strange faces. You stop to consider whether or not you want to meet new people. Challenges remain to being completely comfortable with yourself. You can simply ask a stranger to dance, or you can take the risk of engaging that person in conversation first, just to become acquainted. It demands so much more of you to get to know the stranger personally. You expose yourself even more. Do you want to take the risk? Do you want to make the effort?

The stranger in the shadows is the dark side of you, your false self. Step 7 invites you to become intimately acquainted with what you do not like about yourself. It invites you to find a way to make that feared stranger a friend.

How can that happen? Alcoholics Anonymous gives a clear answer: "Indeed, the attainment of greater humility is the foundation principle of each of AA's Twelve Steps (p.

70)." It also adds, "In all these strivings, so many of them well-intentioned, our crippling handicap had been our lack of humility (p. 71)." Feeling so defeated in your efforts to overcome your character defects, the one weapon needed is humility, a further acknowledgment of your powerlessness to convert yourself.

Humility is truth. It involves seeing and accepting yourself as you are, not as you wish you would be. It is total self-acceptance, with all your strengths and weaknesses. Being humble, you have the capacity to accept whatever happens in your life with a sense of peace.

Driven by anxious expectations, your tendency may be to get caught up in fixed ideas about how you, your life, and your world should be. You want to be the complete master of your life. Your self-will stands in the way of you being humble and progressing in recovery.

Obstacles to Being Humble

There are at least four obstacles to being humble. They are

- great expectations;
- saying "no" to life;
- craving control; and
- being ashamed of weaknesses.

Great Expectations

Anxiety obsessed, you feel helpless in a threatening world. One place to find safety is in your mind. You create the image of a perfect world, entertain high expectations about yourself and others, and work hard to realize your dream. However, your idea of perfection is just an idea, a fantasy, a dream. The more you live in the dream world, the more you separate yourself from the nitty-gritty, often messy experience of the real world. Placing pride in realizing your dreams, you refuse to accept your limitations.

Terry: Expectations and Pride

"I always want everything to be just so. People tell me I have OCD, but I don't care what they think. There's a right way and a wrong way to do things. If you don't do it right, it's not worth doing. That's my philosophy in a nutshell. When I go to work, I do the best job I can and try to be perfect. When I'm home, I want everything neat, clean, and in order. I don't think I'm asking too much. I admit I can become impatient with myself and others when my expectations aren't met. But I take pride in everything I do."

Saying "No" to Life

According to AA, alcoholics are vulnerable to the "three Ps: perfectionism, procrastination, paralysis." Hooked on anxiety, you may hold perfectionist ideas about how you and your life should be. When your performance does not match your idealistic expectations, you procrastinate. Eventually, you give up and become paralyzed. You become disappointed that life is harder than you expected, and disengage, saying "no" to life. Avoiding the inevitable suffering of life, you refuse to accept reality.

Ryan: Lost Child

"I feel like a lost child. I can't make any decisions about my future. School came easy for me, and my parents pushed me to get good grades. Nothing was good enough for them. If I got a B, they'd ask why I didn't get an A. If I got an A, they'd say I should have gotten an A+. I worried about doing well in school. When I entered college at a prestigious university, I barely passed and lost complete confidence in myself. I began procrastinating with assignments, dropped out of tough classes, and finally left college. Now I don't know what I want to do."

Craving Control

Feeling powerless, you seek control over your life and others to feel safe. You secretly entertain a fantasy to be the total master of your life. Like Frank Sinatra, you take pride in doing it your way. You want to eliminate uncertainty and unpredictability. Without realizing it, your fear drives you to act like an all-powerful god, the master of the universe. Any limits to your control arouse panic if your anxiety is extreme. Any detour from the expected puts you in a tailspin. Your self-centered pursuit of control interferes with your humble acceptance of reality.

Raquel: Craving for Control

"I'm a worry wart, always feeling on edge. I feel so out of control with my life and emotions that I think I'm going crazy. The only way I can find some peace is to take charge of situations. My mind is constantly making plans. Nothing is left to chance. I monitor closely what everyone around me is doing. My family accuses me of being a control freak. I see what they mean, but I don't know any other way to cope with my anxiety."

Being Ashamed of Weaknesses

No one escapes the tyranny of your high standards, especially yourself. Believing you are weak and defective because of your anxiety condition, you judge yourself mercilessly. You are ashamed of your weakness. Your inner critic is alive and well, terrorizing your life. Your sense of shame that results from you not living up to your idealized standards is really the reverse side of pride. In your mind, if you are not perfect, you are worthless. The refusal to accept your limitations prevents you from humble self-acceptance.

Christopher: Inner Critic

"I'm so self-conscious when I talk with people that I can't concentrate on what they're saying. Critical thoughts run through my mind that they're judging me and thinking I'm boring. I don't know what to say. I really try to pay attention to the conversation, but I get so distracted. I think I must have attention deficit disorder.

I even see myself as boring because I don't have any interests and don't do anything worthwhile with my life. I'm such a mess. I hate that I care so much what people think of me."

"Humbly asked God…"

What does it take to be humble? Two experiences bring you to your knees and open your heart to a new life: great suffering and great love.

Great Suffering

The Steps/Traditions book expresses clearly this truth: "For us, the process of gaining a new perspective was unbelievably painful. It was only by repeated humiliations that we were forced to learn something about humility. It was only at the end of a long road, marked by successive defeats and humiliations, and the final crushing of our self-sufficiency, that we began to feel humility as something more than a condition of groveling despair (p. 72)."

You felt utter defeat in attempting again and again to gain mastery of your anxiety. All your efforts failed. Your first step on the road to recovery involved admitting your powerlessness over your anxiety and how your life had become miserable and unmanageable because of it. That was just the first humiliation. You experience a second defeat in becoming aware of your character defects and admitting your powerlessness to remove them. Long buried in unconsciousness and ruling your attitudes and behavior, awareness of your faults initially brings you shame. A humble acceptance of them seems impossible.

Great Love

The second experience that humbles and transforms you is great love. Fear is the opposite of love. Fear closes you off from yourself and others while love expands your heart and life. You experience love as a miracle. Love casts out fear. It also humbles you before the greatness and grandeur of life.

Angela: Moved by Love

"My anxiety has always crippled me. I had separation anxiety as a child. As an adult, I was afraid to leave the house. When I was married, I heard so many horror stories from my mother about the pain and danger of pregnancy that I never wanted to have a child. What a shock when I found out I was pregnant! I worried myself sick throughout the pregnancy.

When my baby was born, it was the greatest moment of my life. What a miracle! I can't imagine loving anyone more than my baby. As my child was growing up, I amazed myself at my courage to get out and participate in his events."

Prayer Changes You, Not God

The seventh step invites you to pray to God. Why pray to Him? What does it accomplish? If you do not believe in a personal God, prayer makes no sense. It is having a conversation with nobody, with someone who does not exist.

Even if you do believe in God, how does it make sense? Why do you need to ask God for anything? God, who is all-knowing, already knows what you need. All-loving, He gives it to you. As Jesus says in the "Sermon on the Mount" (Matthew 6:32-33): "Your heavenly Father knows all that you need. Seek first His kingship over you, His way of holiness, and all these things will be given you besides." Nevertheless, Jesus also taught the power of prayer in the same sermon (Matthew 7:7): "Ask, and you will receive. Seek, and you will find. Knock, and it will be opened to you."

How can you make sense of such contradictory advice? The answer involves a deeper look at the nature of prayer.

When I was a child, I was taught that prayer is having a conversation with God. Raised Catholic, I learned many prayers, such as the *Our Father* and *Hail Mary*, which the priests and nuns encouraged me to repeat often. I spoke, and God listened. As I grew older, my prayer became more a free-flowing conversation with God in my own words. I expressed what was going on in my life and felt comfort in knowing that God listened and cared about what I said.

Now as an adult, I realize that God is an invisible, mysterious partner in my prayerful dialogue. As I related in Step 2, God is not so much for me a Supreme Being out there but rather a living Presence within me. The Sacred Presence is closer to me than I am to myself. So, prayer involves the experience beyond words of a Divine Presence within, a deeper entering into the mystery of myself, which is bound to the Mystery of God.

In my Catholic education, I also learned that prayer is a lifting of the mind and heart to God. My teachers suggested that praying changes us more than it changes God, who is always faithful in love. Prayer lifts us out of our ordinary world into God's world.

Now as an adult, I appreciate that my ordinary world and God's are not so separate. The Sacred pervades all life. There is nowhere that God cannot be found. The Divine Presence is everywhere and most especially sensed in the silence of our own hearts.

The act of praying, of asking God specifically for something, transforms us. How does that happen?

Imagine you are attending a symphony. You go because you want something: the pleasure of listening to beautiful music. You consciously intend to be entertained, but as you become immersed in the music, you become captivated by its beauty and power. You are not conscious of the individual notes played or the instruments in the orchestra. You are caught up in the music. You lose yourself. For the moment you are transformed. You become the music. What an exhilarating experience that transcends your initial intention to be simply entertained!

Prayer may begin with a conscious intention. You want something from God and ask for it specifically. However, as you become more immersed in the act of praying, your faith is aroused. You sense God's presence in a new way, outside and within you. You experience at a deep level the power of His love and the tenderness of His concern. In the process, you lose yourself, that is, all your conscious striving. You acknowledge your powerlessness to change yourself through your analyzing and working at your problems. Your self-centeredness begins to dissolve. Humility is born. Whatever you were asking for becomes less relevant because you sense you are being transformed through the praying. You become one with God. Your only desire is to do His will, "to seek first his kingship over you."

Prayer from the heart transforms your consciousness, giving you a new mind and heart to engage in your daily life. It releases the Higher Power that is both within and beyond you. It gives you hope in the midst of defeat while battling your demons.

"...to remove our shortcomings"

You pray to remove your shortcomings as if they are dirt on surface of your psyche that can be swept away without leaving a trace. However, your faults are more like deep stains that penetrate near the core of the person. They are deeply embedded in your unconscious from birth and early childhood. Your faults represent misguided attempts to cope with the pain and emptiness of your life. They are attempts to fill the hole in the soul. You seek happiness, but look in the wrong place. In reality, your hated vices are distortions of your strengths that need to be redirected to attain true happiness. Consequently, the better strategy is to learn to transform, not remove, your shortcomings.

A traditional story illustrates the transforming strategy. Once upon a time, a poisoned tree grew in the middle of a village. All the elders gathered to decide what to do. One group saw only the danger in the tree's presence and recommended, "Let's cut it down before anyone is harmed." A second group countered, "Let's not hate it or fear it. After all, it's part of nature, which is good, and must be respected. We must have compassion for the tree because we share its nature. Let's build a fence around it so we will not get too close and get poisoned." The leader of the group listened to all the arguments and finally spoke up: "This poison tree is perfect, exactly what our village needs. Let's learn its secrets. Instead of destroying it or avoiding it, let's pick the poisoned fruit. Let's investigate it carefully and look for ways to use the poison as medicine to heal ourselves and others." Hearing that wisdom, all the elders stood up to affirm the decision.

This story suggests a path of transformation in three steps. These include the following:

- Don't uproot the poison tree too quickly.
- Investigate carefully the fruit and the roots.
- Turn the poison into medicine.

Don't Uproot the Tree Too Quickly

Your first instinct is to get rid of the bitter fruit of anxiety. You cannot stand the physical discomfort of uptight feelings, queasy stomach, nervous sweating, shallow breathing, and racing heart. The thoughts of doom and gloom enshroud you. So, you undertake various strategies to eliminate the discomfort. You try to distract yourself from your worries by keeping busy. You work at relaxing your body through exercise, deep breathing, and meditation. You make an effort to confront your negative thinking, replacing it with more positive thoughts.

When these efforts do not give the relief you want, your second instinct may be to give up in despair. So, you let your fear possess you. You indulge your worrisome thoughts and let your compulsive behaviors go unchecked. You avoid any persons, places, or activities that arouse anxiety. Your life shrinks, diminishing your pleasure in living.

Remember that your anxious reaction is a symptom of an underlying problem, disguising your character defects and woundedness. If you destroy the fruit, you will not learn about the poison and find a remedy.

Investigate Carefully the Fruit and the Roots

The next step is to examine closely your anxious reaction, a process you began in the fourth step. What you are anxious about reveals what you love and hate. It is a window to your soul. Pay particular attention to the thoughts that arise when you are anxious. Notice also the persisting pattern of thoughts which gather to shape your self-identity.

An anxious reaction lasts for only ninety seconds. The uncomfortable physical sensation comes and goes quickly. What prolongs and intensifies it are negative thoughts and the stories you tell yourself. You imagine catastrophes and dwell on terrible things happening.

The negative thoughts are embedded in stories you tell yourself. Why do you tell yourself such stories if they prolong the pain? The anxious mind cannot tolerate uncertainty. To create a sense of security through understanding, you make commentaries about your life. You manufacture an image of yourself that gives you a sense of identity and purpose. These stories also reveal your woundedness, your efforts to cope, and your poisoned thinking. The following are three typical stories that anxious people tell themselves: being a perfectionist, a caretaker, and a victim. See if you can identify with elements of these stories.

David: Perfectionism

"I make no apologies for my high standards. Actually, I take pride in them. I firmly believe that if anything is worth doing, it's worth doing right. I was demanding of myself in school, graduated with honors, and pursued a medical degree. I became a surgeon. I saved many lives because of my attention to detail, to being exact in my work. My staff complains that I'm often impatient. I agree that my anger comes out when they become careless. I don't tolerate sloppiness.

My father taught me to be a perfectionist in everything I did. I was afraid of his temper but am grateful for his teaching me the right way to do things. He had me wash his car every week. If I didn't do it just the way he wanted, he would make me wash it again, and again if necessary."

If you are a perfectionist, you are idealistic and hold yourself and others to extremely high standards. In many ways "perfectionism" is misnamed. It is really "imperfectionism" because of your focus on what is missing. You are sensitive to the gap, to how reality does not measure up to your standards. Intolerant of mediocrity, you judge yourself and others according to these standards and can be harsh in your criticism at times. From an early age you learned to manage your anxiety by doing the right thing. The need to be right consumes you. The poison circulating through your anxiety is anger, which is aroused when your ideals are not met.

Monica: On Being a Caretaker

"My father drank heavily, and my parents fought all the time. I wanted to fix their marriage and keep peace in the family. As the oldest child, I had the responsibility to care for my younger brothers. When my parents battled, I protected them and assured them that everything would be all right. I enjoyed taking care of them, and they looked up to me like a mother.

When I graduated from high school, I had no difficulty choosing a career. I entered a nursing program. I had a built-in detector that alerted me to what people around me needed. It was fun for me to learn about the human body and ways of taking care of patients. Taking responsibility and caring for patients came naturally to me."

If you are a caretaker, you have a natural instinct to care for others. You are attuned to the needs of others. From childhood, you have learned to connect with people by helping them. You take pride in your ability to help others and may tend to become a rescuer of lost souls. Giving of yourself makes you feel alive. You need to be needed. However, you may tend to neglect your own needs, sacrificing yourself in caring for others. You manage your anxiety, the sense of being powerless, by taking charge in serving others.

A hidden pride poisons your anxious fruit, though. It is a pride that you are superior because you are not as needy as those you help.

Alicia: Feeling Like a Victim

"I'm jinxed. Anything that can go wrong in my life has gone wrong. I've had so many health problems, like I've been cursed with a weak body. I've had trouble with my supervisors at every job I've had. They made ridiculous demands on me, and I refused to be submissive. I'm not afraid to speak up, and that has cost me several promotions. It's all so unfair. I've been looking for another job now but feel trapped because there's nothing available that pays what I need to survive. My relationships? They've been a disaster. I've dated so many loser men that want to take advantage of me that I've given up completely on the idea of getting married.

I can see that I've had to fight for myself since childhood. My parents ignored me completely and only paid attention to my brother, whom they treated like a king. I felt helpless to get any attention from them."

If you see yourself as a victim, you live with a sense of helplessness in a threatening world. You are acutely sensitive to the dangers around you, always vigilant. You mistrust the motives of others, particularly those in authority who have power over you. Because you suffered terrible things in the past, you fear that the painful past will repeat itself in the future. So, you are always on guard. Pessimism and doubt grip your mind. Caution rules your life. You manage your anxiety by being alert and seeking control, clarity, and certainty. However, fear poisons your quest for safety and security.

Turn the Poison into Medicine

In my practice, I spend my day listening to my patients tell me their stories. Each story is fascinating and revealing but still fiction. My patients report to me a few facts embedded in a narrative they create to help understand themselves. I often tell my patients, "That's an interesting way to think about yourself. How did you come to think that way?"

In response, they tell me about the messages they received from their parents and other important people in their lives. I then propose another question that often startles them, "What purpose do you think it could serve for you to think of yourself that way?" Together we probe the possible motives behind the story.

Pay close attention to the stories you tell yourself to make sense of your life. Ask yourself what purpose it might serve for you to tell yourself that story. One way to answer that question is to make a cost/benefit analysis of your life narrative. It will reveal what is a poison and what is a medicine for you. The following is an example of such an analysis:

If you tend to be a *perfectionist*, what are the possible benefits, the medicine, in thinking that way?

- It motivates you to be hardworking, responsible, and conscientious.
- You are not complacent, always pushing yourself to excel.
- You have a strong conscience and high ideals.
- Fairness and integrity guide your actions.
- Your anger energizes you to fight for what you believe is right.

What are the possible costs, the poison, of being a perfectionist?

- You can be narrow-minded and rigid in your thinking, believing you are always right.
- You can be intolerant of those who disagree with you.
- You can be harshly critical of yourself and others.
- You have difficulty relaxing, risking burnout.
- You are easily angered and can indulge a self-righteous anger.

If you can identify yourself as a *caretaker*, what are the payoffs for you in assuming this role?

- It motivates you to be loving and overcome selfishness.
- Others admire you for your generosity, service, and self-sacrifice.
- You take pride in what you do for others.
- You are sensitive to others' needs and value improving relationships.

- Others depend on you, and you are there for them.

What are some drawbacks to identifying with the caretaker role?

- You are so focused on others that you become out of touch with your own needs.

- Your self-esteem depends on the approval of others.

- You can become controlling and manipulative, imagining you know what is best for others.

- You may seek out troubled people to fix.

- You may think yourself superior to others.

If you identify yourself with the *victim* role, what are some advantages for you?

- You are acutely aware of your vulnerability and take steps to protect yourself.

- You are cautious in trusting and loyal when you find someone trustworthy.

- You can be confident and courageous in facing your fears.

- You are willing to fight for the underdog.

- Others may offer you sympathy and want to help.

What are some disadvantages of the victim role?

- You may indulge a sense of helplessness and not take action.

- You may blame others for your problems and not take responsibility.

- Others may try to exploit your weakness.

- Fear and doubt may rule your life.

- Always suspicious, you may isolate yourself for protection.

Everyone develops their own life story as a way of making sense of their various experiences. They experience their lives like an unfolding drama. Their stories also express their self-images, their sense of personal identity, and their perceived strengths and weaknesses.

If you are anxious, your personal story takes on a particular quality. Your automatic negative thinking tends to focus on your weaknesses, overlooking your strengths. You lose a humble, healthy sense of balance about yourself. Further, because of your intolerance for ambiguity, your ideas about yourself become fixed. You give great weight to the stories you tell yourself, seeing them as fact, not mental fiction. You may become lost in your thoughts to distance yourself from your anxious feelings. Your attachment to your life story can take on an addictive quality, restricting your freedom to become fully engaged in your life.

The *Tao Te Ching* poetically expresses an alternative mindset and the consequences of letting go of these fixed ideas:

> The mark of a moderate man
> is freedom from his own ideas.
> Tolerant as the sky,
> all-pervading like sunlight,
> firm like a mountain,
> supple like a tree in the wind,
> he has no destination in view
> and makes use of anything
> life happens to bring his way (59).

Paradox of Effort and Grace

When I was a child learning to pray, I was taught: "Work as if everything depends on you; pray as if everything depends on God." My teachers were aware of the danger in ignoring either side of the equation of effort and grace. If we believe that only our efforts count, we can become arrogant with success or despairing with defeat. If we believe that God does it all, we can become passive spectators to our lives. Prayer prepares us for action, giving us confidence and direction. In turn, action, struggling to make a better life, brings us humbly to prayer.

The fellowship of Alcoholics Anonymous echoes this paradoxical wisdom, encouraging its members both to work the program and surrender to their Higher Power. The *Tao Te Ching* advocates both doing and not doing, letting events unfold naturally:

> Less and less do you need to force things
> until finally you arrive at non-action.
> When nothing is done,
> nothing is left undone.
> True mastery can be gained
> by letting things go their own way.
> It can't be gained by interfering (48).

Recovery from anxiety is like planting a garden and watching the flowers grow. It requires much effort to prepare the garden for growth. You cannot force flowers to bloom, but they will not flourish unless you prepare the ground. You have to till the soil, plant the proper seeds, and pull weeds. Then the sun, rain, and warmth allow the seeds to sprout and show their natural beauty. The hidden power of nature works its wonders. You watch and wait, tending the garden as needed, and witness the miracle of new life.

In the same way, you cultivate the garden of your soul. You remove the weeds of your shortcomings and plant seeds of good works. Prayer, meditation, and spiritual practices nurture the plants. You work at removing any obstacles that interfere with the emergence of your true self, which is naturally good, wise, and sane. The gift of new life cannot be suppressed, if the mind and heart are open and willing. The following are some practices to cultivate an awake mind and heart ready for growth.

Practice: Write Your Life Story

We all have a unique story to tell. We live our lives day after day and create commentaries to explain our experience to ourselves and others. Our experience can be confusing and baffling. We create personal narratives to give meaning to our lives and to connect with others. Intimacy grows in the exchange of our stories through which we share ourselves.

Take a moment to reflect on your life and how it is unfolding. Begin at the beginning. What were your parents like? How would you describe them? What qualities did you love and hate about them? What was their marriage like, and how did they parent you? Review in your mind all the significant people in your life: your siblings, relatives, and teachers. Notice their qualities, how they interacted with you. Did anyone suffer from an anxiety disorder? Gain a sense of their impact on your life.

Next, look at the important events in your life, the turning points. Some events were beyond your control, while others resulted from choices you made. Were there life-changing events, such as the death of a parent, physical or mental illness, the birth of your children? How did you cope? How did you progress through school, your career, and your relationships? What important decisions did you make that changed the course of your life regarding marriage, children, and career? How did you make those decisions? Did you carefully evaluate the costs and benefits, react impulsively, or choose intuitively? How did fear influence your decision-making?

Stand back and observe the flow of your life, with all its fits and starts. What patterns do you notice? What seems to be the trajectory, the direction, of your life? What seems to be the driving forces within and outside you? You can begin to understand your hidden motivations, your desires for possessions, power, or prestige. What were your passions and priorities?

Write in your journal your own autobiography. Be an astute observer of yourself as if you were an historian investigating the life of an important person. Paint a collage of your life with the various events. You will notice that you have always been telling yourself stories about yourself, and these stories have changed over the years. Your self-conscious thoughts are not as solid and fixed as you think. You are also infinitely more than your thoughts about yourself, which cannot fully grasp your mystery.

Practice: Body Scan

Your anxious mind often takes possession of you, and you become lost in your thoughts. You focus on the future and imagine catastrophes occurring over which you have no control. To gain a sense of control, which is really an illusion, you worry. You imagine that worrying will somehow prepare you for the worst, but it only makes you more miserable.

How can you escape the fixed negative thinking of your anxious mind? By returning to your body and listening to its wisdom. Without knowing it, when you become anxious, you disengage from your body and your experience of the present moment. By focusing your attention on your body, you anchor yourself in the present moment and let go of your thoughts about possible future troubles.

The body scan is a traditional Eastern practice that cultivates awareness of the body (1). The procedure is simple:

1) Lie down on your back in a comfortable position. Find a quiet place where you will not be disturbed. Close your eyes to avoid any distractions. Relax and feel the solidness of the floor supporting your body.

2) Focus on the rising and falling of your breath. Your breath signifies life and your connection with the world. Breath is also spirit. Feel yourself relaxing as you pay attention to the rhythm of your breathing. As thoughts arise, do not fight them. Simply acknowledge them and let them pass.

3) Shift your attention to various parts of your body, beginning with the top of your head. Slowly move your awareness through your body to the tips of your toes. Pause to notice any sensations of tension or pain. Note the quality and intensity of the discomfort. Your body, more than your mind, holds emotional pain going all the way back to childhood.

4) Imagine breathing into the various parts of your body as you scan it with the light of your awareness. Feel the lightness of your breath infiltrating and lifting any areas of tightness and heaviness. Stop at areas where you feel pressure and consciously breathe in the tension. Then, breathe out calmness and peace.

5) Finally, be aware of the sense of your body as a whole. Feel yourself united and at peace with your body. Be totally relaxed.

Do this exercise in an unhurried manner for at least fifteen minutes. Afterward, arise slowly to resume your day. Carry with you the freeing experience of being completely in your body and not in your mind. At various times of the day, pause for a moment to pay attention to your body, briefly scanning for any sensations.

In Step 7, you again acknowledge your defeat in attempting to rid yourself of your shortcomings. The experience humbles you and brings you to prayer. Through your own efforts you cannot eliminate your faults and your anxiety, but you can begin a process of transforming them into life-giving virtues.

13

Wounded Healers: Nurturing a Kind Heart

*Step 8: "Made a list of all persons we had harmed,
and became willing to make amends to them all."*

*"Resentments are like stray cats;
If you don't feed them, they'll go away."*

—AA saying

In working the steps so far, you looked inward to become better acquainted with yourself. You realized how much your anxiety blinded you. Like dust in your eyes, it kept you from seeing yourself clearly. You failed to recognize your own basic goodness, sanity, and bravery because you were so preoccupied with your helplessness in a dangerous world. The world seemed a hostile place, abandoned by a loving God.

As your anxious vision cleared, faith in a Higher Power, in Ultimate Reality, in God, was awakened. You also humbly acknowledged the full truth about yourself, seeing both your strengths and weaknesses. You admitted and confessed the character defects that gave rise to your anxious reactions.

Now, tired from all the dancing, you pause to take a breather. You take a seat on the sidelines and watch the others dance. Before, you felt so uncomfortable with yourself and were so preoccupied with trying to relax that you never looked closely at the others in the hall. Now, for the first time, you notice all the other people. They came, like you, because they loved the band, the music, and dancing. They wanted to connect with others, meet old friends, and make new ones.

As you look around the dance floor, you gaze at different individuals. Memories crop up. You have a history with many of the people in the room. Suddenly, pangs of guilt emerge. You recognize that you have hurt some of these people and neglected others by your past behavior. Your heart goes out to them.

The honest and courageous look inward at your anxiety has not been enough to bring you relief. Step 8 invites you to look outward at others, to see them as clearly as you are beginning to see yourself. You are painfully aware of how your fear and anxiety has hurt you. This step encourages you to do something that might surprise you: recognize how your anxiety has harmed others.

Alcoholics Anonymous is unflinching about the need for alcoholics to take this step for a genuine recovery: "Every AA has found that he can make little headway in this new adventure of living until he first backtracks and really makes an accurate and unsparing survey of the human wreckage he has left in his wake (Steps/Traditions, p. 77)."

You may acknowledge that your anxious reactions have strained relationships but may object that it has caused wreckage. You can see how it has wrecked your life in many ways, robbing you of happiness. How has it damaged others' lives?

Answering that question requires that you develop empathy, the ability to walk in another's shoes. Empathy involves you stepping out of yourself and your fixed ideas and seeing the world from another's perspective. If you are anxious and fearful, your attention focused on self-preservation, empathy may be in short supply.

Obstacles to Empathy

There are at least four obstacles to empathy. These include

- anxious self-preoccupation;
- being trapped in the victim role;
- suffering in isolation; and
- prejudiced ideas.

Anxious Self-Preoccupation

Gripped by anxiety, whether worry or a panic attack, your sole focus is on finding relief. Feeling threatened, you are desperate for a sense of safety. In those fearful moments, you cannot think about anyone else. Even afterward, the effects linger in an insecure feeling that you could be assaulted again. So, you arrange your life in a protective mode. Responsibilities are set aside when fear strikes. You can only pay attention to yourself and your need for calm and safety. The impact of your anxious behavior on others eludes you.

Sally: Self-Preoccupation

"I've had panic attacks since I was a teenager. They come out of the blue and paralyze me. My heart pounds and I can't breathe. I think I'm dying. It doesn't matter what I'm doing. The panic takes over. I'm in a state of emergency and only want to find some relief. Fortunately, my husband understands and tries to calm me and gives me medication. He took me to the hospital many times in the past because I thought I was having a heart attack until we both understood about panic attacks.

Afterward, I'm exhausted and have to rest. Then, the panic is followed by worry, the dread that I will have another attack."

Being Trapped in the Victim Role

The danger-detector in your brain runs in overdrive. You view the world as a threatening place and must protect yourself at all costs, even at the price of friendly relationships. If you have been hurt badly enough in the past, especially if you were traumatized, it imprints a powerful memory. You become terrified of being hurt again, of becoming a victim. You are slow to trust others. Your guard is up. Your attention becomes concentrated on signs of danger. The hyper-vigilance interferes with being open to others' feelings.

Jessica: Victim Role in Life

"I was abused as a child and vowed I would never let anyone hurt me again. I'm always alert to people trying to take advantage of me and react quickly. I'm also proactive in protecting myself. I keep a list of people who have offended me and write down precisely what they did. Every now and then I review the list. Once someone makes that list, I never trust them again and keep them at a distance. I also record phone messages and save those which are especially obnoxious. You can't be too careful these days."

Suffering in Isolation

You believe that your anxiety disorder makes you different, sets you apart. Even though a quarter of the population suffers clinical anxiety, you ignore the numbers. You still feel alone with your suffering. You do not understand your irrational fears and expect others will not. Your inner critic torments you for being so weak. Shame prevents you from admitting your pain to others, whom you believe will not understand. In your mind, they will only judge you for being mentally ill. Your lack of compassion for yourself interferes with your ability to empathize with others who have their own life challenges.

Anthony: Feeling Alone with Anxiety

"No one understands how terrified I feel about getting on an airplane. I go into a panic and just cannot do it. My wife and friends encourage me to get drunk and drugged before getting on the plane. They make it sound so easy. They don't understand that I'd have to be drugged the whole trip because I'd be worried about the flight home. I feel like such a wimp because of my fear. I won't let anyone know at work and keep a cool, calm facade. I just refuse to take any business trips that require flying. I believe my coworkers would laugh at me."

Prejudiced Ideas

Fear fixes the mind with many prejudiced thoughts. You may be able to identify the distorted thoughts, the what-if thinking, the exaggerated dangers, the sense of being out of control, but cannot stop the flow. You may tell yourself, "I'm an anxious person. That's just how I think." You may even divide the world of relationships into two groups: either those who threaten you or those who rescue you. Caught up in anxiety, you develop the habit of seeing everything from your own biased point of view. Your fixed ideas block a clear vision of yourself and others.

Reggie: Unclear Thinking

"I've been in therapy for many years for my anxiety and am gaining some under-standing of my anxious mind. When I'm in the grip of fear, I can't think clearly. All I see is danger. All I want to do is escape. I focus on the future and only see gloom and doom. I know my thinking is distorted, but I can't stop the irrational thoughts. I feel like I'm being carried along in a rapidly flowing stream through rocks and tree limbs to a destination unknown. I can only scream in terror and helplessness."

"Made a list of all persons we had harmed..."

Alcoholics Anonymous recommends its members make a list of all the persons they harmed. It encourages them to look backward and outward at their relationships. The benefits are clear, according to AA: "It is the beginning of the end of isolation from our fellows and from God (Steps/Traditions, p. 82)."

You may think that your anxiety only hurts you and nobody else. This step invites you to stop, look, and think again. To make a meaningful list of persons harmed requires a double awareness: first, of your connectedness with others, and second, of the impact of your anxious behavior on others, which is empathy.

All for On and One for All

We are not as separate from each other as we think. However, our culture tells us otherwise. It encourages us to be independent, self-sufficient, "our own person." It further teaches us to be ambitious and competitive, to become "number one." The result is a "me-against-them" attitude that causes alienation.

The spiritual traditions teach an alternative wisdom. Instead of "everyone for himself," it proposes "all for one and one for all." These traditions teach that the way to happiness is through love, which arises from and creates a "we-mentality."

The analogy of the human body expresses unity in diversity. For example, St. Paul explained in his *First Letter to the Corinthians*: "Now the body is not one member, it is many. If the foot should say, 'Because I am not a hand I do not belong to the body,' would it then no longer belong to the body? If the ear should say, 'Because I am not an eye I do not belong to the body,' would it then no longer belong to the body? If the body were all eye, what would happen to our hearing? If it were all ear, what would happen to our smelling? . . . If one member suffers, all the members suffer with it; if one member is honored, all the members share its joy."(12:14-17, 26) We live in intimate communion with one another. For this reason, compassion, developing an empathetic heart, connects us with others and heals our wounds.

Our essential connectedness is stated clearly in the golden rule, to which all the religious traditions subscribe: "Treat others the way you would have them treat you." (*Matthew* 7:12) The love commandment echoes this truth: "You shall love your neighbor as yourself." (*Matthew* 22:39) That means loving your neighbor as another self. There is an inseparable link between how we treat others and how we relate to ourselves. In caring genuinely for others, we care for ourselves; in loving ourselves, we love others.

The opposite also holds true regarding hatred and judgment. "If you want to avoid judgment, stop passing judgment....The measure with which you measure will be used to measure you." (*Matthew* 7:1-2)

We imagine making life-long choices between independence and dependence. The deeper truth is that we are interdependent, mutually dependent on each other. As we are becoming more aware with the current ecological crisis, interdependence extends beyond the realm of personal relationships to include the whole universe. The minerals, plants, and animals are our brothers and sisters. The fate of the natural world determines our destiny as a human race. Our actions shape the future of the universe.

The Hindu myth of Indra's net expresses the interconnectedness of all. The god Indra hangs a net over his palace at the axis of the world which reaches without limit in all directions. A single glittering jewel hangs from each of the countless nodes of the net. The jewels shine like stars in the firmament. If you closely inspect an individual jewel, you discover that it reflects all the other jewels in the net, infinite in number. Each jewel reflected in this one jewel reflects all the other jewels, creating an infinite mirroring process.

For a moment, consider the book you are holding in your hand. How did it come to be? It is made from paper, which comes from trees. The trees come from seedlings which are nurtured by the sun, rain, soil, and organisms in the soil. All the forces of nature collaborate to make the seed grow into a tree which is manufactured into paper. Who manufactures the paper? Crews of individuals cut down the trees, transport the logs, and make the wood pulp into paper. Don't forget the author who reads others' books and draws from their ideas. His thoughts also originate from his own mind that is connected to the consciousness of the world. The publisher, printer, distributor, and bookseller all work together to make the final product available to you. When you stop to think about it, the book you hold in your hand contains the universe.

A Walk through Your Past

"No man is an island." Who you are today has been shaped by your history and your relationships. Only a self-centered pride could say you are entirely a self-made person. Your anxiety reveals what you fear losing. Your fears of being misunderstood, rejected, and abandoned also display your deep longings for connection with others.

Take a few moments to look back in your life and examine your relationships (1). Proceed in three steps/groups: those who benefited you, those who harmed you, and those you harmed.

Those Who Benefited You

Let your imagination transport you back through your life, beginning with your childhood. Think of those who showed you love, attention, and affection. Let the important people in your life come to mind: your parents, grandparents, aunts and uncles, relatives, friends, teachers, and work associates. Hold each of these individuals for a few moments in your mind, one by one, and recall what they did to enrich your life. Allow your heart to fill with gratitude for their generosity and love. Whether these persons are living or deceased does not matter. They are still alive through you in memory and in the ways they shaped your life.

Then, take a few moments to express a heartfelt thanks to them, each individually. Recall what you appreciated most about them and thank them for it. If that person is still alive, consider how you might express your gratitude to them personally.

For building relationships, expressing appreciation is just as important as apologizing. Gratitude for being loved releases the power within you to transform your shortcomings into virtues. Love inspires love.

The earth also gives you the gift of life. In appreciation for the gift received, your heart opens with love and compassion. I begin each day with a prayer of thanksgiving and desire to serve: "As the earth gives us food and air and all the things we need, may I give my heart to caring for all others until all attain awakening. For the good of all sentient beings, may loving kindness be born in me."

Those Who Harmed You

Again take a walk through your past, beginning with childhood. This time, recall those who harmed you and caused you suffering. This may be a painful walk, but take it with the confidence you gained from the memory of those who loved and supported you. Look honestly at your grudge list. One by one, hold in memory each of those persons who caused you pain. Hold them gently. Recall the painful incidents and how the person offended you. Allow yourself to feel the pain and your anger. Watch the hurt, sad, and angry emotions arise and fall away.

In your mind, tell the person how their behavior affected you, how it influenced your life. Imagine what you would say. Then, put yourself in the place of that person. Try to imagine what that person was feeling, thinking, and doing when they harmed you. What motivated their actions against you? Did they realize they were hurting you? Imagine that person listening attentively to you expressing the suffering they caused you. Imagine also what that person would say to you now that you are aware of your suffering.

Your anxiety hides a reservoir of pain. You are so frightened because you have been hurt in the past and fear being hurt again. Anxiety protects you, making you withdraw behind protective walls. It works! Or it seems to.

Be gentle with yourself, then, as you recall painful incidents in your life. Especially, if you were traumatized by physical or sexual abuse as a child, you must be careful in remembering the past. The recollections may be too painful, too overwhelming, and cause flashbacks. If you begin to feel overwhelmed, stop immediately, take a deep breath, and try to calm yourself. Address the painful memories only when you feel strong enough and ready. Be gentle with yourself.

It is important that you allow yourself to feel the full force of the anger that you used to protect yourself from the pain. Your anger protects you for a period of time. However, if your anger prolongs into a simmering resentment, you harm yourself and others. As the AA slogan states: "Having a resentment is like drinking poison and expecting someone else to die." You can release your hurt and anger only after allowing yourself to experience fully the feelings. Eventually, you can come to forgiveness, which is the giving up of your anger and the desire for revenge.

Those You Harmed

Your anxiety clearly harms you, causing you immeasurable discomfort. Your anxious reactions and your efforts to manage them also harm others. Take a few moments to look more closely at the impact of your anxious behavior on those around you.

The Steps/Traditions book states: "To define 'harm' in a practical way, we might call it the result of instincts in collision, which cause physical, mental, emotional, or spiritual damage to people (p. 80)." Your instinct to find safety and security may clash with the needs and desires of those around you. You may harm others both by what you do and what you do not do, sins of commission and omission.

Review your life and think about those you harmed, intentionally or not, by your anxious behavior. Who are they? Consider the following observations and questions:

- Caught up in anxiety, you are preoccupied with finding relief, withdrawing to protect yourself. You may avoid uncomfortable persons, places, and things, causing your life to shrink. How has your withdrawal affected others? Did you ignore important responsibilities, harming those who depend on you? How neglectful have you been?

- In panic with pounding heart, profuse sweating, and labored breath, you think you are dying. You only want relief. Then you worry about another panic attack. So preoccupied with your own safety, how attuned have you been to the needs of others, especially those who depend on you?

- When you are on the worry train, you want to unburden yourself. You seek someone to listen and empathize. What effect has your obsessing had on others?

- Anger is the frequent handmaid of anxiety. When frightened, you may react with anger to regain a sense of power and control. How did you express your anger? Did you express it destructively, causing others to suffer?

- When anxious, you feel out of control with your life. You may compensate by trying to exert power and control over your life situations and others. Did you engage in needless power struggles with others? Were you controlling in your relationships, not respecting the freedom of those around you? Did you pressure others to conform to your expectations and routines?

- Anxiety seeks safety in control, clarity, and certainty. In the extreme, it wants absolute guarantees about outcomes, perfect knowledge, and absolute power. Did you respect the opinions of others when they disagreed with you? Did you force your opinion on them?

- When you feel overwhelmed with anxiety or fear, you can only think about yourself. Your personal comfort becomes paramount. Were you so preoccupied with your safety needs that you ignored the needs of others?

- Fear can consume you, making you isolated in your suffering. Did you abandon others who needed you, not even being aware of their needs?

- If your anxiety is overwhelming enough, it can lead to despair, a sense of hopelessness. How did your negativity affect those around you?

- The anxious mind is ruled by automatic negative thoughts, which leads to criticism of yourself and others. How critical and complaining have you been with others? How has it affected them and your relationships?

- Look carefully at what you fear losing and your excessive efforts to safeguard it. How much did the desire for possessions, power, or prestige control your life? Have you harmed others in your single-minded pursuit of these desires?

When two anxious people get together, they may unintentionally harm each other by their opposing ways of coping.

Stephanie: Marital Conflicts

"When I become upset, I need to talk. My husband tells me I obsess about things and keep repeating myself. He tells me he reaches the point when he can't listen anymore and walks away. I then feel abandoned and get even more upset, needing to talk more. My husband told me that he gets frightened by the intensity of my emotions and needs to withdraw to cope."

Troy: Struggles with His Wife

"I have OCD and have to keep everything in order. My wife is a slob. We're the odd couple and battle constantly about her messes. She buys excessively and hoards things, telling me it gives her comfort. I need to simplify my life. Her hoarding makes me feel out of control."

Carrie: Power Struggle with Her Husband

"I'm a planner and want to know well in advance what we're doing. Otherwise, I get very anxious. My husband is the opposite. He hates planning and lives for the moment, a carefree guy. He complains that I try to control him, and he feels smothered. He said he feels anxious when he's boxed in and has no freedom to move."

One by one, hold in memory those you harmed. Recall the circumstances, the repeating situations, in which you caused that person pain. Bring to mind what you were experiencing during those incidents: your anxiety, sense of desperation, and your selfish pursuit of relief. Put yourself in the place of the person you hurt and feel their pain. What did they experience?

Be gentle with yourself during these recollections. Avoid blaming yourself or refusing any responsibility. Allow yourself to feel genuine remorse, which opens your heart in compassion. Such compassion is the only way to escape the prison of self-absorbing anxiety.

Look at those who benefited you, and move toward gratitude. Look at those who harmed you, and move toward forgiveness. Look at those who harmed you, and move toward remorse.

"…and became willing to make amends to them all"

A famous line in *Love Story*, a popular movie several years ago, declared, "Love means never having to say you're sorry." In contrast, it is the Jewish practice around the high holiday of Rosh Hashanah that people atone for their sins by showing remorse to all those in their social circle. They are encouraged to approach everyone they know and say, "Will you forgive me if I've done or said anything this year that has hurt you?"

Coming to Forgiveness

Step 8 recommends you pursue a middle path between no apology and asking everyone for forgiveness. It suggests a path that is more arduous and beneficial to yourself and others. You are invited to make amends to specific persons for specific deeds. Accomplishing that task requires that you look at the past and your relationships with honesty, humility, and courage, which will help transform your shortcomings and repair your broken relationships.

Step 8 cautions, "It is a task which we may perform with increasing skill, but never really finish." (Steps/Traditions, p. 77) Your goal in exploring your past and your relationships is eventually to come to a whole-hearted forgiveness of yourself and others. Forgiveness means giving up the anger for the harm done and the desire for revenge. Such forgiveness is not accomplished once and for all by a sheer act of will. It involves the whole person, embracing the emotional pain, struggling to understand, and learning to let go. Forgiveness is a process that unfolds over time as your wounds heal.

Coming to forgiveness involves a courageous delving into your past. Your anxiety hides a reservoir of pain that others caused you and that you brought on yourself. Your anxious reactions self-medicate the pain, distracting you from feeling the full force of your suffering. Much suffering is buried in unconscious forgetfulness and the conscious choice not to remember. Anxiety is the symptom that something you dread is buried. It takes courage to poke around in the rubble of your painful past, not knowing exactly what you will discover.

If you were traumatized as a child by physical or sexual abuse or severe neglect, the pain is deeply buried. Many memories are repressed, enabling you to cope. Approach this step with caution. It may be too overwhelming for you to expose the pain. Do so only when you are ready. I advise you to proceed with the help of a therapist.

Coming to forgiveness requires an honest look into your past. As you did your moral inventory, you may have discovered the many ways you deceived yourself and others. You hid behind a façade for social acceptance. Now you are invited to look behind the mask and admit your shortcomings and their impact on those around you. You see the grudges you hang on to and your stubborn refusal to forgive yourself and others. Radical honesty involves giving up the excuses, blaming, and rationalization of your behavior. You may not like what you see. Vices do not paint a pretty picture. Being honest with yourself you take full responsibility for yourself and your actions, which is the only path to freedom.

Finally, coming to forgiveness demands a humble acceptance of yourself and others. Can you accept what you see, even though it contradicts your expectations, wishes, and treasured self-image? When you see your faults in all their nakedness, you balk. Your seething resentment at how others hurt you may be especially difficult to admit. Humbly admitting to yourself and forgiving yourself for your sins frees you from your bondage to them.

Shame, which is the reverse of pride, makes you want to hide your wrongdoing. Only humility, accepting yourself as you are, enables you to face your faults and forgive them. Self-forgiveness, in turn, gives you the courage to expose your imperfections to another and humbly ask for their forgiveness. Through forgiveness, you free yourself from the burden of the past—all the crippling shame, hurt, and guilt.

Paradox of Forgiving and Being Forgiven

When you pray the *Lord's Prayer*, you say, "Forgive us our trespasses as we forgive those who trespass against us." That is a bold request. Consider the implications. You make your being forgiven by God dependent on your willingness to forgive others. Forgiving others, then, takes on an urgency because your salvation depends on your willingness to give up your grudges. It makes you face squarely your tendency to hang on to your hurts and self-righteous anger.

As Jesus hung upon the cross, with his dying breath he prayed, "Father, forgive them, for they know not what they do." His final words reveal the heart of all authentic religion and any open-minded philosophy. Jesus did not condone His murder, pretend that it was okay, or simply turn His other cheek. He faced honestly the evil and chose to break the cycle of violence. Further, He interpreted their evil actions as the result of ignorance.

What did His persecutors ignore? They ignored two facts of life that any clear-sighted person can see. The first fact is that we are all in this together. We have a shared origin and destiny. The narrow-minded believe, "Every man is for himself." Such a view only leads to competition, rivalry, envy, the single-minded pursuit of self-interest, and, eventually, violence. The belief in our separateness nourishes the cycle of violence that will suck us all into its vortex in the end. Only forgiveness, a letting go of the hurt and hatred, can break that cycle.

The second fact is the circle of life: what goes around comes around. What we do to others we do to ourselves. What we receive from others we give back in return. Conversely, what others do to us they do to themselves. They give back what they receive from us. There is a flow in all relationships which produces a mirroring effect. Our great choice is what we want to contribute to that circle of life: either love or hatred. Forgiveness does not ignore the hatred in the world or in our own hearts but embraces it with love and transforms it.

Practice: Write Your List of Persons Harmed

After reflecting on your past and your relationships, write down in your journal three lists: those who have benefitted you, those who have harmed you, and those whom you have harmed. Look first at the list of those who have helped you during your life. Reflect on the persons listed one-by-one and write what you are most grateful for from them. Take a moment to express your gratitude and feel the warmth of kindness you have toward them.

Next, look at the list of persons who caused you pain. Consider for a moment the ways each person on the list caused you suffering. Remember the incidents and allow yourself to feel the pain. Also allow yourself to feel the sadness and anger that accompany the pain. Briefly write one painful incident for each person. Hold each person in your mind and heart and extend to them your forgiveness. If you feel stuck in genuinely feeling the warmth of forgiveness, do not force it. Simply make the conscious intention to forgive the person. If the wound is deep, it may take time to come to a heart-felt forgiveness. You forgive as the wound heals.

Finally, look at the list of persons you harmed. Think about the various ways you injured them, intentionally or not. Reflect on how your anxiety and ways of managing it affected them. Put yourself in their shoes. Write in more detail how you hurt each person on the list. Allow yourself to feel remorse for each of the persons you hurt. Resist the tendency to let your inner critic beat you up. Simply feel the sorrow and make the intention to avoid harming these individuals again.

Practice: Tonglen in Practice

Your anxious mind encourages you to avoid pain and seek pleasure, no matter the cost. You can become content with the meager pleasure of feeling safe and avoid the discomfort of facing your fears and extending yourself. Anxiety can be a sign of growth when it is aroused as you push against the edges of your comfort zone. Your preoccupation with seeking pleasure and avoiding pain can isolate you from others. Self-obsessed, you lack empathy for their suffering.

A traditional Eastern practice to cultivate fearlessness and empathy is "Tonglen," which means "sending and receiving."(2) It counters your natural instinct to flee what is uncomfortable and chase after pleasure. Through this exercise, you receive with openness and compassion your own and others' suffering. Then you send out love and peace. Here are the steps in the practice:

1) Sit comfortably in a quiet place with your eyes closed. Focus on the rising and falling of your breath. Breathe slowly and deeply, sensing peace and relaxation filling your body. With each breath, feel a sense of openness and spaciousness within your heart.

2) Next, still focusing on your breath, imagine that you are breathing in hot, black, dirty smoke that repulses you. Feel your repugnance as you breathe in the burning blackness. As you breathe out, imagine you are exhaling a cool, gentle, fresh breeze that fills the room. Imagine the bright freshness of the great outdoors coming from within you. Breathe in tarry smoke and breathe out fresh air.

3) Now, visualize yourself in pain because of your anxiety and because of the shame and guilt you feel for harming others. Do not avoid feeling the intensity of your suffering as you usually do. Consciously embrace the pain. With each in-breath, feel that suffering as if it were hot, thick, black smoke. Breathe it in deeply, but do not hold on to it. With each natural out-breath, imagine exhaling peace and tranquility, as if it were cool, fresh air.

4) After several minutes of focusing on transforming your own suffering, visualize a person whom you harmed. Allow yourself to feel deeply the pain you caused them and your own remorse. Breathe in their suffering like black smoke; then, exhale a cooling peace. Sense your compassion as you breathe in their suffering and your love as you breathe out peace and joy.

5) Finally, imagine all the living creatures of the world and their suffering. Like you, all want to avoid sorrow and find happiness. Sense your oneness with the whole world. Inhale the suffering of the world, and exhale happiness and peace.

You can use this exercise at any time for even a few moments with anyone you choose. It keeps you present to their suffering and helps develop empathy. The practice helps you nurture a compassionate, fearless heart, confident that the pain you encounter can never destroy you. In fact, the suffering, if embraced, can lead to new life.

In Step 8, you take a step back to look backward and outward. You consider with courage, honesty, and humility all those you have harmed by your anxious behavior throughout your life. With a compassionate heart, you feel deeply the pain you caused and prepare yourself to ask forgiveness and make amends.

14

Finishing Business: Let Your Light Shine

*Step 9: "Made direct amends to such people whenever possible,
except when to do so would injure them or others."*

"Thinking will not overcome fear, but action will."

—W. Clement Stone

Walking the path of recovery, you took steps to understand and be compassionate with yourself. You were a victim of your anxiety disorder. So far, you still risked getting lost in yourself and indulging in self-pity. Then, you began to look outward at your relationships. It may have shocked you to realize that your anxiety and desperate attempts to manage it had a direct impact on others. That realization caused you to feel compassion for those you harmed and remorse for what you did, inadvertently or not.

Unfinished business remains. You ask yourself, "How can I repair the damage I caused? How can I rebuild those strained or broken relationships?"

Still resting on the sidelines of the dance floor, you look around at all the other dancers. It seems for the first time you see them clearly. You have a history with many of your fellow dancers. After reflecting for a moment on that history, you realize that you had both happy and sorrowful times together. Now, your attention is drawn to the painful times when they offended you or when you harmed them. Sadness and remorse well up in your heart.

You know the next step. You have to be the bigger person in seeking reconciliation, but you hesitate, thinking to yourself, "Do I really want to take that risk? After all, I might look like a fool." You stand at a crossroads. The streets are named "Fear" and "Action."

Step 9 invites you to face your paralyzing fear and take courageous action. Fear dominated your life for too long and prevented you from pursuing life-giving activities. That self-protective fear makes you stand still. The compassion for those you hurt and your own sense of remorse prod you to move forward. What will you do?

The Alcoholics Anonymous Big Book makes no mistake about the correct course of action: "Now we need more action, without which we find that 'Faith without works is dead (p. 76)." You need to free yourself from the bondage to your fears and take action. You need to swallow your pride, ask forgiveness, and make amends.

You may notice a hesitation to jump in and make amends. Apologizing is not easy. It may take you out of your comfort zone and arouse anxiety as it does for most people. However, you can look at your avoidant reactions and learn about yourself. Observe closely the ways you run away from uncomfortable situations. Notice your instinctive tendency toward fight, flight, freeze, or faint in the presence of perceived danger. Making amends with another and asking for forgiveness can feel very threatening to you.

Hindrances to Making Amends

There are at least five hindrances to making amends. These include

- Distraction by comfort;
- self-righteous anger;
- lazy withdrawal;
- restless worry; and
- self-doubt & self-blame.

Distraction by Comfort

When anxious, you may notice your tendency to flee from the uncomfortable feeling and seek some pleasure. You cope with your anxiety by distracting yourself with some pleasurable activity. Running away can become a habit hard to break. It can interfere with you pursuing activities that your wise mind knows is better for you and others.

Lori: Distraction

"Whenever I feel stressed out, I go shopping and buy ice cream. That gives me relief. I don't think about whatever is bothering me. Through therapy, I'm learning that when I have the urge to shop or eat sweets it is a signal that I'm feeling anxious about something. I'm trying to stop and pay attention to what is going on in my life. Besides, I don't like what my uncontrolled shopping and eating do to me. I get fat and go broke."

Self-Righteous Anger

When stretched beyond your comfort zone, you may react with anger to protect yourself. But what are you protecting when it comes to apologizing? It is your pride. Your hostile response, then, becomes a self-righteous anger that hides your fear of losing face. It also reveals your attachment to your self-image, which can only lead to more insecurity.

Neil: Anger

"My wife told me I need to apologize to my business partner. Her suggestion out-raged me. I know I had made a mistake and wasn't honest with him about a busi-ness dealing. But he lied to me many times. He needs to apologize to me before I do anything. Why do I need to take the first step? How dare my wife tell me to ask for forgiveness?"

Lazy Withdrawal

In a stressful situation, you may tend to withdraw, afraid you would be overwhelmed if you took action. You feel faint-hearted. However, your buried feelings of guilt will not simply disappear. They will emerge indirectly in a depressed mood. You secretly judge yourself a coward and criticize yourself for being so weak. You may rationalize your sloth-ful behavior, but deep down, you cannot fool yourself.

Greg: Tendency to Withdrawal

"I hate confrontation. If I have a problem with someone, I just try to ignore it or smooth it over. I don't want to deal with it. Even if I'm at fault, I let it go. I believe that time heals all wounds. It wouldn't make a difference anyway if I apologized. That would only embarrass me and add salt to the wound. Actually, I'm afraid the other person would not accept my apology, and I would feel worse. It's better just to ignore it."

Restless Worry

Worry freezes you into inactivity. It can also be a substitute for action. You may engage in magical thinking, assuming that your worry will prevent what you fear from happening. The energy you put into obsessing is then withdrawn from constructive action. You do not take charge of the situation. The consequence of this strategy is that you feel more helpless, and your anxiety increases.

Georgina: Worry:

"When I have a conflict with someone, I obsess about it for days. I worry about the relationship ending and feel helpless to do anything about it. I imagine that person talking about me, about what a fool I was, and then all my friends would reject me. I'm afraid to approach the person to say I'm sorry if I'm at fault. What would that person think? It feels so embarrassing."

Self-Doubt & Self Blame

Self-doubt and spontaneous self-blame may interfere with an honest and accurate self-appraisal. When you do not see your faults clearly, you cannot make effective amends. The wrongdoing may all be in your imagination, exaggerated by your inner critic. You engage in a fruitless battle against yourself. If you make an effort to ask forgiveness, the imagined offended party may not see the problem as you do. Your apology may be off the mark and not result in a stronger relationship.

Robbie: Self-Blame

> *"After a disagreement with someone, I go over and over it in my mind. Eventually, I come to the point that I tell myself that it was all my fault. Then, I feel terrible. I can never see that someone else may share the blame to some degree, as my friends point out. After several days, I may apologize profusely to the person, who often listens with a blank stare as if I did nothing wrong."*

"Made direct amends to such people whenever possible..."

After acknowledging the need to make amends and improve relationships, the next question is how to accomplish this task. How do you make amends? I suggest a three step process: make peace with yourself, change habits, and ask forgiveness.

Make Peace with Yourself

There is an old Latin adage: "You cannot give what you do not have." If you want to bring peace to your relationships, you must begin with yourself. You must make peace with all the warring factions within yourself first. Then, from that firm foundation, you can extend peace to others.

Working through the previous steps, you are well on the road to inner peace. You acknowledged your powerlessness over your anxiety and began letting go of all your futile efforts to control it. In the process, you discovered within you a Power greater than yourself that had been hidden within the darkness of your fears. You also acknowledged that your anxious reactions served a purpose, both beneficial and harmful to you and others. Your anxiety arose from and reinforced character defects, which you identified as distorted desires for possessions, power, and prestige.

Your vices assume many faces and control you in subtle ways.

You make peace with yourself by extending compassion to yourself, by forgiving yourself from the heart. Forgiveness does not mean that you condone your wrongdoing, ignore it, or exaggerate it. It entails an honest, humble, fearless self-appraisal, and a full acceptance of yourself with all your strengths and weaknesses. You gain a glimpse of your basic goodness, knowing that you are better than your bad behavior. Because of your innate goodness, you have nothing to prove and nothing to protect. You are free to be yourself, not enslaved by fear.

Breaking Bad, Making Good

Your bad habits are not as solid as you think. They live on the surface of your life even though they seem deeply-rooted in your psyche. They were learned in childhood from early conditioning as misguided attempts to gain happiness. Society reinforced them.

In contrast, the self you experience in encounters with truth, beauty, and goodness reflects your true nature. Your faults are like silt in a clear glass of water that obscure the light of your deeper inner self. As you came to believe in Step 3, the divine Spirit, the Power greater than yourself, Ultimate Truth dwells within you.

I frequently tell my patients: "You cannot control your thoughts and feelings which come and go on their own. The stream-of-consciousness keeps flowing. You learned from childhood many ways of thinking and reacting. However, you always have control over how much weight you give them. Of course, you always have control over your behavior. You don't have to act on any urges as powerful as they seem."

Pamela: Efforts to Act against Her Compulsive Cleaning

"I get OCD about cleaning. I can't enjoy my kids at home because the only thing I'm thinking about is the mess they're making and having to clean it up. Even when I'm out with my husband, I'm not really there. I'm thinking about cleaning up the messes at home. I'm aware of how my OCD is hurting my family because I'm so emotionally absent. Now, I'm determined not to think about cleaning and stopping myself from cleaning when the kids are home. I was really anxious at first, but I kept resisting the urges. Now, I'm finding out it's not so bad with the messes. I can enjoy my family for a change."

Brad: Controlling His Temper

"I'm a perfectionist and don't tolerate fools. I can't stand when people make me wait for no reason or don't follow through with things they promised. I fly into a rage. My whole life I struggled with my temper. What helped me learn to control it was recognizing that my anger covered my anxiety. It also helped to see the terror in my children's eyes and my wife's resentment at my temper tantrums. Now, I pause when I feel my anger rising and pay attention to what I'm anxious about. When I take that time out, I realize that what I'm so upset about is really no big deal."

Donna: Pushing Herself to Get Out of the House

"I'm terrified of crowds and only feel safe at home. I've missed so many of my children's events because of my fear. Our social life suffers because of my reluctance to go out with friends. I feel sorry for my husband although he doesn't complain. I know my kids miss me at their school events. I'm learning to deal with my panic attacks, realizing that, even though I'm afraid I'm dying, I'm still okay. I talk to myself to help calm me and take deep breaths. Mostly, I push myself to get out. Once out, it's not really so bad."

Watch Yourself

You make amends to those you harmed by facing your bad habits and trying to change them. Your bad habits, or vices, can be transformed into virtues, or good habits. The following four-step process can help transform your habitual patterns:

1) Recognize your habitual patterns.

2) Accept and understand your habits.

3) Do something different.

4) Persist in your changes.

Recognize Your Habitual Patterns

Preoccupied with ridding yourself of the discomfort of your anxiety, you may not notice the many ways you try to cope with it. Like your ancestors in the animal world, in the face of fear your body is wired to protect itself by fighting, fleeing, freezing, or fainting. You focus on the danger and ways to escape it. However, unlike the animals, you have intelligence which enables you to become conscious of your reactions and make choices about them. You can assess the level of the danger, how real or imagined it is, and its source. With some reflection, you can also evaluate the cost and benefits to yourself and others in the way you respond and then alter your behavior.

Exercising your capacity to stand back and observe yourself, you develop your natural skills. As a person, you are immeasurably more than your habitual thinking, feeling, and behaving. Observing yourself honestly, you learn openness and curiosity, suspending your automatic negative thinking and judging. It marks an important step in freeing yourself from the slavery to your habits.

Accept and Understand Your Habits

Your first reaction when you take a close look at your behavior may be: "I don't like what I see." You hate your shortcomings and the weakness they show. You expect more of yourself. Perhaps, you have an ideal image of yourself, a social face, which you project to the world. Your imperfections cause you shame and embarrassment because they contradict your treasured self-image. Your intolerant reaction may reveal a hidden pride.

Acceptance of yourself with all your flaws invites you to become humble, surrendering your perfectionist self-image. You are good enough as you are but just need a little improvement. Your weaknesses can become the avenue through which you develop your strengths if you face them squarely. A full self-acceptance can also help you learn compassion, patience, kindness, and gentleness. Practiced first on yourself, you are prepared to treat others with the same open-hearted acceptance.

The habits you dislike serve a survival purpose. They protect you from wounds of which you are not fully aware. You can gain wisdom in exploring the roots and workings of your habitual reactions. Considering the negative impact of your behavior on yourself and others can motivate you to make changes. As you grow in empathy, your will to change strengthens.

Jared: Facing His Fear of Making Mistakes

"I'm an honor student and love school, but I die a thousand deaths before every big exam. I'm terrified of failing. So, I push myself to study hard. I know I overdo it, but I can't help it. The fear drives me. My performance anxiety has helped me to work hard and get good grades but at the price of my happiness. I don't know how to relax.

I know how I learned to react this way. My father was a taskmaster. Nothing was good enough for him. To gain his approval I believed I always had to prove myself by getting good grades. It horrifies me to think that I'm becoming my father."

Do Something Different

Your anxious mind craves the three Cs: certainty, clarity, and control. The unknown terrifies you. Your need for predictability keeps your habits well entrenched. So you continue with your routines, rituals, and fixed ways of thinking. To change would arouse intolerable anxiety.

Change involves a leap into the unknown, what you fear most. It takes immense courage to make any changes and endure the flood of uncomfortable feelings. Yet, if you can come to believe in the empty and illusory nature of thoughts and feelings, like misty clouds in the blue sky of your consciousness, you may find the courage to experience them fully. No thought or feeling can kill you. Only your stressful reaction to them can cause bodily harm. If you dare to feel the discomfort of anxiety and survive it, you will be immeasurably strengthened. A seed of hope will be planted.

Simply pausing to reflect in the midst of your emotional storm may signify a monumental accomplishment for you. Do whatever you need to do to find a measure of calm so you can relax: breathe deeply, sing to yourself, dance, or exercise. Do not let the anxious floodwaters carry you away. Think about what you can do differently so you are not so controlled by your habits. For example:

- If your temper has the best of you, learn to take a time out and see things from a different perspective. You have the opportunity to develop patience.

- If panic attacks and worry about them dominate your life, learn about their harmlessness and gradually expose yourself to what you fear. You will gain courage in the process.

- If your fears make you withdraw from socializing and other activities, learn to challenge your inner critic and the imagined negative judgment of others. In the process, you will become a more confident and generous person.

- If you freeze into anxious indecision, accept the lack of guarantees for correctness and the tentativeness of every decision. Making decisions in the face of fear and doubt will increase your courage.

- If obsessive thoughts and compulsive behaviors consume you, take the risk to stop indulging them and face your anxiety. You will gain a sense of freedom and strength.

- If automatic negative thoughts and judgments occupy your anxious mind, learn to confront them with your rational, wise mind. Your reward will be wisdom.

- If worries and fixed ideas of coming catastrophes monopolize your thinking, see their emptiness and resolve to let them go. Serenity and tranquility will be the fruit of your labor.

- If you are obsessed with controlling your environment and those around you, shift the focus of your attention to learning self-control instead. The consequence will be that you find serenity, humility, and wisdom.

- If you are a perfectionist, let go of your unrealistic ideals, live the present moment, and find moderation and peace.

- If you despair of ever escaping your anxiety and give up trying, stop to consider the consequences and redouble your efforts. Then, you will discover an unsuspected zeal, strength, and hope within you.

Persist in Your Changes

Transforming bad habits to good ones, vices to virtues, takes time and effort. You can become discouraged by the slowness and inconsistency of the progress. You take two steps forward and one step back. It may take more effort than you were prepared to make. Remember that your anxiety and its supportive habits of reacting possess an addictive quality. Like any addiction, relapses are normal.

Be patient with yourself. Remember also that you are already perfect and changing only the surface behaviors of your life. Your true nature is wise, compassionate, and powerful. Dedicating yourself to recovery, you release an immense Power within to create new life. That Power has only been temporarily short-circuited by your ingrained habits.

Research demonstrates that the brain is more plastic than we realize. It is more capable of change. Learning throughout life creates neural pathways that lead to repeated behavior. Repetitive thoughts, emotional reactions, and behaviors reinforce those pathways.

New learning is possible. You can teach an old dog new tricks. As you open yourself to new experiences and ways of thinking and behaving, the old neural pathways are diverted and new ones develop. These new pathways, in turn, are reinforced with repetition until they lead once again to a new automatic behavior. The challenge of recovery is to remain open to new experience and to growth.

In persisting at making changes, you learn discipline, determination, and self-control. You will also feel joy in the new life and improved relationships you experience.

Two Wolves

There is a story from the Native American tradition about this inner battle with habits. A tribal elder told his grandchildren: "There is a terrible fight going on inside me between two wolves. One wolf represents pride, anger, greed, gluttony, envy, fear, deceit, lust, sloth, and despair. The other stands for humility, patience, generosity, gratitude, serenity, courage, truthfulness, innocence, zeal, and hope. This same fight is going on inside of you and every living person."

The children were amazed by what their grandfather said and sat silently thinking about it. Then one child asked, "Which wolf will win?"

The wise elder responded, "The one you feed."

If you are willing to work with your anxiety and not simply try to get rid of it, your life can be enriched. Through the struggle with your unwanted habits, you acquire virtues that could not be achieved otherwise. Your spirit is freed from the shackles of anxious bondage but not without a fight.

St. Paul calls these virtues the fruits of the Spirit and lists them as love, joy, peace, patience, kindness, generosity, gentleness, faithfulness, and self-control (*Gal.* 5: 22). The Buddhist tradition lists similar traits and calls them *paramitas,* or perfections: generosity, proper conduct, renunciation, wisdom, energy, patience, truthfulness, and determination. The Buddhists also add four limitless qualities: loving-kindness, compassion, joy, and equanimity.

"...except when to do so would injure them or others"

"Drunks cause more damage by their drinking than I ever would by my anxiety," you may protest. You have a point. Alcohol is a dis-inhibitor. It turns off the brain's control center. While intoxicated, an alcoholic can do many crazy things they would never do when sober. They often wreak havoc on the lives of their families, friends, and associates.

For you, your anxiety is an inhibitor. It puts your brain on hyper-alert, making you over-controlled in your behavior. Even though the harm you cause others is less dramatic than that inflicted by some alcoholics, you hurt others nonetheless. Your over-control intrudes upon, manipulates, and neglects others, causing them pain.

Because the damage inflicted by the alcoholic's drunken behavior may be dramatic and far-reaching, Alcoholics Anonymous recommends caution in making amends: "Good judgment, a careful sense of timing, courage, and prudence—these are the qualities we shall need when we take Step 9 (Steps/Traditions, p. 83)."

Such caution may not be necessary for you. Most of your suffering was in quiet desperation. Because your anxiety restrained you so much, you may have harmed others more by what you did not do than by what you did. Nevertheless, the pain you caused others was real. Amends need to be made, mostly by a sincere apology.

How to Ask for Forgiveness

Contrary to the sentimentalism of *Love Story*, mature love means saying you are sorry when you have wronged someone. How can you make an apology from the heart?

First, you need to recognize honestly the impact of your anxious behavior on others. This requires empathy, the ability to step out of yourself and into the shoes of another. That may not be so easy for you because of your instinctive self-preoccupation with your own security. Working Step 8 prepared you for making a sincere apology.

Second, seek forgiveness only when you are ready. It is an intimate act of exposing yourself that may arouse an overwhelming anxiety. Anticipate your fears in approaching each person on your list and how you can keep yourself calm enough to speak from your heart. Of course, you must be sincerely sorry for what you have done. Otherwise, your deceit will only cause more harm.

Third, asking for forgiveness should be done face-to-face, not over the phone, texting, or through email. If you cannot meet with that person because of practical difficulties, you may decide to write a letter. If the person is deceased or unavailable, you may hold that person in your mind, make a sincere apology, and pray for him or her.

Fourth, make your apology specific, not general. Do not say, "Forgive me for whatever I may have done to hurt you." Before the meeting, have a clear idea of specific incidents or behaviors that harmed that person. Do not make excuses for yourself. Do not use your anxiety disorder as a justification for your hurtful behavior. Speak simply, directly, and honestly from your heart as best as you can.

Fifth, allow the hurt party to respond, and then listen. Resist the urge to become defensive if that person becomes critical of you. Your inner critic may be easily activated by any angry response. Most likely, the offended person will be surprised and grateful for your apology and quickly accept it. That person may even try to take some of the blame and ask for your forgiveness. Be open to whatever happens. Do not become fixated on a particular outcome as is your habit. Let it be an intimate moment.

Finally, realize that asking for forgiveness is just one step in the process of healing. Have a firm purpose of amending your own life so that you will not harm that person or anyone else again. Of course, you will not succeed 100%. Recovery is a work in progress, not perfection. Commit yourself to transform your vices into virtues. Learn from your inevitable relapses, allowing them to strengthen you.

Some may ask, "Should I tell the person about my anxiety condition?" You may wonder if that person will think you are making an excuse for yourself. You may also still feel shame about your condition and want to keep it secret. I advise that you decide for yourself. You have the right to privacy regarding your mental health condition. You also have the right to respect your sensitivity about being misunderstood and judged by others. Many, ignorant about mental illness, entertain prejudiced ideas about it. When you become secure within yourself about your condition, you may choose to tell others. Your honest and straight-forward speaking about it may help overcome the prejudiced thinking of many in our society.

Paradox of Darkness and Light

It is darkest just before dawn. Suddenly, the sunlight bursts forth above the horizon, its brilliance dispelling the darkness. The light shines with such splendor and majesty. The darkness obscured the light for a period of time but could not contain it. The force of light inevitably broke through and overcame the darkness. Night would again return but so would the irrepressible light. We behold a great paradox in nature: from darkness comes light.

As a child of nature, your life synchronizes with the rhythm of the universe. Your journey of recovery began in the darkness. You admitted your powerlessness to overcome your own the dark night of anxiety. So, you began a search for enlightenment. In your search, you realized that you looked for light in all the wrong places; that only lead you down dark alleys. Praying for faith, you saw glimpses of the light, but it remained hidden beyond your grasp. Then, it dawned on you that you had to give up your grasping for illumination and let it happen.

Gradually surrendering your will power, you entered an unfamiliar place called "not being in control." Contrary to your expectations, your anxiety increased as you became more involved in your recovery. You confronted your own heart of darkness, admitting, confessing, and surrendering your shortcomings. Painfully, you recognized how you harmed others and sought ways of making amends. In the process, you humbled yourself, letting go of all your self-defeating strategies to manage your anxiety.

Recovery leaves you in a place of darkness, a place of powerlessness, uncertainty, and ambiguity. You are confronted with your greatest fears, summed up in the word *unknown.* Where can you turn for help? Only by embracing fully the darkness of the unknown, surviving the experience, and learning to relax with it will the light enter your life. A Power greater than yourself sustains you. Through that survived dark night experience, your light will shine like a radiant sunrise.

Practice: Walking Meditation

Restlessness rules your body and mind, and you cannot sit still. Your agitated body provokes worries about your health; your obsessive mind makes you physically tense. You cannot relax. Invitations to be quiet and sit still place an intolerable demand on you, making you feel even more overwhelmed.

Walking meditation is an effective way to work with your restless body and mind (1). It is a deceptively simple practice of walking and being aware of what you are doing. The exercise can benefit you by channeling your restless energy into a slow walk and focusing your wandering mind on the present moment. Your anxious mind wants to escape your body. This practice brings you back to it. Here is the procedure:

1) Choose a place to walk where you will not draw attention to yourself or be distracted. It might be your bedroom, living room, or backyard. You need just enough room to walk slowly in a circle or back and forth and not be disturbed.

2) Stand still for a moment and breathe deeply. Be aware of the sensations of your standing body. Feel yourself relaxing with each breath. Try to put aside the racing thoughts in your mind. Don't try to stop them because it will not work. Simply let them pass as you focus on your body.

3) Begin to walk slowly. Your restless anxiety urges you to walk quickly to some destination, matching your movements with the speed of your thinking. Resist the urge to move quickly. Walk without a destination. Just simply walk and be mindful of your movements. Feel your mind and body slowing down.

4) As you walk, focus your attention on your feet taking each step. Do not look around or watch your feet. Look ahead without seeing what is around you and turn your inner eye to the physical sensations of walking. Be aware of each foot lifting, shifting weight to the other foot, making contact with the floor, moving from heel to toe, and bending your toes. Notice the cycle of your gait: the lifting, moving, weight shifting, and floor contact. Observe how your walking is a controlled falling forward and catching yourself. As you make contact with the floor, sense the groundedness of your body on the earth.

5) Your restless mind makes you feel insecure, ungrounded. When your mind wanders way from the movement of your feet and legs, gently bring it back to the present activity. You are cultivating an inner observation of your body, not allowing yourself to become lost in your thoughts that travel rapidly to the past and future. You can only live in your body in the present moment.

6) Once you are comfortable focusing on the movement of your feet and legs, you can include attention to your breath. Notice how you automatically synchronize your breathing with your steps, perhaps three steps for each in-breath and another three steps for each out-breath. Sense how your breath fills your body, making it alive.

Perform this practice for a specific period of time, 10-15 minutes in the beginning. You may increase the time as you become more relaxed and comfortable with this exercise. You can also practice mindful walking when you are running errands. If you have a destination, walk a bit more slowly but not so slowly as to draw attention to yourself. Instead of thinking about your to-do list, concentrate on the movement of your feet and legs and your breathing. Gently let go of other distracting thoughts. You may surprise yourself at how doing errands can be relaxing and enjoyable if not so anxiety-driven.

Practice: Loving-Kindness Extended

At the end of the chapter on Step 5, I recommended a loving-kindness meditation, called *metta*. I suggested you first extend loving-kindness to yourself. You can also extend this practice to loved ones, neutral people, to enemies, and to the whole world. To help you make amends and rebuild your relationships, I suggest you extend loving-kindness to those you harmed.

1) Sit comfortably in a quiet place. Close your eyes and focus on the rhythm of your breath. Breathe deeply from your abdomen, and allow the muscles of your body relax. Sense the warmth of your breath entering the tension of your muscles and loosening the knots.

2) Once you relaxed, hold in your mind one person you have harmed. Allow yourself to feel the pain you caused that person. After a few moments, shift your attention to your feelings of sorrow and regret for the harm you caused that person. Do not indulge your inner critic and beat yourself up. Feel your remorse and desire to make amends.

3) Then, select and focus your attention on phrases that address the pain and turmoil you caused that person. Express them as heartfelt wishes for that person. For example, say to yourself: "May he/she be happy." "May he/she be free from all suffering." "May he/she feel content with their life." "May he/she experience peace and joy." Add whatever wishes best express your deepest desires in the moment.

4) Repeat three or four phrases to yourself for a period of time. Repeat the phrases slowly and thoughtfully for about 10 minutes. Coordinate the repetition of the phrases with the rise and fall of your breathing. Allow the words to sink into your mind and body.

5) Review your list of those you harmed. One by one extend wishes for happiness and freedom from suffering for each of them. Perform this practice whenever you have the available time. It does not have to be done in one sitting.

This exercise can help you develop empathy for others and heighten your motivation to make amends. You can also extend loving-kindness to those on your list who harmed you. Extend to them your forgiveness.

Step 9 moves from the contemplation of Step 8 to action on behalf of others. You recognize your habitual patterns and their impact on others. Empathy and remorse motivate you to ask forgiveness. You also begin the life-long process of transforming your faults into virtues, which can benefit others. In the process, your anxious self-obsession dissolves into a desire to improve your relationships.

15

Eyes Wide Open: See More Clearly

Step 10: "Continued to take personal inventory,
and when we were wrong, promptly admitted it."

"The key to change…is to let go of fear."

—Rosanne Cash

You may have hoped that recovery would be a quick sprint to the finish line of anxiety relief. Unfortunately, it turned out to be a marathon, requiring more time, effort, and endurance than you expected. That should not be a surprise. You likely struggled with your anxiety condition for many years and tried various strategies to find relief. Perhaps you hoped that working the steps would provide the solution to your suffering. But no quick fix came.

You spent a long evening dancing. You are tired. It was fun meeting new people, dancing, and enjoying the music. The night both energized and exhausted you. Initially, you were reluctant to come to the dance, afraid you would not fit in. You were self-conscious about your dancing, imagining that everyone would be watching you. But you took the risk. You let yourself go and surprised yourself at how much fun you had. You relaxed and connected with so many people. As the evening progresses, people keep asking you to dance. You are so tired. How can you keep the good feeling going?

True Wisdom and Power

Having completed the first nine steps, you learned some important lessons. First, no person or situation makes you anxious. They have no power over you. As you look around and observe other people, you notice that they respond differently than you to challenging situations. They do not appear to be so easily overwhelmed. They are not so fearful.

Somehow, they can remain calm. You can only conclude that your fear comes from you. It is your way of reacting that causes you distress.

Second, you learned that you cannot change people, your personal history, or many of your life circumstances. You have no power over them. To manage your anxiety, you may have become a "control freak." You tried to impose a predictable order on your environment and those around you so you could feel calmer. You blamed your family history for your misery, wishing the past were different. All these efforts failed. You faced your limits, learning humility.

Third, through your repeated failures to eliminate your anxiety, you learned that you cannot control your own thoughts and emotions. Therapy and self-help books may have encouraged you to abandon your negative thinking and replace it with positive thoughts. Yet, the harder you tried to push down those anxious reactions, the more they pushed back and dominated your mind. They seemed to have a life of their own. Admitting powerlessness and defeat, you began to let go and accept the free flow of your consciousness.

So what can you change? You can manage your own attitudes and behaviors. You can take charge of your own life and change your attitude toward your anxious condition. Instead of fighting it, you can embrace it, work with it, and learn its wisdom. You do not have to be the slave of your fears and let them dictate how you live. Instead, you can face your fears and realize their emptiness. That realization enables you to make choices based on freely-chosen values.

You experienced the truth of AA's *Serenity Prayer*: "Lord, grant me the serenity to accept what I cannot change, the courage to change what I can, and the wisdom to know the difference." Working the steps and paying close attention to your experience you learned both your limits and your possibilities. You can only take responsibility for your own life, your own reactions, and your behavior. In the process, you gain serenity, courage, and wisdom as antidotes to fear.

The Serenity Prayer resonates with a more ancient wisdom, that of the *Tao Te Ching*:

Knowing others is intelligence;
knowing yourself is true wisdom.
Mastering other is strength;
mastering yourself is true power (33).

These verses suggest a two-phase recovery that guides the AA program. The first is a step back to observe yourself closely to learn wisdom. The second is a step forward in choosing to act, rather than react, gaining a sense of self-mastery. The steps alternate between contemplation and action, a graceful back-and-forth movement.

Obstacles to Continuous Self-Appraisal

With Step 10 you shift to practical day-to-day living to achieve true wisdom and true power. The Step/Tradition book underlines its importance: "Then comes the acid test: can we stay sober (calm), keep in emotional balance, and live to good purpose under all circumstances? (p. 88)."

An essential practice to developing inner peace is acquiring the habit of accurate self-appraisal. Working steps four and five, you already faced many inner resistances to making a continuous and regular self-examination. Other obstacles also intrude:

- impatience with progress;
- poor work ethic; and
- expectation of guarantees.

Impatience with Progress

Because real dangers exist, some measure of anxiety will always be present as a warning signal. If you have an anxiety disorder, though, your reactions become excessive and crippling. Working the steps, you experience an ebb and flow to your fearful reactions. You may feel progress in managing your anxiety and hope for a cure. However, like any addiction, you can experience relapses, periods of feeling overwhelmed. Then, discouragement sets in. You may want to give up.

Lois: Impatience with Her Progress

"I've battled my anxiety many years. I've been terrified of leaving home since I retired from being a teacher. I'm afraid of having a panic attack, embarrassing myself, and not having anyone to take care of me. When I worked as a teacher, I felt in control of my life and the classroom. School and work became a safe haven for me. But since I've been home with my husband, I won't leave without him. He has become my refuge.

I've been working with my therapist to face my fear of having a panic attack and feel like I'm making progress. Then, I have a relapse and can't leave home. It's two steps forward and one step backward. I'm so discouraged I want to give up."

Poor Work Ethic

Some people fight against their uncomfortable emotions, feel defeated, and give up. Others prefer not to fight, go with the flow, and drown in their emotional storms. The middle path of working with your thoughts and feelings requires effort, constant vigilance, and disciplined action. When you have a lifelong struggle with anxiety, you may become lazy and refuse to make the effort. As AA constantly reminds its members, "You have to work the program." There are no quick fixes. There are no shortcuts.

Darrell: Laziness

"I've been shy and self-conscious as far back as I can remember. My parents took me to a psychiatrist who diagnosed me with severe social anxiety. I never followed through with my family's recommendations that I go to counseling and take medication. Since I was a teenager, I drank and smoked marijuana instead to calm myself. My family complained about that. They told me how much I needed help and

should push myself to get out of the house and socialize. Frankly, I'm not interested. What they suggest is just too much work."

Expectation of Guarantees

Your desire for perfection may paralyze you. You are scared stiff. If you want absolute certainty, clarity, and control, you may avoid making decisions that would benefit you. You wait to decide, gathering more and more information until you feel secure. How much information is enough? The problem is that if you are looking for a guarantee of success you will procrastinate forever. You will never take the risk to involve yourself in any project or practices that can help you recover.

Lindsey: Need for Certainty

"What I fear more than anything else is the unknown. I work hard to eliminate as many unknowns in my life as I can. I ask a million questions until I understand something completely. I plan everything I do to the last detail. Routines guide my life. Some people call me OCD about all this, but I don't care. I know what I need. Sometimes, I have trouble making decisions because of how much I need to know to feel secure. I also want a guarantee that what I decide to undertake will succeed. That's not always realistic. But I'll never give up my desire for it."

The Triad of Recovery

You are now entering a new phase of your recovery, the ongoing, life-long management phase. Fortified by the wisdom and power gained in working the steps so far, you look forward to your continuing recovery. Your recovery from addiction to anxiety will always be a work in progress. "We shall look for progress, not for perfection," the Steps/Traditions book admonishes (p. 91).

Moving forward requires a fine balance of doing and not doing, of effort and waiting for grace, to transform negative habits. Too much effort results strain and discouragement. Too little effort leads to passive resignation.

What will a balanced recovery take? The Twelve Step program suggests a balanced attention to three practice areas: "Trust God; clean house; help others."

This triad of practices is not something new. They are rooted in ancient religious traditions, passed on from generation to generation. Jesus told His disciples that some demons can only be cast out by prayer, fasting, and almsgiving. In His "Sermon on the Mount," He explained prayer as a trustful opening of the mind and heart to God and dedication to following His will. Fasting is not simply abstaining from food. It symbolizes a willing self-renunciation of any distorted desires that interfere with doing God's will. Almsgiving to the poor represents the generous willingness to serve others and not only oneself.

Islam, which means "surrender," carries on this tradition. Islamic beliefs are summarized in the five pillars of Islam. Three of those pillars concern praying regularly toward Mecca, fasting during the month of Ramadan as a sign of self-renunciation, and giving to the poor. These practices lead to the dying of the old self enslaved to bad habits and the rising of a new self, guided by virtuous living.

These last three steps summarize the previous nine and apply them to daily living.

"...to take personal inventory..."

Step 10 begins by recommending a daily practice of the fourth step, but instead of taking a "moral inventory," it recommends a "personal inventory." What qualifies this inventory as personal is that it is a deeper examination of consciousness that recognizes both strengths and weaknesses. Your inner critic engages in routine fault-finding missions that undermine your self-esteem. This tendency toward negative self-judgment needs to be balanced by an appreciation of your basic goodness, innate sanity, and natural bravery.

Unchaining Melodies

As children listening to lullabies, we grow up learning songs that enchant, comfort, and guide us. You may not notice these songs in your head because you are as accustomed to them as the air you breathe. If you pay close attention, however, you can hear familiar refrains. You personalize popular songs, adapting them to apply to your life interests.

One adapted refrain is, "All I [not you] need is love." This music expresses your desire for love, acceptance, recognition, prestige, praise, and approval and your belief that being loved is absolutely essential for your happiness.

A second common refrain you may hear is, "I do [not did] it my way." This tune expresses your need for power, control, and self-sufficiency. You believe that being powerful is the path to true contentment.

You may pick out a third refrain, "I've got [not He's got] the whole world in my [not His] hands." You believe that comfort, health, possessions, achievements, and success will guarantee you happiness.

These melodies, taught and reinforced by the culture, influence how you react spontaneously to the people and situations you encounter on a daily basis. The tunes fill your mind, blocking out other dissonant music and focusing your attention on specific desires. These "I" tunes express your unique perspective on life. Interacting with your world, they cause a chain reaction within you which becomes habitual.

A saying from an unknown source (1) describes the links in the reaction chain and their connections:

Watch your thoughts; they become words.
Watch your words; they become actions.
Watch your actions; they become habits.
Watch your habits; they become character.
Watch your character; it becomes your destiny.

I would add two more links at the beginning of the chain, physical sensations and emotions.

You have a power within you that you may not fully appreciate. It is the power of your consciousness which is in immediate contact with Reality. From a Christian perspective, your consciousness is the "Inner Witness," the meeting point of the human spirit and Divine Spirit of Truth (*Romans* 8:16). Your anxious mind obscures the clarity of your natural consciousness but cannot overcome it. In fact, with your attention, you can focus your mind like a searchlight on yourself. Your clear awareness can loosen your bond to the chains of your anxious reacting.

Step Back: Observe Your Habitual Reactions

To break the chain of habitual, automatic reacting, you first need to take a step back and observe yourself closely. Your natural tendency will be to judge critically what you see. It is important to withhold your judging and just notice your urge to do so. Simply observe your own mind, the flow of sensations, feelings, and thoughts.

The Steps/Traditions book recommends a "spot-check inventory, taken at any time of the day, whenever we find ourselves getting tangled up (p. 89)." Whenever you feel yourself becoming overwhelmed in a situation, pause and observe yourself before taking any action. The sooner you can catch yourself reacting, the better chance you have of halting the avalanche of thoughts, feelings, and behaviors.

Here you take a zoom lens look at your experience. Notice each of the links in the chain one-by-one:

Body Sensations: What are you sensing in your body now? Observe any tension in your body, its location, the quality of the pressure you feel. Do you feel any pain? Is it sharp, dull, periodic, or persistent? Notice your breathing, how deep, shallow, slow, or rapid it is. Pay attention to your heart rate. Scan your body and note any sticking points: light-headedness, dry mouth, choking, queasy stomach, sweating, trembling, restless limbs. When you are anxious, your body becomes activated for fight or flight. Your body may alert you before your mind of a perceived danger.

Emotions: What are you feeling now? The four main emotional groups are sad, mad, glad, and scared. Which state is predominant for you at the moment? Notice any subtle variations in your mood, its fluctuations, and combinations of feelings. How intense is the feeling? Pay attention to its ebb and flow. Feelings generally last about 90 seconds if not prolonged by the stories you tell yourself.

Thoughts: What thoughts are running through your mind at the moment? Notice the automatic thoughts that arise explaining to yourself the cause of your physical sensations and emotions. Note how your interpretations generate emotional reactions of fear, anger, sadness, or shame. Be aware of the shifting shapes of your negatively-biased thoughts that arise spontaneously in your mind. Observe their ongoing parade: worries about what can go wrong, regrets about past behavior, self-critical thoughts, and preoccupations about being in danger. Notice the impact of these thoughts on your mood.

Thoughts arise expressing your beliefs about how the world works. Everyone wants to avoid suffering and find happiness, developing belief systems about how to achieve these ends. Pay attention to your own beliefs that correspond with the above melodies: "All I need is love," "I do it my way," or "I have the whole world in my hands." These songs reflect your longings for prestige in others' eyes, power over your environment, and comforting possessions. Note the intensity of the music, your enthusiasm for your belief that the object of your desire is either necessary or nice for your happiness. Notice also how the degree of your attachment to your desire generates fear and anxiety about losing what you crave.

Words: How do you talk to yourself and others? What kind of words do you use, ones that build up or tear down? Note the words you use in conversation. Do you tend to shame, blame, and correct others? Or do you express kindness and compassion? Do you gossip or speak more about yourself? Do you tend to criticize and complain or compliment and praise? Do you say directly what you want or do you say what you think people want to hear? Do you speak the truth honestly from your heart to the benefit of others? Or is your speech deceitful, manipulative, and self-serving? Do you speak the truth in love? In conversations, do you also listen with an open mind and heart? Your words are windows to your soul and more powerful than a sword.

Actions: How do you treat yourself and others? You may keep yourself so busy managing your anxiety that you just react in situations. You do not stop to consider carefully what you really want and how best to respond. Imagine yourself a spectator watching the drama of your life unfolding. What do you see? Do you act like a hero or a villain? What is the impact of your behavior on others? Does your behavior bring happiness or cause suffering? Do you treat others the way you wish to be treated? Does your behavior correspond with your values? Your actions repeated over time become habits

Habits: What habitual patterns of feeling, thinking, and behaving do you observe? When you are anxious, you instinctively manage it by fighting, fleeing, or freezing. These responses become ingrained habits, often unconscious, from childhood conditioning. Do you tend to engage in power struggles to feel secure, acting aggressively with others? Do you habitually disengage in the face of conflict and withdraw into your own world for safety? Do you become frozen by clinging to others or to fixed ideas to protect yourself? These ingrained habits of reacting mold your character.

Character: What stories do you tell yourself about who you are? You naturally reflect on your life experience and create an image of yourself in your own mind. That self-image gives you a sense of meaning, purpose, and identity. "This is who I am," you tell yourself. Listen to the theme songs that play through your mind. Notice the stories you tell yourself that give you a sense of identity. Many who are anxious see themselves in various roles: perfectionists, caretakers, workaholics, victims. You play out character roles in your personal life drama.

Destiny: Observe the pattern of nature around you. Good seeds produce good fruit while bad seeds produce bad fruit. You reap what you sow. What you observe in nature also applies to you. Your choices have consequences, some foreseen and others not, creating your character and your destiny. Your future is in your hands.

The great spiritual teachers were astute observers of the world and human nature. They knew intimately the laws of cause and effect and showed the way to authentic happiness. The Buddha taught: "Everything has mind in the lead, has mind in the forefront, is made by mind. If one speaks or acts with a corrupt mind, misery will follow, as the wheel of a cart follows the foot of the ox....If one speaks or acts with a pure mind, happiness will follow, like a shadow that never leaves (*Dhammapada* I: 1-2)." Jesus proclaimed, "Your verdict on others will be the verdict passed on you. The measure with which you measure with will be used to measure you (*Matthew* 7:2)."

You cannot overcome your unhealthy habits by will power and strenuous effort. You already tried that and failed. Only self-awareness, which is open and non-judgmental, can free you from the slavery to your automatic reactions. When you observe closely your reactions, you realize that they are less substantial than you thought. Your sensations, feelings, and thoughts come and go, like morning mist. They are as solid as a cloud. You alone give them substance and weight by putting faith in them. You may mistakenly believe your feelings embody irresistible urges and your thoughts express absolute truth.

When you stop to notice how your mind works, you gain a glimpse of your true self in its basic goodness, wisdom, and power. You can stand back from the passing clouds and sense yourself as the spacious blue sky of unlimited consciousness. The bright light of awareness dispels the darkness of illusion. Then, the once enslaving feelings and thoughts, even the anxiety, fall from you like chains of dead weight. You realize that you have nothing to prove and nothing to protect about yourself. The awareness releases all the energy that was bound up with your self-protective, self-centered faults.

"...and when we were wrong promptly admitted it"

Step 10 further recommends that action follow your personal reflection. Like steps five and nine, you admit your faults to another and make amends. The step suggests a practice helping to transform the energy released from your unhealthy reactions into positive habit energies.

Step Forward: Choose and Act

If you want to transform unhealthy habits into wholesome ones, you need to stay in the present moment. Step 10 says you have to act "promptly," without dwelling on the past or future. "There are two days in every week which we have no control over—yesterday and tomorrow. Today is the only day we can change," a well-known AA saying advises.

Nina: Difficulty Living the Present Moment

"My mind runs wild when I'm anxious, and I can't help it. I know it's crazy how my thoughts jump from the past to the future and back again. It's almost like I have attention deficit disorder because I can't focus on the present. I'm so nervous at parties, but I force myself to go because I don't want to be a loner. Afterward, and even during the party, I keep reviewing in my mind what I said and did and how stupid I must have looked. Then, I jump to the future and worry about what my friends will think about me when I see them again. I'm driving myself crazy."

If you observe your mind closely, you learn that you cannot change your spontaneous physical sensations, emotional reactions, and thoughts. They come from your unconscious, the emotional programming from your childhood. Undoubtedly, you demonstrated to yourself repeatedly your powerlessness over your anxious reactions. However, you can choose how much weight you give to those anxious thoughts and feelings. Of course, you are always free to decide how to act. There are no irresistible urges, although you may think that is the case.

You can choose to act in a way different from your usual habits and plant seeds for the growth of new habits. Therein lies your true power.

To accomplish this, Step 10 gives specific advice: "In all these situations, we need self-restraint, honest analysis of what is involved, and willingness to admit when the fault is ours, and an equal willingness to forgive when the fault is elsewhere (Steps/Traditions, p. 91)." When anxiety is aroused, you need to restrain yourself from your automatic protective reactions. Take the pause that refreshes, stopping to think about what is going on within you in this situation. AA wisdom suggests, "The seven Ts—take time to think the thing through." Ask yourself, "What is the real danger here? Am I exaggerating it? What is the most beneficial response to make now?"

Based on the honest, humble, courageous personal inventory you made, determine the boundaries of your responsibility. If you realize you harmed the other person by your action, do not delay in accepting responsibility and apologize. If you were hurt by the other person, resist your urge to stew about it. Acknowledge the hurt and try to resolve the misunderstanding.

If there is no immediate resolution, do not hang on to the hurt and anger. Remember, the AA saying, "Having a resentment is like drinking poison and expecting someone else to die." Forgive from your heart as soon as you can. Refuse to drink the poison.

If you think independently and care about people, misunderstandings are inevitable. Making the effort to resolve the conflicts quickly and with charity plants the seeds for a new life. Taking positive action helps overcome your anxious sense of powerlessness.

As much as you instinctively hate your anxiety because of the discomfort it brings, a hidden wisdom is present. In your anxiety, you sense the enormity of life beyond your grasp and control. You appreciate its mystery and live in awe and fear of it. Your best efforts will never eliminate the unknown. Rather, the more you learn, the more you become aware of what you do not know. Wisdom comes in acknowledging your ignorance.

You learn humility in acknowledging your powerlessness to orchestrate your life completely. "The best laid schemes of mice and men..." Much is beyond your control. Your anxiety makes you vigilant. It is a constant reminder to be aware. You can become, not only safe, but enlightened.

Paradox of Dying and Living

Jesus said, "I solemnly assure you, unless the grain of wheat falls to the earth and dies, it remains just a grain of wheat. But if it dies, it produces much fruit (*John* 12:24)." What happens in nature happens in us. The moment we are born we begin to die. Our days are numbered. Death is present in every moment of our lives. What distinguishes us from the rest of nature is that we are conscious of the end and try to make sense of it.

If you are anxious, you want certainty, guarantees about the future. However, the only certainties in life are death and taxes, as the saying goes. Yet, the certainty of dying does not offer comfort. Instead, living under the specter or death likely haunts you, underlies all your fears, and generates much of your anxiety. Fearful of loss, you know there will come a time when you will lose it all.

Only confidence that new life comes from dying can offer comfort. The paradox you face each day is: we live to die and die to live. How can that be? What dies in us? What lives on? Living in time, each moment is new. The past dies, and a new moment in time is born, only to pass away.

One patient, an anxious man, had a ritual at the beginning of each therapy session. He asked me, "What's new?"

I assumed my role in his routine, responding, "This moment is new. What's new for you?" I invited him to confront his reluctance to live in time, letting go of the past to embrace the present moment.

In recovery, the unhealthy habits of the old self die through a gradual process of recognizing them and letting them go. Attachments keep you stuck and need to be dropped like the dead weight they are. The energy of your vices does not simply evaporate. Instead, it is transformed through effort and grace into life-giving habits. Your willfulness, being preoccupied with yourself, becomes a willingness to embrace others in love.

Just as you cannot force the grain of wheat to grow, you cannot create a new life for yourself through sheer will power. You can cultivate the soil through disciplined practice. However, the fruits of a liberated life flourish through surrendering to a Higher Power that dwells both within and beyond you. Will power, the desire to have absolute control over your life, must die for you to be free and genuinely happy.

Practice: An Evening Inventory

The Steps/Traditions book recommends, in addition to the spot-check inventory, a regular evening inventory-taking. It suggests drawing up "a balance sheet for the day" in both red and black ink. Your anxiety draws you to the negative. An accurate balance sheet of your life must also include the positive: what you have done right.

A Japanese practice called *Naikan*, which means "looking inside," can be helpful for this balanced accounting at the end of the day (2). The practice invites you to reflect on the past twenty-four hours of your day and ask yourself three questions: 1) What have I received? 2) What have I given? 3) What difficulties have I caused?

What have I received?

Your natural anxious instinct focuses on what is missing, not on what is present. Your glass is always half empty, never half full. Because you pay so much attention to what you do not have or fear losing, you ignore what you already have. Your life is full, and you do not even recognize it. At the end of the day, pause to reflect on all the good things you received. Contemplate the simple pleasures: kindnesses from those you encountered, a joyful moment with the family, a call from a friend. Noticing your blessings can inspire an attitude of gratitude to offset your preoccupation with things going wrong.

What have I given?

When you are anxious, you try to rearrange your world to feel more secure. You may expect others to adjust their lives to your sensitivities. Self-preoccupation and a sense of entitlement may creep into your life. To confront this tendency, it is important to consider what you did for others. Note even the simple things: a friendly greeting at the store, listening to a friend's troubles, doing your work with a joyful heart. Noticing your own spontaneous generosity can increase your self-confidence that you have much to offer.

What difficulties have I caused?

Your harsh self-critic can make you either exaggerate your faults or hide them in shame. True humility invites you to see yourself accurately and recognize the impact of your behavior on others. At the end of the day, honestly admit to yourself how you may have harmed others. Allow feelings of remorse to rise in your heart. That will motivate you to find a way to repair the damage, both to yourself and the other person.

Practice: The Five Remembrances

Anxiety-driven, you hate change. Change is your enemy because it creates uncertainty. You long for something permanent, reliable, and predictable. To ease your sense of insecurity, you create rituals, routines, and fixed ideas on which to lean. You try to manipulate your world to feel secure. You look for some solid ground on which to stand firm. When these strategies fail, you may go into a terrifying freefall.

The Buddha taught his followers that happiness comes only from accepting the facts of life. The most basic fact is that change is constant. Everything is impermanent, in constant flux. He encouraged his disciples to live responsibly by embracing things as they are, not as they wished they would be. He reminded them that only their actions, their ongoing consequences, last. To help them accept the truth of impermanence, he invited them to meditate regularly on what are called "the five remembrances."

1) I am of the nature to grow old. There is no way to escape growing old.

2) I am of the nature to have ill health. There is no way to escape ill health.

3) I am of the nature to die. There is no way to escape death.

4) All that is dear to me and everyone I love are of the nature to change. There is no way to escape being separated from them.

5) My actions are my only true belongings. I cannot escape the consequences of my actions. My actions are the ground upon which I stand.

Take some time each day to reflect on these five facts of life. Your immediate reaction may be that these remembrances are depressing and will only bring you down. But think more carefully. They express fundamental truths of your experience about aging, health, change, and death. Accepting these facts of life can help change your perspective and appreciate the wonder of your life. They remind you to live the present moment fully. Your time is precious because it is so limited. Despite all the changing circumstances of your life, you still have freedom to choose how you want to act. Your actions, over which you have control, are the firm ground on which you stand.

The practice of the five remembrances concretizes the *Serenity Prayer*, distinguishing what you can and cannot change. You can only change your own behavior, which affects your destiny. Embracing the complexity of your life, you gain serenity, courage, and wisdom.

Practice: Write Your Own Obituary

Have you ever taken a walk through the cemetery? What did you notice? Within yourself, you may have observed a mixture of feelings, sadness, fear, and even peace. Looking around, the place was likely serene, with trees, vegetation, and flowers. People walked around slowly, reflectively, and grieved for their loved ones. The graves had markers, mostly stone monuments and some brass plates. On the markers, you saw inscriptions of people's names, the beginning and end dates of their lives, and a memorial saying. Some were labeled "father" or "mother," "husband" or "wife," and an adjective added, mostly "loving." These stone memorials suggested permanence in the midst of the shifting sands of the person's life who was buried there.

Despite your immediate reaction, the cemetery is a place of hope and new life, not despair and death. Bodies are ceremoniously buried as a testament that something of the person lasts: the soul, the spirit, the memory.

A grave marker presents a brief resume of someone's life. Consider for a moment your own curriculum vitae and what obituary you would want written for yourself. How do you want to be remembered? You are a unique person, never to be duplicated again in the history of the world. Your actions outlive you in the impact you make on others and in their memory of you. What contributions do you want recalled to your family, to your work, and/or toward bettering the world? What difference did you make in the world during your brief lifespan? You spend your life shaping your character through your choices. What adjectives would you like remembered about you, your generosity, wisdom, and dedication? What stories would you like people to repeat at your funeral?

After pondering your life, write your own obituary in your journal. This is not a morbid exercise. Rather, it is a hopeful one. You will live on in your deeds. Use your reflections about the end of your life as a motivation and guide to make those values a reality today.

With Step 10, you continue the work you began to clean house. You step back to observe your habitual reactions. Then, you step forward to act consciously in ways that correspond to your cherished values. In the process, an inner transformation happens. The old self dies.

16

Being Present: Love More Dearly

*Step 11: "Sought through prayer and meditation
to improve our conscious contact with God, as we understood Him,
praying only for knowledge of His will for us and the power to carry it out."*

"If the only prayer you say your entire life is 'Thank you,' that would suffice."

—Meister Eckhart

Fear never stands still. It is always running but never really getting anywhere. It flees the present moment, experiencing it as terrifying. You then dwell on past hurts and worry about future harm, all to create the illusion of safety. Anxious thoughts of danger disturb you, so you keep busy to distract yourself. What you fear most is the unknown. To fill the void, you create scenarios of catastrophe. Better an imagined negative outcome than an uncertain future. You keep running, exhausting your mind and body, until you collapse. The utter defeat can motivate you to begin recovery, finally to stop, look, and listen.

The evening grows late. You are tired and take a moment to rest. You sit down away from the dance floor and crowds so you will not be disturbed. Sitting there, you simply want to absorb the evening: the sights and sounds. What a splendid time you had, so much more enjoyable than you imagined! Anxious thoughts consumed you before the dance, tempting you to stay home, but you took the risk, coming despite your fear. Your reward was a surprisingly enjoyable evening. You met many interesting people. The music captivated you, and you forgot yourself in the rhythm and movement of the dancing. You became the music and the dance. Now you are savoring the moment, feeling more alive than you have in a long time.

Step 11 expresses the second major theme of the steps: "Trust God." It invites you to continue deepening your relationship with your Higher Power, with God, that you began in the previous steps. In steps two and three, you came to believe in a Higher Power and turn your life over to God's will. In Step 7, you prayed for God to remove your faults.

The Steps/Traditions book underlines the benefits and necessity of prayer for your continued growth: "We want the good that is in us all, even in the worst of us, to flower and grow. Most certainly we shall need bracing air and an abundance of food. But first of all we shall want sunlight; nothing much can grow in the dark. Meditation is our step out into the sun (p. 98)." Actually, it is a step into the present moment with full awareness.

Obstacles to Meditating

Your anxiety keeps you in darkness, in a mindset of doom and gloom. Many of your thoughts and behaviors keep you out of the sunlight. You avoid taking the time and making the effort to meditate. You may be

- tormented by thoughts;
- constantly busy; and/or
- living in another time zone.

Tormented by Thoughts

Fixated on anxiety, you tend to become lost in your thoughts. Negative thoughts enslave you, and there is no escape. They take on the full weight of reality. You believe what you think is absolutely true, making you a prisoner of these fixed negative ideas. The mental noise interferes with you quieting your mind and body for meditation. Inner silence is the fertile soil for the enlightened awareness of meditation.

Bryan: Tormenting Thoughts

"Stray thoughts take over my mind from time to time, and I can't get rid of them. From out of nowhere, the thought comes that I'm going to die at a certain time. I'm filled with dread and can't sleep. I stay awake until that deadline passes and I'm safe. Sometimes, other stray thoughts get mixed up with my thought of dying. I think that I'm going to hurt somebody and that I will kill myself.

I'm a gentle person, never violent. Those thoughts disturb me to no end. I know they're irrational, but I can't shake them out of my mind."

Constantly Busy

Anxiety takes over your body, making you agitated and restless. Your body is wired to be activated for fight or flight when you sense danger even though your mind may not consciously recognize a threat. Your body knows before your mind. That tendency to stay in constant motion interferes with you quieting yourself for prayer and meditation. Meditating requires that you sit still, be quiet, and listen. That may seem like an impossible task for you in your anxious state.

Lorraine: Restlessness

"I simply cannot sit still. My leg twitches and shakes. When I try to relax, my mind also races, and I feel even more nervous. So, I get up and get busy cleaning or doing something. Even when I'm sitting down, I have to fidget with something or my anxieties take over. Sometimes, I literally wring my hands for no reason when I'm not doing something to occupy my mind."

Living in Another Time Zone

Your anxious mind is a scattered mind. It never settles into one time zone. Instead, it entertains past regrets and mostly focuses on future worries. What it avoids is the present time because it is never enough for you. Something is always missing. Your inner critic tells you what you did in the past was not good enough. Your projected fears imagine that you will lose what you value in the future. Meditation encourages you to be fully present in the present moment, accepting yourself as already perfect. Your anxious mind resists that challenging task.

Leonard: Struggle to Stay in the Present Moment

"I've become interested in Eastern philosophies and am taking a Yoga class. I understand the need to stay in the present moment, but I'm finding it nearly impossible to do. My mind jumps around like a monkey swinging through tree branches. It grabs on past memories, and I dwell on regrets. Then, it grabs onto something on my "to do" list, and I start planning and worrying. My mind never seems to settle on what I'm doing in that moment."

"Just do it!" That phrase from Nike advertising expresses our culture's mantra. We are encouraged to look toward the future and make it better. The idea of continual progress seduces us, "Make it better and better every day in every way." That future, we believe, will only be created by hard work and constant effort. We use our brain power to create, plan, and build. Our fast-paced, success-driven, future-directed culture breeds anxiety and restlessness. When is there time for stillness, solitude, and quiet reflection?

"Sought through prayer and meditation..."

Prayer and meditation are difficult for anyone living in our restless culture that spawns so many addictions. The various religious/spiritual groups in our culture, including AA, take up the challenge of calling us to pray. We learn to pray in different ways, according to our religious background, temperament, and season of our life.

Teach Us How to Pray

I was raised Roman Catholic. Observing my own spiritual history, I noticed different ways of praying at various times in my life.

Saying Prayers

My parents first taught me to pray as a young child. Each night before going to bed, Mom or Dad would kneel down with me at the bedside. They taught me to make the sign of the cross and fold my hands. Then, together we said: "Angel of God, my guardian dear, to whom God's love commits me here. Ever this night be at my side, to light and guard, to rule and guide." Then, we asked for God's blessings on various people and ended with the sign of the cross. That bedside prayer inspired confidence in me that God loved me, watched over me, and protected me from any dangers.

In grade school, the nuns taught me more prayers to recite. We learned the *Our Father*, the *Hail Mary*, and the *Glory Be*, prayers taken from the Scriptures. We recited them carefully in class and put them together to pray the rosary. Reciting these prayers, I gained a sense of belonging to a faith community with a solid tradition. Initially, I merely memorized the words, but gradually I let their meaning penetrate my heart. I felt closeness with God.

Talking with God

Attending high school retreats, I was taught another way of praying. Instead of using the community's words, I was encouraged to speak to God from my heart in my own words. "Be spontaneous. Tell God whatever you are feeling. Speak to Him from your heart, as you would a close friend," my religion teachers urged me. I experienced God as an intimate Friend and sought a personal relationship with Him. In prayer, I expressed to God my deepest desires and secrets I would tell no one else. He was my Confidant.

Listening from the Heart

While in the college seminary, we each had a spiritual director and regular conferences. The spiritual director instructed us about different forms of praying. What impressed me most at this time was a shift in my prayer from speaking to listening. Hearing what God was saying to me in the depths of my heart was more important than what I was telling Him. I learned the importance of being still and silent. I also learned to read the words of Scripture slowly and reflectively, letting the words penetrate to my core. "Be still and know that I am God," (*Psalm* 46:10) became the theme of my daily meditation. I came to appreciate God's mysterious, unshakable presence in my life.

Being Still

Solitude, silence, and stillness have become the hallmarks of my prayer and meditation for the last several years. Jesus's response to his disciples' inquiring about how to pray makes more sense to me. He taught, "When you pray, go to your inner room, close the door and pray to your Father in secret. And your Father, who sees in secret, will reward you." (*Matt.* 6:6) The inner room is within myself, where God is closer to me than I am to myself. I sense Him living and praying through me. I try to live the words of St. Paul urging his congregation to "pray constantly." My prayer and life are not so separate. Frequently, I pause during the day to be consciously aware of God's enduring Presence.

I looked outside my Christian upbringing to the Eastern traditions that promoted the value of contemplation centuries before Christianity. Their wisdom showed a path to serenity and peace similar to the way of Christ. For example, the *Tao Te Ching* advocates emptying the mind to find peace:

> Empty your mind of all thoughts.
> Let your heart be at peace.
> Watch the turmoil of beings,
> but contemplate their return.
> Each separate being in the universe
> returns to the common source.
> Returning to the source is serenity.
> If you don't realize the source,
> you stumble in confusion and sorrow (22).

...to improve our conscious contact with God as we understood Him..."

The Steps/Traditions book underlines the positive benefits of regular prayer and meditation. The experience of those who practice validates its benefits: "All those who have persisted have found strength not ordinarily their own. They have found wisdom beyond their usual capacity. And they have increasingly found a peace of mind which can stand firm in the face of difficult circumstances....Perhaps one of the greatest rewards of meditation and prayer is the sense of belonging that comes to us. We no longer live in a completely hostile world. We are no longer lost and frightened and purposeless (pp. 104, 105)." Conscious contact with God is the sunlight that dispels the darkness of your fears.

Half Life to Whole Life

Carl Jung, the noted Swiss psychologist, observed that there are two halves to life, often divided by a mid-life crisis. The crisis usually occurs between ages thirty-five and forty when disillusionment sets in. Depending on your life experiences, it can happen at any age. The crisis launches you on a spiritual path that defines the second half of life.

In the first half of life, you are engaged in building the outer structure of the house you call your life. You want the house to be comfortable and attractive to those who view it. How others perceive you is important. You expend great energy in building your family, your career, your status, and your wealth. The pursuit of progress drives you to work hard. You want a better life for yourself and your family. Investing so much of yourself in the project, you instinctively identify with the house you are building, making it the source of your security, self-esteem, and happiness.

When a crisis comes that shakes the foundation of your house, you face a choice. That crisis can take many forms. Your health begins to fail or loved ones die, and you sense for the first time your mortality. One day you will die. Your marriage or some significant relationship fails, and you feel lost and lonely. Disillusionment grabs you as you climb the ladder of success, and you ask yourself, "What does it all mean?" The specter of death, of losing all that is important to you, terrifies you.

You can choose to redouble your efforts to repair the house. Or you can look for new ways to make a home.

In the second half of life, you gain wisdom in realizing that everything passes. You turn your attention from the outer structure of your life inward, searching for what really lasts. You ask yourself what is really important to you. What do you value? How do you want to invest your limited life energy? What difference can you make in your world? Accepting the inevitable losses in life, you seek what endures and is of ultimate importance.

The founders of the great world religions each faced their own mid-life crisis before beginning their second half of life missions. Siddhartha Gautama, a prince in a small northern India kingdom, was being groomed to be king. At age twenty-nine, his world was shaken when he ventured outside the secure confines of his palace and encountered suffering he never knew existed. His life changed direction. He then longed to dedicate himself to the relief of suffering. For six years he studied, fasted, and meditated. While meditating in solitude and silence, he faced his demons and became enlightened, discovering the four noble truths to relieve suffering. He became the "awakened one," the Buddha.

Moses was a shepherd in Egypt. He was a Jew, and his people were enslaved by the Egyptians. He heard the cries of his people, and it turned his life around. While praying in the desert, he encountered a burning bush. In that bush, he experienced God's Presence who revealed His name, "I Am Who I Am." Moses achieved a new identity and mission in that mysterious meeting. He was called to set his people free.

For thirty years, Jesus of Nazareth worked as a carpenter building wooden objects with His father. He felt the suffering of his people subjected to the cruelty of their Roman occupiers. After being baptized in the Jordan River by His cousin John, He went off into the desert for forty days to fast, pray, and be tempted. He emerged with a new identity and message: "Reform your lives; the kingdom of God is at hand." He immediately went to His hometown synagogue, announcing, "I came to set captives free."

Muhammad of Mecca had a secure life. He was married, had a family, and ran a successful business. Yet, something was painfully missing in his life. His hometown was corrupted by the pursuit of wealth in the business of idol worship. Muhammad often went out into the desert to pray. One day, when he was about forty years old, he encountered an angel of God in a cave who ordered him to recite to his people the words of Divine Revelation. Initially confused and fearful, he gathered his courage to proclaim, "There is no God but God [Allah]."

Compassion for their people drove these men to search for a way to relieve suffering. They let go of their normal, conventional lives. Turning both inward in prayer and meditation and outward in preaching and giving to the poor, they found the path to true happiness. They invited their followers to share their experience, surrender their old lives, and embrace a new life. Unlike conventional religion which demands assent to a belief system, rights-and-wrongs, dos-and-don'ts, the founders pleaded for a new consciousness.

The Choice: Cave or Mountain

As much as you detest your anxiety condition, it presents you with an opportunity to begin a new life, the second half of your life. You are well acquainted with suffering, disillusionment, and defeat in your struggles with fear. Now, you face a choice. The suffering can make you retreat into yourself or expand your mind and heart. You can choose to remain in your dark mental cave or go up to the mountaintop where you will see more clearly and love more dearly. Through prayer and meditation you make conscious contact with God, your Higher Power, Ultimate Reality, and achieve a new consciousness. You view life with a wide-angle lens.

If you remain in your dark mental cave, you will be a prisoner of your anxious mind. The anxious mind has its own operating system, with the following characteristics:

- Biased toward the negative, imagining worst case scenarios.

- Tending to compare, judge, and criticize in a negative direction.

- Engaged in rigid, either-or, black-or-white, all-or-none thinking.

- Avoiding present experience, regretting the past and worrying about the future.

- Intolerant of uncertainty and ambiguity.

- Possessed by will power, unwilling to give up control.

- Obsessed with personal security in a threatening world.

If you venture up to the sunlit mountaintop in prayer and meditation, you will develop your wise mind. The wise mind, also called the contemplative mind, operates on another system, with the following qualities:

- Unbiased, open-minded, focusing on the totality of experience.

- All-centered, accepting that everything belongs.

- Discriminates, but sees the connections of all things, their wholeness.

- Experiences the present moment fully.

- Embraces the mystery of life, accepting uncertainty, not knowing, as a path to exploration.

- Willing to surrender to the truth.

- Sees our shared destiny and has compassion for all.

"...praying only for knowledge of His will and the power to carry it out"

When you pray in solitude and silence, you discover the answers to two questions: Who am I? What should I do? You acquire knowledge of your true self hidden beneath all your fears and worries. You also become empowered to live according to the deepest desires of your real self.

Finding Truth, an Inside Job

My patients come to me in distress, seeking relief from their suffering. Often, their greatest complaint is that they do not know themselves or what they want to do in life.

Alicia: Lack of Self-Knowledge

"I've been anxious my whole life. There was always something to worry about. I worried about my own health and my family's. I worried about finances, crime, terrorists. You name it, and I worried about it. If I didn't worry, I don't know who I would be. Somehow, I believe there is a person buried beneath all my fears who is crying to be heard and released. But I don't know how to reach that person."

My patients come to me as a psychologist because they consider me an authority on the workings of the mind. "Please tell me what to do," they plead.

I respond, "Who do you think is the expert on you?"

They say, "I know I should be, but I don't know myself."

I assure them I will accompany them on this wonderful journey of exploration and instruct them, "It's easier than you think. Just pay attention to yourself."

For many that is something new. They never paid close attention to themselves. Instead, they kept themselves busy reacting to the events and people in their lives or looked outside themselves for direction.

"The glory of God is man (the person) fully alive," an ancient wisdom teaches. God's will is your happiness, which is living a full and meaningful life in accordance with who you are. Consequently, the tasks of knowing yourself and knowing God's will for you overlap. In discovering who you are, you sense the presence of God, your Higher Power, Ultimate Reality. In prayerfully seeking to know God's will, you meet yourself at the core of your person.

How do you know God's will and yourself?

Steps in Active Decision-Making:
Discerning God's Will (Deciding for Your True Self)

Step 11 states clearly that you have to stop, be quiet and still, and listen. God comes to you disguised as your own life. In taking your life seriously, conscientiously making daily decisions, you encounter His presence and guidance. If your inner critic has taken control of your thinking, you may not trust that you can come to know yourself and what God wants for you. An act of faith, as you initially made in steps two and three, is needed. You need to believe not only in God's goodness but also in your own innate goodness, sanity, and wisdom.

Consider some decision you are making about your life and follow these steps:

Trust your ability to know yourself and God.

As helpless as you may feel, you still have control over your behavior. Your actions express and shape who you are. Instead of just reacting, think about some important decision that is weighing on you. It may concern a proposed change in your life regarding a relationship, a job, or your state in life.

Hold a decision in your mind.

Hold that decision in your mind with the intention of seeking guidance on the best path to take. Resist the urge you might feel to make a quick decision and react. Allow yourself to relax with the question.

Listen to your innermost thoughts, feelings, and desires.

Retreat to a quiet place where you can be alone without being disturbed. Sit in a relaxed position. Focus on your breathing and allow the rush of thoughts to pass. When your mind and body are calm, hold the question about what to do in your mind. Notice the thoughts, feelings, and desires that congregate around that question. Pay attention to the subtle stirrings of your heart. You will notice many competing urges. Observe the intensity of the urges. Just take note of them.

Analyze the costs and benefits.

After spending time listening to yourself, begin to analyze with your rational mind the competing thoughts, feelings, and desires that emerged. Take two pieces of paper and draw a line down the middle. On one sheet of paper, write the advantages of remaining where you are without taking action on one side, and the disadvantages on the other. Try to be honest with yourself. Write freely, letting your thoughts flow. On the second sheet of paper, write the advantages of making the change on one side, and the disadvantages on the other. Consider carefully the costs and benefits of your proposed decision.

Analyze the decision in the context of your life history.

Before making the decision, especially if it is an important one, reflect on the proposed action in the context of your life. Step back and look at the flow of your life up to this point. Ask yourself if this decision is more consistent or inconsistent with your life history. Consider what values have guided your life and whether the proposed action is compatible with those values. Allow for something new emerging in your life and observe its trajectory.

Make a tentative decision and notice the feeling.

After this thorough review, consulting with your wise mind, make a tentative decision. Notice how sitting with the decision feels. Persistent turmoil indicates that you are not yet ready to make the decision. A sustained feeling of inner peace normally follows a wise decision even though you may feel some anxiety in carrying it out. Feelings of peace, courage, strength, and consolation emerge from following the guidance of your true self. Feelings of anxiety, sadness, confusion, and inner disturbance arise from letting your false self control your decision-making.

Repeat the process if you are not at peace.

If you do not experience inner peace, repeat the procedure at a later date. Repeat the practice as often as you need until you arrive at a place of serenity.

The Power of Acceptance

When anxious, you expend so much energy fighting with yourself. Exhausted, you feel even more powerless, which, in turn, increases your anxiety level.

Blair: How Anxiety Wore Him Out

> *"My worry exhausts me, but I don't know what to do about it. When I'm anxious, I feel so restless I can't sit still and begin pacing. My mind keeps going round and round about problems and what I should be doing. My muscles tense up, my lips quiver, and my jaw clenches. I'm in the middle of a battle, and I know it's only with myself. The worry saps so much of my energy, I don't have anything left to deal with the problem."*

If you learned to relax, you would be amazed at how much energy would be released. It is like golf. Occasionally, you amaze yourself at how far you hit the ball when you are relaxed and do not try to kill it.

Resting in the openness of your wise mind through prayer and meditation, you relax. Instead of fighting against reality, you see and accept things as they are. Instead of living in a fantasy world shaped by your wishful "shoulds," you embrace life as it is. You get off the mental grid. You avoid the inevitable collisions with reality.

There is a hidden power in acceptance. The energy wasted in trying to orchestrate your world to feel secure is unbound. You experience that unbound energy as liberating, a Power greater than your old self. Actually, it is the power of your true self being released.

You experience a new freedom in your relationships. "I love you just the way you are," becomes your theme song. You refuse to engage in power struggles with others. You give up the manipulating, criticizing, and cajoling to make people behave the way you want. When you allow others to be themselves, you feel liberated to be yourself. There is no longer any need to protect or prove yourself to gain acceptance. You love yourself just the way you are, realizing your deep-down perfection.

You view the circumstances of your life as neutral conditions in which to grow and thrive. As St. Therese, the little flower, advised, "Grow where you're planted." When your anxious mind perceived the world as threatening, you either ran scared or fought back. You saw enemies lurking around every corner. Hyper-vigilance drained you. Now, with your contemplative mind, you sense a vital connection with the whole universe. Outer events and circumstances no longer threaten you or exert power over you. Being content with yourself, you take charge of your life. You are free to be yourself.

You make peace with yourself. Aware of your basic goodness, you accept your short-comings as part of who you are. You no longer engage in a war against yourself, a war that only tears you apart and wastes your energy. You no longer view your anxiety as an enemy to be vanquished. Loving your enemy means foremost loving the imperfect person you see in the mirror.

That radical self-acceptance releases a power that enables you to transform the energy of your faults into virtues. You can identify with St. Paul who gained wisdom, humility, and strength from his weaknesses. He wrote, ". . . to stop me from getting too proud I was given a thorn in the flesh, an angel of Satan to beat me and stop me from getting too proud!

About this thing, I have pleaded with the Lord three times for it to leave me, but He has said, 'My grace is enough for you; My power is at its best in weakness.' So I shall be very happy to make my weaknesses my special boast so that the power of Christ may stay over me....For it is when I am weak that I am strong."(*I Cor.* 12: 7-10)You gain strength in accepting, rather than fighting against, your weaknesses.

Paradox of Blessing and Curse

Because it is so painful, you consider your anxiety a curse. It is your thorn in the flesh that you beg God to remove. You may see yourself as a victim of your condition and ask, "Why me?" Your search for a cause only leads to dead ends. You may blame God, fate, your parents, or your defective mind. There is plenty of blame to throw around because you feel so targeted for misery and helpless to defend yourself. Cursing the day you were born with your condition only leads to an emotional hangover of apathy, anger, and bitterness.

Your anxious mind has tunnel vision, blind to the whole. Darkness dominates. It can only see the pain your anxiety causes you. However, your contemplative mind, bathed in sunlight and nourished with prayer and meditation, sees your condition differently. It views your life as a whole, from a larger perspective. While not ignoring the suffering your anxiety causes, it also sees your anxiety condition as a hidden blessing.

What is the blessing of anxiety? If you embrace it with loving acceptance, fear can enlighten you. "The fear of the Lord is the beginning of wisdom," the *Bible* points out. Anxiety and fear bring you to your knees. You learn your limits and gain humility. The world is beyond your grasp and control, a place of mystery inspiring fear, wonder, and awe. You can withdraw in fear or surrender to the mystery, give up your efforts to control, and open up your mind and heart.

The suffering of anxiety can launch you on a spiritual path to growth and serenity. Confronted with the pain of anxiety, you have a choice about your relationship to it. You can reject it and become embittered. Or you can accept it, learn from it, and become compassionate toward others who suffer in a similar way. Many alcoholics end up thanking God for their condition because it allowed them to discover AA and turn their lives around. Seeing your condition also as a blessing can inspire gratitude and the generous desire to help others.

Practice: Write a Gratitude List

Anxiety-obsessed, you develop the mental habit of focusing on what is missing in your life and what you might lose. What you ignore is what you already possess. Your wise, contemplative mind provides you with a glimpse of the fullness within the emptiness. You are and have more than you imagine. You are already perfect although you may need some improvement.

Alcoholics Anonymous suggests with its wise sayings ways to transform the addictive mind. "The only way to have gratitude is to live in the now, not in the past or the future." "Every day is a gift; that's why we call it present." "Count your blessings."

Psychological research today, spurred by a movement called positive psychology, validates the AA wisdom. Research shows that about 50% of our potential for life satisfaction is genetically influenced. We reflect our parents' temperamental level of contentment. Surprisingly, favorable life circumstances account for only 8-15% of a satisfied state of mind. More than a third, 35-40%, of our happiness is connected to our voluntary attitudes toward our lives (1). As Abraham Lincoln observed, "Most folks are about as happy as they make up their minds to be."

Take some time to reflect on two gratitude questions.

The first question: What are you most grateful for in your life? Make a review of your life from childhood. Notice all the positive influences that made you the person you are today. You survived and thrived because of the love and support of many people. Think about all those who benefited you. Take note of your good qualities and consider all those who were role models for you and encouraged you to develop your abilities. Consider all your blessings: health, abilities, career, material possessions, friendships, loving relationships, and so forth. Then, write in your journal what you are grateful for.

The second question: How has your anxiety benefitted you? Retrace in your mind the history of your anxiety with a mindset different than your usual. Focus on the positive. Observe what you learned about yourself in struggling with your anxiety, especially an awareness of your attachments. Notice how your anxiety has motivated you to look more deeply into your life and pursue a spiritual path to find meaning in your life. Take note of the good habits that resulted: humility, honesty, courage, compassion, and so forth. Write in your journal what you discovered about yourself.

Practice: Centering Prayer

Habituated to anxiety, you are restless in body, scattered in mind, and storm-tossed emotionally. You cannot sit still because you are so restless, tense, energized for defensive action. Your mind wanders toward the negative, bouncing back and forth from a regretted past to a worrisome future. You feel cast upon a stormy sea of emotions, unable to calm yourself and navigate your life. How can you find serenity in body, mind, and emotions?

Your anxious agitation really occupies only the surface of your life. You feel like you are swimming desperately in stormy waters to keep from drowning. Relief can come from going deeper to the tranquility of the bottom of the ocean. Your spirit must move downwards into its silent depths to find its center. Your center is where the spirit of your true self and God's Spirit meet.

Father Thomas Keating, a Cistercian monk, developed a method of prayer to foster a contemplative attitude in your daily life. It is an attitude of being fully present in each moment of your life, aware of God's loving presence. His prayer method is called "Centering Prayer," which opens your mind and heart to deepen your relationship with God (2). These are the guidelines for the prayer:

1) Choose a sacred word as a sign of your intention to surrender yourself to God's presence and action in your life. Spend some time in prayer and reflection to find a word that inspires you. It might be a word from Scripture, such as Father, Lord, Jesus, Mother Mary. It might be a word that expresses your highest aspirations, such as *Love, Trust, Faith, Courage, Hope, Peace,* and *Let Go.* Choose a word that has a personal meaning for you, expressing your desire for communion with God.

2) Go to a quiet place where you will be alone. Sit comfortably with your eyes closed. Close your eyes to focus your attention on the stillness within you without outer distractions. Be relaxed, sitting with your back erect. Breathe deeply. Then, introduce your sacred word and repeat it to yourself slowly. Let the repetition help you focus on your center where you sense God's loving presence.

3) Allow yourself to enter more deeply into the silence within you. Thoughts, feelings, sensations, and desires will inevitably arise. Do not fight them. Simply let them pass and keep your attention focused on the sacred word. During the prayer, even the sacred word may disappear. Gently let that pass also.

4) At the end of the prayer time, spend a few moments in silence. Sense that you are resting in God, and God is dwelling within you. Then, slowly open your eyes and resume your activities with an uplifted mind and heart.

Spend at least 20 minutes in centering prayer. You can extend the time as you become more comfortable with the stillness and silence. Throughout the day during your normal activities, take a moment to center yourself and be fully present as you were during the prayer time.

I add one word of caution. If you have been traumatized, an extended period of silence may be overwhelming for you because of the painful memories that may emerge from deep within your unconscious. Stop the practice if you are feeling overwhelmed. Return if and when you are ready.

With Step 11, you cultivate your relationship with God, your Higher Power, Ultimate Reality, through prayer and meditation. Taking a step back, you become more aware of who you are and what you are meant to do. Silent reflection energizes you to undertake your unique mission in life.

Dennis Ortman, Ph.D.

17

Gifts Shared: Follow More Nearly

Step 12: "Having had a spiritual awakening as the result of these steps,
we tried to carry this message to the anxious,
and to practice these principles in all our affairs."

"Inaction breeds doubt and fear. Action breeds confidence and courage.
If you want to conquer fear, don't sit home and think about it.
Go out and get busy."

—Dale Carnegie

Anxiety makes you shrink from life. You cower in fear. Not being in control presents the greatest threat. To feel safe and secure you avoid persons, places, and things that challenge your sense of mastery. You even avoid feelings that arise from your unconscious. The unknown terrifies you so you create fixed ideas about how the world should be and hide behind them.

Healing can come only from your willingness to step out of your comfort zone, to become engaged with life and with others.

The evening draws to a close. The music has stopped, and the band is packing up its instruments. Lights turned up, you look around the room at the faces of all the people you met. People approach you and say, "I had a great time dancing with you and getting to know you." You smile and nod in agreement. Quiet satisfaction swells within you. You remember how hesitant and nervous you were to come to the dance. You think about the many risks you took in asking others to dance. You also risked getting to know them and letting them know you. The music still resounds in your head, and your body feels its rhythms. You prepare to take another step—into the outside world. How can you keep the experience of the dance alive and share it with others?

Step 12 expresses the third major theme of the steps: "Help others." It encourages you to put into daily practice what you began in Step 9, making amends and building relationships. Reaching out to others, the step promises, is the only path to a joyful life. The Steps/Tradition book states: "The joy of living is the theme of AA's twelfth step, and action is the key word. Here we turn outward toward our fellow alcoholics (sufferers) who are still in distress. Here we experience the kind of giving that asks no rewards (p. 106)." Yet, there is an unexpected reward, a loss and a gain--the loss of your anxious self-obsession and the gain of surprising joy.

Taking action to help others is the natural fruit of the previous eleven steps. Service of others aligns with all the ancient spiritual traditions. Jesus remarked, "Yet I am in your midst as the one who serves you." (*Luke* 22:27) He invited His followers to care for the poor and reminded them that they would be judged in the end on how they served "my least brothers." Muhammad reserved a portion of his income for the poor and made almsgiving one of the pillars of Islam. Buddha taught, "Even as a mother protects with her life her child, her only child, so with a boundless heart should one cherish all living things." (*Metta Sutra*) The way to happiness is serving others.

You likely consider your anxious reaction with all the physical, emotional, and mental discomfort it causes as the problem. However, it is not really the problem, only a symptom. What, then, is the real problem? Your fear and anxiety reveal what you cling to so desperately. You imagine that your happiness depends on it. The self-centered clinging to what will never bring you lasting happiness is the real source of your misery. The desperate desire becomes your addiction. It is a knot that must be untangled for you to be free.

The AA Big Book expresses clearly the heart of addiction, which is also the heart of anxiety: "So our troubles are basically of our own making. They arise out of ourselves, and the alcoholic is an extreme example of self-will run riot, though he or she does not think so. Above everything, we alcoholics must be rid of this selfishness. We must, or it kills us (p. 62)!"

What applies to the alcoholic also applies to you in your anxiety. You become preoccupied with your own safety and security. In the grip of fear, you think only of yourself, no one else. However, the medicine can be found in the illness. You have a choice. You can escape your self-enclosed prison by choosing to be as concerned about others as you are about yourself.

Anxious people are born, not made. You were born with a brain on high alert, most likely inherited from your parents and reinforced by your home environment and culture. While much of your anxiety is not of your own making, you have a hand in creating some of the problems it causes you. How you choose to relate with your nervous discomfort influences the quality of your life.

You can choose to let the anxiety control your life, or you can decide to become its master through constructive action. The choice is yours.

Obstacles to Taking Action

There are three obstacles to taking action. They are

- Being a perfectionist.

- Being a loser.

- Being a victim.

Being a Perfectionist

If you tend to be a perfectionist, you may easily become stuck in your recovery from anxiety. You find safety in rituals and routines. Your comfort zone can be quite restricted. What you fear most is failure. In your habitual black-and-white thinking, you either excel at something or are a miserable failure. There is no gray area. You want to master whatever you undertake and must be confident of success. Overcoming anxiety requires you to stretch yourself by engaging in unfamiliar activities. Facing situations with unknown outcomes, your perfectionism may lead to procrastinating, and then to paralysis.

Jerome: Perfectionism

"I'm a card-carrying perfectionist. That's who I've been my whole life. Being a perfectionist helped me to be an honor student and class valedictorian. It also helped me get a job at a prestigious law firm. I can't stand to lose at anything. I work day and night, whatever it takes, to win a case. I prepare to the last detail. My stubbornness and need to win both help and hurt me. I don't try new things and don't engage in activities unless I know I can be good at it. If I can't master something, I don't even try. Failure's not an option."

Being a Loser

If you take on the identity of a loser, you likely fear success more than anything else. Your life becomes a self-fulfilling prophecy. You believe you will fail at anything you do, and your efforts lead to predictable results. Unconsciously, you find ways of sabotaging yourself. You may become stuck in your recovery because deep down you fear success. Your self-pity only disguises your deeper fear. Recovery involves actively making changes in your life which would terrify you, taking you into unknown territory.

Anita: Loser Identification

"I have a big "L" engraved on my forehead. It's my scarlet letter. Whatever I try seems to fail. I was born with asthma so I could not become involved in sports. I had a learning disability so I had trouble in school, barely graduating high school. My jobs have all been minimum wage, and I've bounced around from job to job. I have no career goals. What's the use? I'd fail, anyway. And my relationships? They've all been disasters! I never dated anyone I could count on. No wonder I'm such a loser."

Being a Victim

If you have been hurt by some event in your life, you naturally become cautious about being hurt again. "Harmed once, shame on you; harmed twice, shame on me." If you were deeply enough wounded, you may bear a permanent scar. You live in terror of being wounded again and do not trust others or yourself. Over time, you may come to identify yourself with the role of a helpless victim. You see yourself as weak and helpless in a threatening world. Your sense of helplessness and fear of any potentially harmful change keep you stuck.

Louise: Taking on the Victim Role

"After my husband left me for another woman, I haven't been the same person. Initially, I blamed myself because I wasn't a good enough wife. Then, I became enraged with him. Now, I'm nervous all the time. I'm terrified to date because I don't trust that any man will be faithful. I feel so wounded and frightened I think I would just fall apart if I became involved with a man who cheated on me again."

Suffering from anxiety, you may let your fears define you. You take on a fixed identity to provide an illusory sense of stability in an uncertain world. Without realizing it, you may come to cherish that identity because it gives a meaning and purpose to your life. However, any fixed identity is a trap. It prevents you from being open to the totality of your experience. It also interferes with your recovery.

"Having had a spiritual awakening as the result of these steps..."

What does it mean to have a spiritual awakening?

The Steps/Tradition book offers a helpful definition: "When a man or woman has a spiritual awakening, the most important meaning of it is that he has now become able to do, feel, and believe that which he could not do before on his unaided strength and resources alone. He has been granted a gift which amounts to a new state of consciousness and being (p. 106-107)." The awakening is to a new level of consciousness that releases a hidden power from within.

Your spiritual awakening came about as a result of working the steps. Anyone addicted has fallen asleep. Some may awaken suddenly, in a dramatic fashion, like St. Paul who was bathed in light and fell to the ground blinded. Most likely, you struggled with anxiety for many years until you admitted defeat to yourself. You wavered in finding strength in your faith. You also wavered in recognizing and admitting the shortcomings your fears exposed. When you finally achieved a measure of peace, you suffered many relapses, as most addicts do. Even though awakened, you never felt completely secure in your recovery.

Progress, not perfection, motivates you now. You keep constant vigilance, learning humility along the way.

The Great Awakening: Inhale

The awakening is like taking a breath of fresh air for the first time. Anxiety tenses your body and constricts your breathing. Your body and mind awaken with the breath of a new spirit.

Cynthia: Spiritual Awakening

"I've always been a spiritual person. I learned to pray when I was a child and found comfort in praying my whole life. I never hesitated to ask God for favors because I

always believed He cared and listened to me. When I began having panic attacks in high school, I did what was natural to me. I prayed. I begged God to spare me this trial. I felt His presence and protection. I still have occasional panic attacks and worry about the next one coming. When I pray, a confidence grows inside me that I'll survive the terror of these attacks. So, I keep on going."

Albert Einstein famously remarked, "The significant problems we face cannot be solved on the same level of thinking we were at when we created them." What new kind of consciousness awakens for recovery? It is a new awareness of who you really are beneath the surface of your anxious reactions.

You learn several truths about yourself:

1) You are not who you think you are.

2) You are more than you think you are.

3) You are less than you think you are.

4) You heal through the power of forgiveness.

You are not who you think you are.

Change and the uncertainty it brings provoke anxiety. To cope, you develop fixed ideas and behaviors to give you a sense of stability. You hold beliefs about how the world works and who you are in that world you perceive as threatening. You entertain ideas about what you need to do to be safe. Without realizing it, pride sneaks in. You entertain the firm belief that if you think something is true, such as a situation of danger and your helplessness, it absolutely must be true.

Believing so adamantly in the truth of your negatively-biased thinking, you lose contact with your immediate experience, running away from the present moment. You become a slave to your ideas, losing your freedom to flow with life.

You are more than you think you are.

Trapped in the dark cave of your fears, you see yourself as a helpless victim. Darkness and dangers surround you. You think of yourself as a defective person because of your anxiety condition. It defines who you are. Thrashing about helplessly, you grasp at whatever is available to provide a measure of safety and security. You cling to relationships or blindly pursue power, prestige, or possessions as guarantees of happiness and peace. Since the future holds no hope for you, you become lost in your pessimistic thoughts of the present.

In your spiritual awakening, you venture to the sunlit mountaintop, escaping the darkness of the cave. What do you see? You see a larger, brighter world that extends beyond the reaches of your vision. It is an open, spacious, luminous world. You are part of something bigger than yourself. You are connected to a larger whole, not as isolated, broken, and separate as you thought. Everyone is your brother and sister, not an enemy. You live in a vast universe, and the energy, life, and power of the universe dwells in you. In religious terms, you live in God, and God dwells in you. You are a child of the light, and the darkness of fear cannot overcome you.

You gain a glimpse of your deeper self that resides beneath your surface anxiety. You are not your fears. You are infinitely greater. Within your core you possess a basic goodness, brilliant sanity, and innate bravery. What a marvelous freedom you have, if you open your mind and heart to the experience!

You are less than you think you are.

Your anxiety disguises a will to power. Outwardly, you feel weak, helpless, and vulnerable. You imagine that if you had absolute control, certainty, and clarity about the future you would feel safe. Secretly, you desire all-knowing and all-powerful, godlike qualities. You try to rearrange your world and engage in predictable activities to exercise that power.

The sunlight from your mountaintop experience, your spiritual awakening, exposes the shadows in your fearful thinking. Because you put so much faith in the validity of your thoughts, you did not realize its cave-like quality. As the AA slogan states, "Fear is the darkroom where negatives are developed." In the bright light of your new consciousness, the negative bias and its impact of your life are revealed. You cannot hide your self-centered attempts to find happiness in chasing after health, love, money, status, power, and so forth. The enlightened mind exposes the dark, insubstantial, shadow-like nature of these pursuits.

Aware of how fleeting the things you fear losing really are, you become free. You realize you are already complete. As the wisdom of the *Tao Te Ching* expresses it:

Be content with what you have;
Rejoice in the way things are.
When you realize there is nothing lacking,
The whole world belongs to you (44).

You heal through the power of forgiveness.

Your anxious mind battles with itself and others. It wants to rule with its fixed, black-and-white, right-and-wrong ideas about how the world and you work. In contrast, your wise mind, which has been to the mountaintop, sees the whole. It perceives that everything belongs even if it initially does not seem to fit. Curiosity, openness, and acceptance govern its thought process. The wise mind recognizes that you are both more and less than you think and embraces the apparent contradiction.

Awakened spiritually, you do not overlook your shortcomings, pretending you are perfect. You recognize them, admit them, and work to correct them. You realize that deep down you are better than your harmful behavior. The sense of your own basic goodness motivates you to act in ways true to yourself, making amends for your faults. Embracing your own inner contradictions with love, you forgive yourself. Recognizing your own failings, you are more patient with others who are imperfect. You are more willing to forgive them. Seeing from a larger perspective, you can live large.

"...we tried to carry this message to the anxious..."

Andrew: Gratitude in Recovery

"My anxiety has caused me so much pain I never thought I could be grateful for it. It took me a while to recognize that my queasy stomach and shakiness were really anxiety and not just some physical problem. Once I was diagnosed with an anxiety disorder, my eyes were opened. I began to see a similar problem in many of the people in my life. My wife and I play off each other because we manage our anxiety in opposite ways. As I'm immersed in my own recovery, I'm becoming more compassionate with myself and more patient with others. As I'm learning to cope with my own anxiety, I sincerely want to help others."

Free to Be Yourself: Exhale

Your spiritual awakening inspires gratitude in you. Even though you have worked hard with the steps, you realize that your recovery is a gift freely given. You begin to exhale the spirit you received, extending the breath of new life to others. If you hold that breath in, you know you will suffocate.

The fellowship of Alcoholics Anonymous was founded as a peer organization, alcoholics helping other alcoholics. Bill Wilson, the founder of AA, was a hopeless drunk (1). He failed countless times to become sober and became depressed and suicidal. By happenstance, he met a childhood friend who had turned his life around and given up drinking. Intrigued, Wilson wanted to know his secret. The man responded, "I've got religion." Inspired by that message of hope, Wilson eventually had his own spiritual experience and achieved a lasting sobriety.

Overwhelmed with gratitude for the gift of sobriety, Bill Wilson sought to pass on the message. He met with other struggling alcoholics and formulated the Twelve Steps for recovery, based on his personal experience and research on spiritual traditions. He believed that alcoholics could understand each other in ways that no one else could. They shared an experience with alcohol that bonded them. He created a fellowship, a place for alcoholics to meet and support each other. A key to recovery, he discovered, was overcoming the self-centeredness that spawned the addiction. Helping others was the way out.

Anxiety-possessed, you can understand a fellow sufferer like no one else. While others may stigmatize and become impatient with anxious people, you have empathy. You can be a blessing to others who share your affliction. Sharing what you learn in your recovery can help set them free. It will bring you joy and further your own recovery. You have a wonderful gift to give that can help relieve the suffering of many.

"...and to practice these principles in all our affairs"

Awareness helps free you from bondage to your anxiety condition. Seeing yourself more clearly, you can then pursue what is meaningful in your life. You can address the question: What am I meant to do?

Russell: Newfound Freedom from Anxiety

"Anxiety ruled me most of my life. When panic struck, I felt helpless, fearing for my life. I saw doctors and went to therapy for years. That all helped to turn down the volume on my anxiety. But what helped most was my coming to accept my condition as just an annoying part of my life. I try not to give my fearful feelings more power than they deserve. I act in spite of my fear. The more I do it, the less power it has over me. I feel freer to pursue what's really important in my life."

What do you value most in your life? What makes you feel alive as a person?

Caught up in anxiety, you lack energy to pursue the question and the ability to act. Fear interferes with your living a full life. It imprisons you. Your only concern in moments of extreme anxiety is your personal survival. Little else interests you. Of course, that makes sense. In the hierarchy of needs, safety and security are at the base of the pyramid. Unless you feel safe, you cannot pursue your higher needs, such as self-esteem, belonging, achievement, and self-actualization.

After your spiritual awakening and the lessening of your fear, you are free to explore and pursue what is important in your life. You can let consciously chosen values guide you instead of your anxious reacting to situations.

Listen closely to yourself and observe the trajectory of your life. Ask yourself what you value most. What do you want your life to stand for? What kind of person do you want to be? Look at all the different areas of your life: intimate relationships, family, friendships, community, career, education, leisure, health, and spirituality. Which areas have the highest and the lowest priority for you? What are your wishes, dreams, and hopes for each of these areas? Notice the sense of freedom you feel in consulting with yourself to answer these questions.

Your responses to these questions reveal the core of who you are, much more than your fearful reacting.

To overcome the self-obsession that accompanies your anxiety, you will need to consider how you want to help others. One of the great values of religious communities is the encouragement they offer for service to others. Their traditions provide concrete suggestions on how to implement the commandment to love one another. The works of mercy from the Catholic tradition suggest ways of helping others for your consideration:

Corporal works of mercy:

- feeding the hungry
- giving drink to the thirsty
- clothing the naked
- sheltering the homeless
- visiting the sick
- ransoming the captive
- burying the dead

Spiritual works of mercy:

- instructing the ignorant
- counseling the doubtful
- admonishing the sinner
- bearing wrongs patiently
- forgiving offenses
- comforting the afflicted
- praying for the living and the dead

Life is difficult. Many opportunities are presented for you to show kindness and compassion if you are aware and willing. How to serve, though? According to your temperament!

Many people come to me complaining, "I feel lost. I don't know what I want to do with my life." They see themselves as a ship without a rudder. I tell them, "You need to ask yourself two simple questions. What do I like doing? What am I good at?" I point out that the answers to those questions usually overlap, suggesting a mission and direction in life.

Knowing yourself helps you decide how you can be a channel of peace and love to others. You can only serve others in ways that are natural for you, given your personality and temperament. Carl Jung, a noted Swiss psychologist, developed four basic personality types, echoing Eastern wisdom. Each type indicates a preferred path to self-fulfillment and service of others.

Note which path most resonates with your self-awareness:

The way of action: Those who pursue this path actively engage in the affairs of the world. They love to work hard and tend to be pragmatic in their approach to life. Outgoing and confident, they seek to influence the course of events, not sitting on the sideline as spectators. Success and achievement motivate them. They live in the present moment, relying on their instincts and intuitions to survive and thrive. They want to make a difference in the world.

Bill and Melanie Gates and Warren Buffet initiated a program called "The Giving Pledge." They approached billionaire entrepreneurs around the world and asked them to make a pledge to give away half their wealth to help the poor. The Gates' give ninety-five percent, while Buffet pledges ninety-nine percent. One hundred and fifty of the most wealthy signed up. The group formed a committee to decide how best to raise awareness of world problems and to use the funds.

Inspired by action-oriented people like the Gates' and Buffet, you may be inclined to join civic or church groups to improve social conditions. You look for ways to share your time, talent, and treasure that will make a difference in the world. You may also promote various social causes, to protect the unborn, to eliminate hunger and poverty, or to protect the environment, for example. Making positive changes in your community and the world motivates you to action.

The way of knowledge: Those who pursue the way of knowledge are rational thinkers. They stand back to observe, analyze, and understand their world. They use their discriminating judgment to discern what is true and what is false. Seeking the unvarnished truth moves them. Reflective, introverted personalities, they firmly believe that knowing the truth will set them free. Some accuse them of lacking feeling. However, they possess a deep passion for knowledge and desire to share their acquired wisdom.

Recently, some celebrities stepped forward to reveal their personal struggles with mental illness. Scott Stossel, an editor and author, wrote a moving account of his life-long battle with anxiety. His book, entitled *My Age of Anxiety* (2), presents his own and the medical community's efforts to understand and find relief for this painful condition. Jane Pauley, the news anchor person, revealed her recent diagnosis of bipolar disorder. These courageous individuals spoke out to confront the social stigma of mental illness and give hope for recovery.

Like Stossel and Pauley, you may be inclined to help others by sharing your experience and knowledge. The spiritual works of mercy, particularly those that involve instructing, counseling, and comforting, attract you. Actively involved in your own recovery from anxiety, you have an opportunity to inspire hope in others who suffer the affliction of mental illness. You can help overcome the culture's ignorance and fear of these disorders.

The way of devotion: Those who follow this path are devoted to love. Their lives revolve around their important relationships. They seek to love and be loved above all else. Emotionally expressive, they want to improve relationships and are deeply committed persons. Their heart, rather than their head, guides them in their decision-making. They possess a deep appreciation of the communion of all living beings, dedicating themselves to creating unity.

Jim and Laura Smith, devoted parents, raised four children. Both decided that their priority in life would be to raise a loving family. They dedicated themselves to the needs of their children and sacrificed many other opportunities for themselves. Through their hard work and generosity, they put all their children through college and helped establish them in careers.

This familiar story expresses the way of devotion. You may be more interested in close personal relationships and issues close to home. What motivates you is cultivating loving relationships. You prefer to invest your time, energy, and resources in helping the people close to you. Rather than involvement in groups, which you experience as impersonal, you want to be involved with people face-to-face. Even though you recognize clearly how everyone is interrelated, you choose to help people one at a time.

The way of contemplation: Those who follow the contemplative way live in awe and wonder at the mystery of life. They know in their heart that life is a mystery to be lived, not a problem to be solved. Tending to be introverted by nature, they relish solitude and silence. They pay close attention to their inner life and rely on their intuitions to understand others. They live in close contact with the beyond that is within.

Your admission of powerlessness over your anxiety has launched you on a spiritual path. Over time you may accept your condition as a gift that opened up your mind and heart in ways that would not have occurred otherwise. Your suffering deepened your sense of the Mystery of life. For this you are grateful. Looking around at others in your culture, you realize that many live on the surface of life, distant from the Center and Source. Your spiritual awakening can benefit others if you are willing to share what you experience.

You can also make your job a calling. Everyone has to work for a living. Money does not grow on trees unless you win the lottery. You spend a good deal of your time and energy working. That time can be a source of either happiness or misery, depending on your attitude toward your job. You can think of your work in several different ways. First, you can consider it a job that pays you money so you can do what you really enjoy doing. Second, you can see it as a career in which you advance, develop skills, and gain status. Finally, you can view it as a vocation, your personal calling to make a difference in the world.

Recognizing clearly our interdependence, no job is worthless or less important than any other job. Whether you wear a white or blue collar really makes no difference. Each work makes its own unique contribution to building up and sustaining society. How you think about your work affects greatly your self-esteem, sense of meaning, and level of satisfaction.

The workplace provides many opportunities for you to benefit others:

- Recognize that your work provides a valuable service.
- Take pride in the job you do.
- Be conscientious about your job, not taking shortcuts.
- Be kind and friendly with your coworkers and clientele.
- Show patience, especially in demanding situations.
- See your work as a path to spiritual growth.

Paradox of Giving and Receiving

Anxiety-attached, your fear of losing something precious makes you hold on tightly. You live with a clenched fist. What do you fear losing? The list is endless: your health, a loved one, your possessions, your good image, and so forth. You entertain the belief that if you hang on tightly enough you will be secure. You also imagine that if you give up something, it is lost forever. Your anxious mind follows a zero-balance way of thinking. There is only a limited supply of whatever you desire, and once it is used up, it is gone.

The twelfth step of recovery insists on turning away from yourself to help others. The step confronts you with a paradox: "We give it away to keep it." That statement confounds the logic of your anxious mind. It also challenges your self-centered urge to protect yourself at all costs.

How can it be that by giving yourself in love that you find yourself? "Faith chases away fear," an AA slogan proclaims. The wisdom of this paradox can only be grasped by a different consciousness than the one that led you down the path of anxiety. You are invited to believe that the love you extend in helping others comes from an inexhaustible Source. That Source is God, your Higher Power, Ultimate Reality. That well will never run dry. "God is love, and he who abides in love abides in God, and God in him," the *Bible* teaches

(*I John.* 4:16). Jesus Himself gave the example of undying service and said, "Anyone among you who aspires to greatness must serve the rest."(*Matthew* 20:26)

Trust also your own experience rather than your biased mind. When you give yourself wholeheartedly in love, without expecting anything in return, the rewards are astonishing. You feel an inner joy and peace. Often, by the law of attraction, the person who receives your love responds with love. It creates a bond of intimacy between you and the person. Even if you do not receive appreciation or gratitude, you know in your heart you were true to yourself. In being yourself, you experience great joy and freedom.

Practice: Meditate on the Prayer of St. Francis

Awakened spiritually, you are aware of how your anxious addiction has enslaved you. Your nervous reacting distances you from yourself and others, making you preoccupied with your own safety. Reflecting on the prayer often associated with St. Francis of Assisi, a medieval saint who gave up all his possessions to follow Christ, can inspire you in your recovery.

The prayer confronts directly your self-centered tendencies, inviting you to become more other-centered. The first half of the prayer encourages sensitivity to those who are suffering and the ways you can bring them peace.

The second half of the prayer invites a shift in perspective, a larger consciousness. Instead of chasing after your desire for comfort, understanding, and love to satisfy your own needs, you can be attentive to the needs of others. By comforting, understanding, and loving them you gain new life for yourself.

Withdraw to a quiet place to reflect on the words of St. Francis' prayer. Read the words slowly and let them penetrate your heart. If a phrase captures your attention, ponder it for a few moments. Let your reflecting fade into silence, letting the truth and power of the words fill your inner space. After a period of time, end your meditation with the intention to live what you prayed.

"Lord, make me a channel of your peace--
that where there is hatred, I may bring love—
that where there is wrong, I may bring the spirit of forgiveness—
that where there is discord, I may bring harmony—
that where there is error, I may bring truth—
that where there is doubt, I may bring faith—
that where there is despair, I may bring hope—
that where there are shadows, I may bring light—
that where there is sadness, I may bring joy.

Lord, grant that I may seek rather to comfort, than be comforted—
to understand, than be understood—
to love, than to be loved.
For it is in self-forgetting that one finds.
It is by forgiving that one is forgiven.
It is by dying that one awakens to Eternal Life."

The first eleven steps culminate in the twelfth step, a call to action. Your spiritual awakening loosened the bond of your anxiety, freeing you to pursue what you value most in life. Serving others is the key to overcoming the self-obsession of your anxious addiction.

Epilogue:
From the Cave to the Mountaintop

"Perfect love casts out all fear."

—I John 4:18

Nancy's Story Continued

Disappointment haunted Nancy after the aborted birthday/anniversary surprise dinner for Rick. She could not stop thinking about it. Sleepless nights followed. His drinking had spoiled many other occasions, but this was different somehow. Nancy sensed that something was shifting inside her, but she could not put it into words. She felt depressed, but she could not measure the depth of her loss.

Rick apologized profusely the next day as he always did. "I'll make this up to you, honey," he vowed. Following her script, she responded, "You know what your drinking does and that you need to stop." And he said for the thousandth time, "I promise I will."

So, they resumed their normal routine. Rick returned to work, and Nancy stayed home to care for the house and their child. Yet, something interrupted the flow of normality as if a huge boulder were thrown into the river of her life. Nancy could not shake the worrisome thoughts that ran through her mind. She entered a dark tunnel, and the future seemed black and bleak. She shook inside and could not relax. She could barely motivate herself to do her usual chores. Her mind was elsewhere, and restlessness possessed her body.

After a restless, sleepless week, Nancy called her friend Laura for lunch. When they sat down together at the restaurant, Laura immediately asked, "Is something wrong? You don't look yourself." Nancy had always prided herself at her ability to keep a calm façade. She hid her emotional turmoil from others, and even tried to fool herself that she was okay, just feeling the normal stress of life. This time, Nancy told Laura in detail the events of the birthday/anniversary dinner that did not happen. She complained again about Bill's drinking.

Then she said, "Something else is going on in me that I don't understand. What happened that night with Rick was nothing new. I've lived with worry and dread my whole life, long before I married Rick. That night it reached the point where I couldn't stand it anymore. I hit bottom. I complain about Rick's drinking, but I think I have my own problem. Worry is taking over my life as much as alcohol is taking over Rick's." Nancy felt immense relief telling someone what she felt too ashamed to tell anyone before.

Laura listened, and her heart went out to her friend. "I'm not surprised. I could see how unhappy you've been. I've been seeing a therapist for the past year. He may be able to help." Nancy took the card with the psychologist's name and number and put it in her purse.

For the next week, Nancy mulled over whether or not to make an appointment. She felt ashamed that she married a man with a drinking problem but felt even worse that she was so irrationally anxious. She had been curious about anxiety disorders for a long time, watching TV shows and browsing in the self-help section in bookstores about the condition. Her desperation finally overcame her shame. She made the call.

Dr. Richardson was compassionate and caring. He listened attentively to Nancy's story, asking a few questions for clarification. At the end of the session, he told her, "I think you've been anxious your whole life and have found ways to cope. But now you have reached your limit, triggered by the birthday disappointment. Let's try to understand what's going on with your anxiety." He recommended that they meet weekly and that Nancy see a psychiatrist for medication to help ease her anxiety and help her sleep. He also recommended a support group that met at a local church. "It will help you deal with your anxiety and your husband's drinking," he said.

At first, Nancy hesitated about going to a support group. Then, she recalled the many people on the Oprah show she heard talk about how much groups helped them. Since she had already taken an out-of-character risk in seeing Dr. Richardson, Nancy told herself, "I'm going all the way."

The next night she told Rick she was going to a self-help meeting but did not elaborate. He didn't ask, and she didn't tell. She had been petrified with fear the whole day but was determined, "I can do this." She felt like she was jumping out of her skin as she entered the room with a sign on the door "Emotions Anonymous." The dozen people sitting at the table in the small room smiled at her and warmly welcomed her.

As she took a seat, the warmth and care of the people in the room began to melt her fear. She said her name, and everyone responded, "Welcome, Nancy." She listened attentively as each individual told their heart-wrenching stories of emotional turmoil, struggles to find relief, and the peace they gained through the group. Nancy somehow found the courage to tell them about her battle with worry. She felt understood and accepted. At last, a glimmer of hope. When the meeting ended with the *Serenity Prayer*, Nancy sensed she found a place and a path to find relief from her anxiety.

A Tale of Two Minds

Your anxiety, as painful as it is, is not your problem; it is only a symptom of the real problem. It is a signal and guide post to what really interferes with your living a full life.

Your anxiety reveals what you cling to desperately, what you fear losing, and what you believe you cannot survive without. Actually, your fearful insecurity arises from faulty thinking, a deeply engrained belief system that your happiness and wellbeing depend on having certain things. Your distorted ideas are the real problem. Anxiety, like all addictions, is a disease of the mind.

This book is the tale of two minds. One mind enslaves you while the other liberates you. One shrinks your life while the other expands it. These two minds, which everyone possesses, compete with each other. Anxiety addicted, you experience the full intensity of that inner battle because both foes are so strong.

Your anxious mind dwells in the dark cave of your narrow-minded, security-seeking thinking. The walls of the cave are made of up of all your thoughts of danger within and outside yourself. You have tunnel vision. All you can see are threats, outside forces trying to take away your peace, happiness, and security. What moves you is the exhausting quest for survival, safety, and security. Thoughts of danger and helplessness paralyze you, keeping you from moving out of the darkness and into the sunlight. As the AA slogan puts it, "Fear is the darkroom where negatives are developed." The negatives trap your naturally free spirit.

Your wise mind lives on a sun-drenched mountaintop and can see in all directions forever. Its view is unlimited, spacious, and clear. The bright sun illuminates everything around you so you can see the world and yourself in all its glory. From the heights, your vision is unobstructed. Nothing is hidden. Both the bright and shadowed spots stand out, the beauty and ugliness of the world. Looking around with your panoramic view, you can see how everything is related, fits together to create a picture of wholeness. Even the darkness and light merge. The fresh air makes you feel alive and well. All is one: true, good, and beautiful from the mountaintop view.

Within the cave, you hang on tightly to your ideas for a sense of safety. They are your refuge against the terror of the unknown, but on the mountaintop, you hold your thoughts gently and let your spirit soar to the heavens. You feel free to get out of your head and into your life.

Ancient and modern wisdom both proclaim the power of freedom from the weight of your fixed ideas. For example, the *Tao Te Ching* teaches:

> The mark of a moderate man
> is freedom from his own ideas.
> Tolerant like the sky,
> all-pervading like sunlight,
> firm like a mountain,
> supple like a tree in the wind,
> he has no destination in view
> and makes use of anything
> life happens to bring his way (59).

Allowing the wise mind, not the anxious mind, to guide your life gives you resilience in the unavoidable troubles of life. Your openness and breadth of vision make you tolerant of difficulties, seeing a path of growth through them. Your firm belief in the goodness of life gives you strength in adversity. Your flexibility enables you adjust to new circumstances.

You recognize and embrace the wondrous Mystery of life, realizing the awesome opportunities. As Gabriel Marcel famously said, "Life is a mystery to be lived, not a problem to be solved."

The Power of Paradox

The Twelve Steps express the wisdom of the wise mind. Everything belongs. All experience, even the painful and unwanted, can lead to growth. The wise mind embraces all of life, seeing the deeper connection within what seems contradictory on the surface. That is the meaning of paradox, which opens the mind and heart to new meanings.

The movement of recovery expresses a central paradox of the Twelve Steps: "The way down is the way up." Recovery happens through a series of humiliations. There is no other way. You experience anxiety as a humiliation, a shameful weakness that defeats you. The more you try to overcome it, the more you fail, even if you have some successes along the way. When you admit your powerlessness over your anxiety, you take the first step toward recovery. Acknowledging your powerlessness, you look beyond yourself, undertaking a spiritual search.

The spiritual path takes you to places you have avoided your entire life. You make a fearless moral inventory, recognizing the faults that underlie your anxiety. Another humiliation. You are further humbled by confessing honestly to another person the exact nature of your shortcomings. It does not end there. Then, you unpeel the onion, looking more deeply at the root causes of your vices. You realize the extent of your self-deception and inability to remove those faults. Humbly, you ask God's help. Your descent continues. Recovery demands making amends. So, you seek ways of making the wrongs right and humbly ask for forgiveness.

The work of recovery is the fruit of both effort and grace, depending on yourself and others, including the Other. One Zen teacher warned, "Avoid the spiritual journey. It is one insult after another."

The surprising destination of recovery is another paradox: "You become who you are." Your true self was lost under the clutter of your anxiety. Recovery is the systematic dismantling of your false self, supported by your anxious mind, and the releasing of the energy of your true self in a life of virtue.

Live the Questions

Your anxious mind wants guarantees and clear and certain answers. That demand restricts your life. Instead, your wise mind shows the way to a full life. It is open to the mystery of life, embracing the unknown and the possibility of newness. It entertains questions, seeking ever more profound answers.

The Twelve Steps put your life in question. They encourage deep self-reflection. In many ways, the steps are a modern formulation of Jesus's "Sermon on the Mount." In His word to worriers, He asked several pointed questions. Stopping to think about them when you are feeling anxious can help you disengage from your automatic fearful reacting. Ask yourself:

- Why do I worry so much?

- What does my worry accomplish?

- What do I worry about?

- What do I treasure most?

The Twelve Steps also reflect an earlier wisdom expressed twenty-six hundred years ago by the Buddha in his four noble truths for the relief of suffering. Let me restate those truths, apply them to the experience of anxiety, and suggest the questions that arise from them.

The first truth, the diagnosis: Suffering from anxiety is natural and inevitable. Because of our intelligence, we are sensitive to the threats around us and can foresee negative outcomes. We live in a world of constant change, requiring ongoing adjustments. We long for permanence, but know we will grow old, get sick, and die.

The second truth, the cause: Much anxious suffering comes from our fear of losing what we hold dear. Our anxiety reveals our attachments. We cling to many things, such as health, relationships, possessions, believing they will provide safety and security in our ever-changing world. The more tightly we hang on, the more fearful we become of losing it.

The third truth, the prognosis: There is a way to lessen anxious suffering through acceptance and letting go of attachments. Freedom comes from seeing and accepting reality as it is, not as we wish it to be. Giving up the futile effort to change reality brings relief. Surrendering to a Power greater than ourselves sets us free to be true selves.

The fourth truth, the treatment: The path to freedom involves releasing the power of the true self. The Twelve Steps provide guidance on the path to freedom. They can be summarized in three themes. First, trust God. Through prayer and meditation we improve our conscious contact with God, gaining confidence, wisdom, and gratitude. Second, clean house. Through a regular personal inventory, we learn honesty, humility, and courage. Finally, help others. Through caring for others, we overcome our innate self-centeredness and learn compassion and generosity.

The questions of Naikan naturally follow as a daily practice:

What have I received from others?

What have I given to others?

What troubles and difficulties have I caused others?

Hope springs eternal. From the ashes of your anxious suffering can arise a new, more fulfilling life. Working the steps, you can transform your anxiety-driven routines to a value-directed life. You then enjoy the fruits of a tranquil spirit, caring relationships, and freedom to be yourself.

ENDNOTES

Introduction

1. R. Kessler, P. Berglund, O. Demler, et al., (2005). "Lifetime prevalence of age-of-onset distribution of DSM-IV disorder in the National Comorbidity Survey Replication," *Archives of General Psychiatry* no 63 (2005):593-602.

2. K. Merikangas, J. He, M. Burstein, et al., (2010). "Lifetime prevalence of mental disorders in U.S. adolescents: Results from the National Comorbidity Survey Replication—Adolescent Supplement (NCS-A),"*Journal of the American Academy of Child and Adolescent Psychiatry* no 49 (2010): 980-989.

3. All quotes from the *Tao Te Ching* from Stephen Mitchell's translation, *Tao Te Ching* (New York: Harper Perennial Classics, 2000).

Chapter One

1. D. Regier, M. Farmer, D. Rae, et al., "Comorbidity of mental disorders with alcohol and other drug abuse. Results from the Epidemiologic Catchment Area (ECA) Study," *Journal of the American Medical Association* no 264 (1995):2511-2528.

Chapter Three

1. See Thomas Keating, *Divine Therapy and Addiction* (New York: Lantern Books, 2009), 4-9.

Chapter Four

1. All the Big Book quotes are from *Alcoholics Anonymous: The Big Book*, fourth edition (New York: Alcoholics Anonymous World Services, Inc., 2001).

2. All the Steps/Tradition quotes are from *Twelve Steps and Twelve Traditions* (New York: Alcoholics Anonymous World Services, Inc., 2012).

Chapter Five

1. *Ecclesiastes Rabbah on Ecclesiastes 5:14*, quoted in Joshua Boettiger, "I have not taken from this world a single thing," *Parabola* no 39 (2014):19.

2. All Bible quotes are from *The New American Bible* (New Jersey: Thomas Nelson, 1971).

Chapter Seven

1. See Jon Kabat-Zinn, *Full Catastrophe Living* (New York: Bantam Books, 2013), 54-74.

Chapter Eight

1. Richard Rohr, *Breathing Under Water* (Cincinnati: St. Anthony Messenger Press, 2011), 20.

2. See Joseph Goldstein, *Insight Meditation* (Boston: Shambhala, 2003).

Chapter Ten

1. Coleman Barks, *The Essential Rumi* (London: Penguin, 2004), 109.

2. See Sharon Salzburg, *Loving-Kindness* (Boston: Shambhala, 2002).

3. See Thomas Keating, *The Heart of the World* (New York: Crossroad Publishing Company), 47-55.

Chapter Eleven

1. Shantideva, *The Way of the Bodhisattva*, trans. Padmakara Translation Group (Boston: Shambhala, 1997), verse 48.

Chapter Twelve

1. See Jon Kabat-Zinn, 75-97.

Chapter Thirteen

1. See Gregg Krech, *Naikan: Gratitude, Grace, and the Japanese Art of Self-Reflection* (Berkeley: Stone Bridge Press, 2002).

2. Pema Chodron, *The Places That Scare You* (Boston: Shambhala, 2001), 55-60.

Chapter Fourteen

1. See Jon Kabat-Zinn, 123-131.

Chapter Fifteen

1. Quoted in Richard Rohr, *Breathing Under Water* (Cincinnati: St. Anthony Messenger Press, 2011), 103.

2. See Gregg Krech.

Chapter Sixteen

1. Martin Seligman, *Authentic Happiness* (New York: Free Press, 2002), 45-61.

2. Thomas Keating, *Open Mind, Open Heart* (New York: Bloomsbury, 2006).

Chapter Seventeen

1. Bill Wilson's story is recounted in *Alcoholics Anonymous: The Big Book*, 1-14.

2. Scott Stossel, *My Age of Anxiety* (New York: Alfred A. Knopf, 2014).

Suggested Readings

Alcoholics Anonymous: The Big Book. Fourth edition. New York: Alcoholics Anonymous World Services, Inc., 2001.

Alexander, William. *Ordinary Recovery: Mindfulness, Addiction, and the Path of Lifelong Sobriety*. Boston: Shambhala, 2010.

Bien, Thomas, and Bien, Beverly. *Mindful Recovery: A Spiritual Path to Healing from Addiction*. New York: John Wiley and Sons, 2002.

Brach, Tara. *Radical Acceptance: Embracing Your Life with the Heart of a Buddha*. New York: Bantam Book, 2003.

Brantley, Jeffrey. *Calming Your Anxious Mind: How mindfulness and compassion can free you from anxiety, fear, and panic*. Oakland: New Harbinger Publications, 2007.

Chodron, Pema. *The Places That Scare You: A Guide to Fearlessness in Difficult Times*. Boston: Shambhala, 2001.

Dodd, Lance. *The Heart of Addiction*. New York: Harper-Collins, 2002.

Germer, Christopher. *The Mindful Path to Self-Compassion: Freeing Yourself from Destructive Thoughts and Emotions*. New York: Guilford Press, 2009.

Goldstein, Joseph. *Insight Meditation: The Practice of Freedom*. Boston: Shambhala, 2003.

Griffin, Kevin. *One Breath at a Time: Buddhism and the Twelve Steps*. New York: St. Martin's Press, 2004.

Grof, Christina. *The Thirst for Wholeness: Attachment, Addiction, and the Spiritual Path*. New York: HarperCollins, 1993.

Jacobs-Stewart, Therese. *Mindfulness and the 12 Steps: Living recovery in the present moment*. Center City: Hazelden, 2010.

Kabat-Zinn, Jon. *Full Catastrophe Living*. New York: Bantam Books, 2013.

Keating, Thomas. *Open Mind, Open Heart*. New York: Bloomsbury, 2006.

Keating, Thomas. *The Heart of the World: An Introduction to Contemplative Christianity*. New York: Crossroad Publishing Company, 2008.

Keating, Thomas. *Divine Therapy and Addiction: Centering Prayer and the Twelve Steps*. New York: Lantern Books, 2009.

Kornfield, Jack. *The Wise Heart: A Guide to the Universal Teachings of Buddhist Psychology*. New York: Bantam Books, 2008.

Krech, Gregg. *Naikan: Gratitude, Grace, and the Japanese Art of Self-Reflection*. Berkeley: Stone Bridge Press, 2002.

May, Gerald. *Addiction and Grace: Love and Spirituality in the Healing of Addictions*. New York: HarperCollins, 1988.

Merton, Thomas. *New Seeds of Contemplation*. New York: New Directions Publ., 1972.

Orsillo, Susan, and Roemer, Lizabeth. *The Mindful Way through Anxiety*. New York: Guilford Press, 2011.

Peele, Stanton. *The Meaning of Addiction: Compulsive Experience and Its Interpretation.* Lexington: D.C. Heath and Company, 1985.

Peltz, Lawrence. *The Mindful Path to Addiction Recovery: A Practical Guide to Regaining Control over Your Life.* Boston: Shambhala, 2013.

Rohr, Richard. *Breathing Under Water: Spirituality and the Twelve Steps.* Cincinnati: St. Anthony Messenger Press, 2011.

Salzburg, Sharon. *Loving-Kindness: The Revolutionary Art of Happiness.* Boston: Shambhala, 2002.

Seligman, Martin. *Authentic Happiness.* New York: Free Press, 2002.

Shapiro, Rami. *Recovery—the Sacred Art: The Twelve Steps as Spiritual Practice.* Woodstock: SkyLight Paths Publishing, 2013.

Stossel, Scott. *My Age of Anxiety: Fear, Hope, Dread, and the Search for Peace of Mind.* New York: Alfred A. Knopf, 2014.

Trungpa, Chogyam. *Smile at Fear: Awakening the True Heart of Bravery.* Boston: Shambhala, 2009.

Twelve Steps and Twelve Traditions. New York: Alcoholics Anonymous World S

Select MSI Books

Self-Help Books

A Woman's Guide to Self-Nurturing (Romer)

Anxiety Anonymous: The Big Book on Anxiety Addiction (Ortman)

Creative Aging: A Baby Boomer's Guide to Successful Living (Vassiliadis & Romer)

Divorced! Survival Techniques for Singles over Forty (Romer)

Living Well with Chronic Illness (Charnas)

Publishing for Smarties: Finding a Publisher (Ham)

Survival of the Caregiver (Snyder)

The Marriage Whisperer: How to Improve Your Relationship Overnight (Pickett)

The Rose and the Sword: How to Balance Your Feminine and Masculine Energies (Bach & Hucknall)

The Widower's Guide to a New Life (Romer)

Widow: A Survival Guide for the First Year (Romer)

Inspirational and Religious Books

A Believer-Waiting's First Encounters with God (Mahlou)

A Guide to Bliss: Transforming Your Life through Mind Expansion (Tubali)

El Poder de lo Transpersonal (Ustman)

Everybody's Little Book of Everyday Prayers (MacGregor)

Joshuanism (Tosto)

Puertas a la Eternidad (Ustman)

The Gospel of Damascus (O. Imady)

The Seven Wisdoms of Life: A Journey into the Chakras (Tubali)

When You're Shoved from the Right, Look to Your Left: Metaphors of Islamic Humanism (O. Imady)

Memoirs

Blest Atheist (Mahlou)

Forget the Goal, the Journey Counts . . . 71 Jobs Later (Stites)

Healing from Incest: Intimate Conversations with My Therapist (Henderson & Emerton)

It Only Hurts When I Can't Run: One Girl's Story (Parker)

Las Historias de Mi Vida (Ustman)

Losing My Voice and Finding Another (C. Thompson)

Of God, Rattlesnakes, and Okra (Easterling)

Road to Damascus (E. Imady)

Still Life (Mellon)

Foreign Culture

Syrian Folktales (M. Imady)

The Rise and Fall of Muslim Civil Society (O. Imady)

The Subversive Utopia: Louis Kahn and the Question of National Jewish Style in Jerusalem (Sakr)

Thoughts without a Title (Henderson)

Popular Psychology

Road Map to Power (Husain & Husain)

The Seeker (Quinelle)

Understanding the People around You: An Introduction to Socionics (Filatova)

Humor

Mommy Poisoned Our House Guest (C. B. Leaver)

The Musings of a Carolina Yankee (Amidon)

Parenting

365 Teacher Secrets for Parents: Fun Ways to Help Your Child in Elementary School (McKinley & Trombly)

How to Be a Good Mommy When You're Sick (Graves)

Lessons of Labor (Aziz)

CPSIA information can be obtained
at www.ICGtesting.com
Printed in the USA
LVHW052303310322
714844LV00005B/363

9 781942 891000